HERDER'S
SOCIAL AND POLITICAL
THOUGHT

Oxford University Press, Ely House, London W. 1

GLASGOW   NEW YORK   TORONTO   MELBOURNE   WELLINGTON
CAPE TOWN   SALISBURY   IBADAN   NAIROBI   LUSAKA   ADDIS ABABA
BOMBAY   CALCUTTA   MADRAS   KARACHI   LAHORE   DACCA
KUALA LUMPUR   HONG KONG   TOKYO

HERDER'S
SOCIAL AND POLITICAL
THOUGHT

FROM ENLIGHTENMENT
TO NATIONALISM

By
F. M. BARNARD

CLARENDON PRESS · OXFORD

© *Oxford University Press* 1965

FIRST PUBLISHED 1965

REPRINTED LITHOGRAPHICALLY 1967 (WITH CORRECTIONS)

PRINTED IN GREAT BRITAIN
BY EBENEZER BAYLIS AND SON LIMITED
THE TRINITY PRESS, WORCESTER, AND LONDON

TO THE MEMORY OF
ALBERT AND GISELA MECHNER,
HELGA AND RACHEL

ACKNOWLEDGEMENTS

I should like first to acknowledge a long-standing debt to Professor Asa Briggs for his teaching, understanding, and encouragement during and since my days at Oxford.

My thanks are also due to Professors Bruce Miller and Alexander Gillies for their advice when I first conceived the idea of writing this study over seven years ago; to Professor Christopher Hughes, who read earlier drafts, for his helpful criticism; and last but by no means least to Sir Isaiah Berlin, for several valuable observations that he made after reading the book in manuscript.

I am most grateful to the German Academic Exchange Service for enabling me to spend a period of research in Germany and to all those at German Universities who helped to ensure that it should be fruitful.

I also wish to thank the Editor of the *Journal of the History of Ideas* for his permission to include in Chapter VI material from my article on 'Herder's Treatment of Causation and Continuity in History', which appeared in June 1963.

Messrs. Peter Greaves and Thomas Richards were kind enough to read the manuscript and to suggest a number of stylistic improvements. To them as also to Mrs. Margarete Whittome, who typed it, and to Miss Janet Fyfe, who helped to compile the index, I owe a debt made all the greater by the unrewarding nature of the task they had so readily undertaken. What I owe to my wife, however, is more than I can put into words.

My debt to European and American scholarship is evident from the acknowledgements made throughout the book. But I should like to pay tribute here to one man who, above all, has helped me towards a deeper understanding of the issues with which the book attempts to deal: Ernst Cassirer. In his life and writings he stood for what was best in the traditions of the European Enlightenment.

December 1964   F.M.B.

NOTE

A German translation of an earlier version of this book has been published under the title *Zwischen Aufklärung und Politischer Romantik* by Erich Schmidt Verlag, Berlin 1964. The present book has been substantially revised and in parts extended.

TABLE OF CONTENTS

BIOGRAPHICAL NOTE AND CHRONOLOGY
OF HERDER'S PRINCIPAL WORKS[1]

Johann Gottfried Herder was born on 25th August 1744 in Mohrungen, a small East Prussian town. After attending the local grammar school Herder had hopes, but little prospect, of pursuing further studies, for his parents could not afford to support him at a university. A chance encounter with a Russian army-surgeon (who was quartered with his regiment in the town during the winter of 1761–2 on returning from the Seven Years War) was to help Herder realize his ambitions. For the Russian offered to take him to Königsberg and assist him to study medicine. Herder, in return, was to translate a medical treatise for him into Latin. Herder soon found, however, that he was not suited for a medical career. He chose theology instead, and managed to support himself by teaching and coaching.

The years in Königsberg (1762–4) proved of decisive importance in the shaping of Herder's mind. Although he had formally registered to study theology, his main interests lay outside theology. Undoubtedly this was in large measure due to the fascination which Kant's lectures had for him. In those days Kant still lectured on a great variety of subjects, covering not only logic, metaphysics, and ethics, but also astronomy, mathematics, and geography. Indeed, it was Kant's course on geography, in which he gave special attention to the correlation between meteorological, physical, and human factors, that aroused Herder's greatest interest. Kant also introduced Herder to Rousseau and to the English empiricists, Hume in particular. But it was, above all, Kant's personality, his cheerfulness, humour, and complete humility, that made a lasting impression on the eighteen-year-old student. Many years later, when Kant and Herder had become estranged, Herder still recalled with gratitude Kant's teaching, and paid him tribute in the most moving and generous terms.

[1] Two excellent biographies of Herder have appeared in English in recent years, one in England, the other in America. They are *Herder*, by A. Gillies, Basil Blackwell, Oxford, 1945; and *Herder, his Life and Thought*, by Robert T. Clark Jr., University of California Press, Berkeley and Los Angeles, 1955.

Herder's interest in European literature, in particular English literature, received further encouragement towards the end of his studies from another remarkable personality: Johann Georg Hamann (1730–88). In some ways Hamann supplemented Kant's influence on Herder. He impressed on him, as Kant had done, the value of experience (in contrast to metaphysical dogmatism), and the limitations of reason in man's total experience. But to some extent he also counteracted Kant's influence, by his extreme hostility to the ideas of the English and (even more so) of the French Enlightenment. For several years Herder's thought revealed an uneasy desire to reconcile the opposing elements in Kant's and Hamann's teachings.

The years 1764–9 found Herder in Riga, where he took on an appointment as teacher and preacher. One of the chief reasons for his departure to Riga, which was then (as now) part of the Russian Empire, was to evade military service in the Prussian army. Herder hated what he called the 'dullness' and 'mechanical regimentation' of Frederick's Prussia. By contrast, he was enormously impressed by the political vitality of this self-governing city. He never tired in later years of praising its 'republican freedoms' and the civic pride of its inhabitants. Riga became for Herder what the political image of Geneva had been for Rousseau.

Herder was ordained in 1767 and so successful was he as a preacher that he was offered the post of minister at Riga's two principal churches. He was equally successful as a teacher at Riga's Cathedral School. Indeed his reputation as a teacher and, increasingly also, as a writer was such as to bring about a call to St. Petersburg. Herder, however, declined this invitation in response to the request of his many friends and literary admirers in Riga, who urged him to stay. At the age of twenty-three he published his first book, the *Fragmente über die neuere deutsche Litteratur*, which was acclaimed as a major contribution to literary criticism.

Herder was, however, too restless, too anxious to gain wider experience, to settle down to a comfortable living in Riga. Just as suddenly and abruptly as he had decided to leave home for Königsberg, he now (May 1769) decided to leave Riga for France.

During the sea voyage Herder kept a diary, known now as his *Travel Diary (Journal meiner Reise)*, which, however, remained unpublished during his life-time. This diary is a most useful documentary source, for it provides the key to his subsequent work. It also reveals the clue to Herder's chronic dissatisfaction with himself throughout his remaining life. For it was during this voyage that Herder began to realize the gap that separated his aspirations from their likely realization. But, then, his aspirations were on the grandest possible scale. He not only aimed at making his name in the world of letters; he was equally resolved to make his mark in the active life of public affairs. It is of interest that during that period he is still, politically, far more interested in Russia than in Germany. His utmost political ambition is to draw up a new constitution for Russia and to reform her educational system. This interest in Russia and the Slavonic world as a whole recurs in subsequent writings and reaches its climax in his most outstanding work, the *Ideen zur Philosophie der Geschichte der Menschheit*, in which he declares the future of Europe to lie in the hands of the 'tireless, peaceful Slavs'.

The first time Herder thought of himself consciously as a German was upon his arrival in France. The longer he stayed, the more German he grew in outlook. Herder had begun to be known in France and was introduced to a number of eminent writers, such as Diderot, d'Alembert, and Barthélemy. But he none the less did not enjoy his stay. He sensed an air of decay; he considered French culture to be on the decline. French social and political life aroused his gravest misgivings. He was thoroughly depressed. When an invitation reached him in Paris to become tutor and travelling companion to the son of the Prince of Lübeck and Holstein, he left at once and without a shred of sorrow.

Herder arrived at Eutin, the capital of Holstein, in March 1770. He was to accompany the Prince's son on a journey to Italy. He stopped on the way in Hamburg, where he met Lessing among others, and in Darmstadt, where he met Caroline Flachsland, his future wife. By the time (end of July 1770) he and his charge reached Strasbourg, however, Herder had grown tired of his position, which frequently gave him the feeling of being deliberately humiliated. Another reason for his resignation and for his desire to stay in Strasbourg was an eye complaint from which he had suffered since childhood and which he hoped an operation at the renowned Strasbourg Faculty of Medicine would cure. Here, in Strasbourg, began Herder's life-long friendship with Goethe. 'In the darkened room of Herder's inn . . . was born the literary revolution of Germany. . . . Herder taught Goethe to be himself. And through Goethe he spoke to the whole of the rising generation.'[2]

The friendship with Goethe was to determine Herder's final destination: Weimar. For it was Goethe, who as minister at the court of Duke Karl August of Weimar, induced the Duke to offer Herder

[2] A. Gillies, *Herder*, Oxford, 1945, p. 19.

the posts of Superintendent of Schools, Chief Pastor, and Court Preacher. Herder was at the time of the offer (1776) in Bückeburg, where, after leaving Strasbourg, he had accepted the post of Chief Pastor to the Count of Schaumburg-Lippe (April 1771). Goethe knew that Herder was not happy in Bückeburg and that he was negotiating over a university post in Göttingen. He now persuaded Herder to accept the Weimar offer, and Herder did. Yet for the rest of his life Herder wondered whether he had made the right decision. None the less, in Weimar he stayed, and in Weimar he died, in his sixtieth year, on 18th December 1803.

Herder was an impressive personality. His presence had a magnetic effect on those who met him. The younger generation was particularly attracted to him, and his house in Weimar became almost a place of pilgrimage to visitors as far afield as Crabb Robinson from England, or Georg Müller, the Swiss theologian and brother of the famous historian. His extensive correspondence, too, bears witness to the considerable range and variety of his intellectual contacts. And yet, throughout most of the years in Weimar, especially after the estrangement with Goethe and Kant, Herder suffered from an acute sense of isolation. He saw himself ignored, misunderstood, exploited. 'I stand alone', he writes in a letter of that period.[3] Partly, no doubt, this feeling of isolation can be attributed to Herder's extreme sensitiveness, which caused him to mistake criticism for hostility. But it cannot wholly thus be accounted for. His sharp pen as a critic, his unorthodox views as a theologian, and his republican sympathies during the French Revolution, created many enemies and made him suspect to the Court circles. Financial worries, waning health, and the heavy duties of his office, could not but exacerbate his melancholy feelings. Above all, the lifelong eye-trouble gave to a voracious reader like Herder continuous cause for anxiety and irritation. But, in spite of these adverse circumstances, Herder continued writing right up to the end. Although he became more and more embittered and dissatisfied, he never ceased to take an interest in what went on around him, and never failed to offer help and encouragement to those that turned to him. For he was, by nature, a warm-hearted man, endowed with a rare capacity for empathy and a distinctly generous disposition. What he unfortunately lacked, but greatly admired in others, was the ability to laugh at misfortunes.

[3] The letter is dated 29 April 1801, and is addressed to Thomas Thorild (1759–1808), an author who taught at the University of Greifswald. (Wilhelm Dobbek, *Herders Briefe*, Weimar, 1959, p. 423.)

'Sense of humour' was not an expression for which he had much liking.[4] But one cannot help wondering whether Herder's sense of personal tragedy was not at bottom the result of a real want of this precious quality.

HERDER'S PRINCIPAL WORKS
(IN CHRONOLOGICAL ORDER)

1767:   *Ueber die neuere deutsche Litteratur. Fragmente.*
1769:   *Kritische Wälder.*
         Journal meiner Reise.
1770:   *Plastik.*
1772:   *Abhandlung über den Ursprung der Sprache.*
1773:   *Von deutscher Art und Kunst.*
1774:   *Auch eine Philosophie der Geschichte zur Bildung der Menschheit.*
         Aelteste Urkunde des Menschengeschlechts (Vol. I).
1775:   *Ursachen des gesunkenen Geschmacks bei den verschiedenen Völkern da er geblühet.*
1776:   *Aelteste Urkunde des Menschengeschlechts* (Vol. II).
1778:   *Vom Erkennen und Empfinden der menschlichen Seele.*
1780:   *Vom Einfluß der Regierung auf die Wissenschaften, und der Wissenschaften auf die Regierung.*
1781:   *Briefe, das Studium der Theologie betreffend.*
1782–3: *Vom Geist der Ebräischen Poesie.*
1784–91: *Ideen zur Philosophie der Geschichte der Menschheit.*
1787–98: *Zerstreute Blätter.*
1793–7: *Briefe zu Beförderung der Humanität.*
1794–8: *Christliche Schriften.*
1799:   *Metakritik.*
1800:   *Kalligone.*
1801–3: *Adrastea.*
1802:   *Cid.*

---

[4] See Herder's letter to Jean Paul of 15 July 1801. (Dobbek, op. cit., p. 425.)

INTRODUCTION

This study attempts to trace the transition from an age in which terms like 'state', 'nation', and 'society', were still compatible with a view of association that could dispense with 'ideology' to one in which this increasingly ceased to be the case. By 'ideology' we mean here a political doctrine grounded in, or underpinned by a comprehensive, though essentially non-political, conception of man and his place in the universal order of things.

Up to the middle of the eighteenth century the area of 'common interests' was still widely defined in strictly individualist and pragmatic terms. The notion of 'contract' served as a reminder that rules of political association were a reciprocal arrangement intended to promote the interests of the contracting parties. The limits which it imposed on the freedom of the individual were only accepted on the understanding that the loss of freedom was more than offset by the gain of security and/or other advantages. At any given time the calculation of loss and gain could prompt men to invoke this notion either to buttress or to challenge the legitimacy of established political authority.

᠔ But could the notion of a social contract also serve as a criterion for determining the territorial limits of a given political authority? Those who came to question the accepted view of the State as simply a territorial unit comprising a number of individuals owing allegiance to a common sovereign, increasingly felt that it could not. Hence the questioning of the accepted view of statehood led to the search for a principle that would meet this requirement.

The context in which this search took place was almost entirely non-political. Those who wished to challenge the accepted view of political association turned to the arts and to literature, to folk-lore and traditional customs, to history and the study of language, resolved to find in these cultural spheres the true bond of social and political union. They had little or no interest in the administrative theories of the political jurist or in the practical experience of the professional administrator. For they were convinced that what brought men together to form a social and political whole was not organization imposed from outside, but their inner consciousness of sharing a common cultural heritage./ Governments came and went, administrative rules were made and unmade, but the consciousness of shared communal traditions endured like the indestructible force of nature.

It is hardly surprising, therefore, that the outcome of the search found expression in a doctrine compounded of two essentially non-political ingredients: the ethical concept of 'self-determination' and the cultural concept of *'Volksgeist'*. Underlying this doctrine and reinforcing it was the variously developed notion of organism. This notion, to be sure, was of older vintage than the concepts of self-determination and national consciousness or *Volksgeist*. But the growing prestige of the natural sciences—biology in particular—helped to give it a significance and prominence which it had not enjoyed hitherto.

The effect of this formidable combination of essentially non-political ingredients first became apparent in the wake of the French Revolution. It has been variously judged ever since. To some it appeared so disastrous that they came to advocate 'a return to the point where the Eighteenth Century had left off'.[1] Germany in particular, the country which has given birth to this ideological 'combination', has more than revealed the perils that are inherent in it.[2] On the other hand, many a suppressed national group came to see in the new doctrine of nationhood and statehood a source of inspiration and hope. Members of subject nations began to take a renewed interest in their cultural heritage and to derive from it a sense of dignity and self-respect which they had well-nigh been in danger of losing.

However, it is not the main purpose of this study to assess the effects of the new conception of political association, but rather to trace its origins in the writings of its first major exponent, Johann Gottfried Herder. In particular we wish to elicit those features of his theory of community which in a substantive sense differ from subsequent organicist interpretations of the State.

---

[1] Albert Schweitzer, *Kultur und Ethik*, *Kulturphilosophie*, Part II, München, 1923, p. XVI.

[2] Even before the worst excesses had time to materialize, Ernst Troeltsch correctly recognized the trend, when in 1925 he wrote: 'The political thought of Germany is marked by a curious dilemma. . . . Look at one of its sides, and you will see an abundance of Romanticism and lofty idealism; look at the other, and you will see a realism which goes to the verge of cynicism and of utter indifference to all ideals and all morality. But what you see above all is an inclination to make an astonishing combination of the two elements—in a word, to brutalize romance, and to romanticize cynicism.' ('Naturrecht und Humanität in der Weltpolitik', in *Deutscher Geist und Westeuropa*, ed. by Hans Baron, Tübingen, 1925, p. 18.)

Herder was not a systematic writer. Vast though his literary output was (Suphan's edition of Herder's works contains no less than 33 volumes), many of his works were fragmentary both in content and form. Even the work for which he is best known to English readers, the *Ideen zur Philosophie der Geschichte der Menschheit* (1784–91) remained uncompleted.[3] His political ideas, in particular, are rarely worked out systematically. More often they are found scattered throughout his writings, sometimes within the most unexpected contexts. In order to present these ideas in some coherent form, the topical rather than the chronological approach seemed to me the more appropriate method of presentation. *What* Herder had to say on any given subject, therefore, rather than *when* he came to say what he did, will be our principal consideration. At the same time I have tried to indicate, whenever the occasion demanded it, the effect of changing circumstances upon the formation and development of his ideas. The first chapter, too, is intended to provide some historical perspective to our exposition.

Like Max Weber over a century later, Herder was preoccupied with the problem of social relations in a world that increasingly came to resemble for him a vast machine in which men were like cogs, whose lives were governed by the inexorable operations of mechanical bureaucracies. But, unlike Weber, Herder not merely wished to dissociate the 'mechanical' from the 'political', but also all elements of centralized power and of élitist rule. In this respect he also went beyond Justus Möser (1720–94), who was by far the most outstanding eighteenth-century advocate of traditionalism and community association. For whereas Möser still confined political participation to the few (those who held property), Herder envisaged a political community in which all citizens, individually or in groups, co-operated within some sort of pluralist scheme where power and control were not centralized but widely diffused. At the same time, however, he also differed from those who before and after him aimed to distinguish between co-operation and coercion, and between 'administration' and 'politics'. For Herder did not recommend the abolition of states in favour of some international organization or 'world government'; indeed he opposed the latter, arguing that international tension was likely to increase rather than abate in the wake of its creation. The existence of independent nation states was for him as natural and necessary as the alternation of day and night; it was something men

---

[3] The work was translated into English during Herder's life-time (by T. Churchill) and published in 1800 (with a second edition in 1803), under the title of *Outlines of a Philosophy of the History of Man*. It is still the only English translation in existence.

had to accept and to which they had to adjust themselves as best as they could. They had to learn to live together as men *and* as members of national communities. 'Cosmopolitanism' was at best a blithe illusion and at worst an invitation to international chaos or enforced uniformity. But if, as Herder wished to maintain, the design of nature was a world of autonomous nation states, the question arises how states could emerge or survive without the cohesive power of central governments.

This was the very question to which Herder sought to provide an answer. His problem was no less than to discover what Bertrand de Jouvenel has called the *vis politica*, the 'natural' cohesive force of political union.[4] Not 'man' *versus* 'citizen': this was an unreal distinction, a distinction made by those who mistakenly contrasted man in a state of nature with man in civil society. But rather: mechanical 'power' *versus* organic 'force'. *This* was a real distinction, a distinction which in Herder's view led to the heart of the matter.

The main chapters of this study seek to trace the attempts which Herder made to discern the *vis politica*, the prime force of spontaneous political association. The terms in which his quest took shape were conceived, however, in a wider, more expansive sense than that in which the word 'political' is often understood. To pay heed to this wider—essentially cultural, psychological and 'familial'—conception of politics, we are employing the adjective 'socio-political' rather than the less cumbersome 'political'.

It is not surprising that a theory which sought to elicit the 'organic' continuum of political association could not dispense with a philosophy of history. Indeed, Herder's theory of community and his philosophy of history are so closely interwoven that it is almost misleading to treat of the one in separation from the other. The key-note of Herder's philosophy of history—as of the epistemological assumptions underlying it—was the principle of inter-relation. In the light of this principle Herder attacked what he considered to be the more facile forms of rationalism: abstractionism, *a priorism*, the doctrine of psychological 'faculties', and the philosophical dualisms of the Cartesian School. Above all, he wished to dethrone 'reason' from its position of supremacy and deny its existence as an isolated 'faculty' superior to, or isolated from the other activities of the mind.[5] More positively it helped him to

---

[4] Bertrand de Jouvenel, *Sovereignty*, Cambridge, 1957, p. 21.

[5] From this it has sometimes wrongly been inferred that Herder advocated 'irrationalism' and that he diametrically opposed all that the Enlightenment stood for. Robert T. Clark's scholarly study *Herder, his Life and Thought* (1955) is a timely corrective to that view.

evolve a *method* which, in spite of its undeniable defects, constitutes a major contribution to the study of history and human affairs generally.

Although many of Herder's ideas have lost none of their relevance to current debates on man and society, it is exceedingly difficult (and possibly pointless) to classify them in terms currently fashionable. Do they reveal Herder as a positivist or an intuitionist, as an essentialist (Professor Popper's substitute term for 'realist'[6]) or a nominalist, as a functionalist or an historicist, as an individualist or a holist? Even if we attempted an answer to this series of questions, it would not necessarily enhance the cognitional status of Herder's ideas, since few of these terms have a generally agreed meaning. But supposing they had, and supposing we were pressed to apply them, we would have to say something like this: Herder, on the whole, wrote *as if* he were a positivist, for he wished to see the methods of the natural sciences employed in the study of human affairs. At the same time he realized, however, that the study of human history demanded a different kind of interpretative 'understanding' than the study of natural history. He argued *as if* he were a nominalist, since he did not conceive of *Volk* as a substantive entity or as a *thing* with a corporate existence of its own over and above, or separate from the individuals who composed it. *Volk* was a relational *event*, a historical and cultural continuum. None the less, he would not have denied this continuum an ontological reality of its own. Whilst he had his 'fatalist' moments, he wished to maintain a functionalist position (in Professor Merton's sense[7]) rather than an historicist one (in Professor Popper's—not entirely consistent—use of the term). For he thought of man as a morally autonomous being capable of choosing between alternative courses of actions, even though he also considered him as part of a given socio-historical continuum. Finally, if we classified Herder as a holist, we would also have to remember that his 'holism' comprised multiplicity and diversity as well as unity.

But the reader may well have doubts about the value of such an exercise. I share these doubts. I have, therefore, refrained from fitting Herder's ideas into categories that would tend to obscure rather than clarify their meaning or misleadingly suggest that Herder was a far more consistent and systematic thinker than he really was. It would not, I feel, detract from his intellectual achievement—for such it was in

[6] Karl R. Popper, *The Poverty of Historicism*, second edition, London, 1960, p. 27.

[7] Robert K. Merton, *Social Theory and Social Structure*, revised and enlarged edition, Free Press of Glencoe, 1957; see especially ch. I ('Manifest and Latent Functions'), pp. 19–82.

spite of ambiguities and unresolved perplexities—if what Herder once said of Lessing were to be said of him as well: 'He was no . . . . . . ist, whatever letters we choose to put before the ending.'[8] For Herder meant it as a compliment.

[8] XVI, 494. (All references are to the Suphan edition of Herder's *Werke*, 33 vols., Berlin, 1877–1913.)

I

HERDER'S GERMANY: THE *AUFKLÄRUNG*

IF WE are told that Emperor Maximilian I added the words 'of the German Nation' to the old title of the 'Holy Roman Empire' in order to assuage a growing national restlessness in the German-speaking lands of the Empire at the turn of the fifteenth century,[1] we are inclined to accept this statement without a shrug. Likewise we find it plausible that men such as Ulrich von Hutten or Martin Luther could never have rallied behind them such a formidable wave of support had they not been able to appeal to an emergent national consciousness. Such is the force of our habit to think in terms of nationalist categories. That Maximilian I could have been prompted by essentially dynastic considerations or that Hutten and Luther could have acted from the conviction that they were accomplishing God's will in the defence of Truth seems a somewhat inadequate historical explanation to the twentieth-century mind. Yet two hundred years ago the national principle as it is understood today was unheard of. The German Empire was not quite so obvious a monstrosity if viewed against the background of the eighteenth-century European scene. Most states were the outcome of wars, dynastic arrangements, or sheer accident. No government thought of invoking the principle of nationality as the rightful source of its power and authority to rule. Whatever the term 'nation' signified—and it rarely had a precise meaning—it certainly did not mean the bulk of the people occupying a common territory and speaking a common tongue.

If then 'Germany' was not exactly a political monstrosity, it was nevertheless a patchwork of considerable economic and political complexity. The different systems of coinage, the numerous customs restrictions and governmental interferences with trade and industry, the poor state of the roads, and the general lack of security reduced the volume of trade to a minimum.[2] Whilst Spain, Holland, France and

[1] See E. R. Huber, *Deutsche Verfassungsgeschichte*, Stuttgart, 1957, vol. I, pp. 3-4, and G. Barraclough, *The Origins of Modern Germany*, Oxford, 1949, pp. 362, 368. Also Ernst Cassirer, *Freiheit und Form*, Berlin, 1916, p. 10. Elie Kedourie, by contrast, in his excellent study (*Nationalism*, London, 1960, 2nd ed., 1961) rightly challenges the projection of nationalistic elements into a pre-nationalist era.

[2] H. Dietze, *Geschichte des deutschen Handels*, Leipzig, 1923, p. 83. There were ten

England were acquiring overseas colonies, Germany was only slowly recovering from the ravages of the Thirty Years War. To effect the economic and political reconstruction which the country needed within the broader framework of the Empire would have required from its emperors a single-mindedness of purpose which was sadly lacking in these as in more propitious times of the past.

Although the imperial crown was elective, in practice it was claimed as an hereditary privilege by the Habsburg dynasty. This, more than any other factor, paralysed the political development of the Empire; for the Habsburgs were Habsburg first and foremost and whatever was deemed by them of dynastic priority was of infinitely greater political moment than any other consideration. This, more than any other factor, too, led to the loss of their political authority first over the German and later over the Austrian Empire. Herder summed up shrewdly the chronic political malaise of the Habsburgs when he wrote: 'This dynastic greed (Herder calls it *Habgeist*, playing on the common prefix of '*Habgeist*' and '*Habsburg*') was unfortunately the inherited policy of the House of Habsburg.'[3]

The Empire was composed of some three hundred more or less independent political units. By the treaty of Westphalia (1648) the sovereign rights of the princes were, in theory, limited by the rights of the Empire. The princes were supposed to observe the laws of the Empire and only depart from them whenever imperial law abstained from enforcing its own legal claim. They were to owe allegiance to the emperor in time of war and were not to enter into any alliance directed against the emperor. These limitations, however, were ignored from the outset. In the War of the Spanish Succession, Bavaria did not hesitate to join forces with France. In the War of the Austrian Succession, the Empire, as a corporate body, remained aloof. In the Seven Years War, Prussia successfully challenged what remained of the might and authority of the Empire. A number of the larger states maintained their own foreign representation and acted as independent powers in European politics. Several territories, too, became associated with non-German lands by virtue of coming under the tutelage of princes who were rulers in their own right over lands lying outside the boundaries of the German Empire. This was so with the Habsburg emperors themselves who combined under one crown the lands of Austria,

---

standards of silver coinage and, on the Rhine alone, between Strasbourg and the Dutch frontier, thirty customs stations. See also W. H. Bruford, *Germany in the Eighteenth Century*, Cambridge, 1935, p. 161.

[3] XVII, 54; see also H. v. Treitschke, *Deutsche Geschichte im neunzehnten Jahrhundert*, ed. by H. Heffter, Leipzig, 1934, vol. I, pp. 17–19.

Bohemia and Hungary as well as possessions in Italy, the Netherlands and Poland. The elector of Hanover ascended the English throne in 1714, whilst the elector of Saxony became associated with the Polish crown. Parts of the northern territories came under Swedish and Danish sovereignty; Alsace was annexed by France.

We cannot attempt here to trace the history of the many petty states that made up the eighteenth-century map of Germany. Their variety in size and form of administration, their changing political and economic fortunes, their strains and stresses in their relations with one another make this a most bewildering and complex subject of study. There was, however, one feature common to them all: the personal absolutism of their rulers. But even in this respect there were differences of degree. Much depended on the personal character and capabilities of the ruler. He was, in practice, the source of all legislation and also the last court of appeal in matters of internal jurisdiction. If he wished, he could make use of a particularly odious privilege, that of *Kabinettjustiz*, whereby he could by-pass the ordinary process of law. An irresponsible and despotic ruler could thus deprive his subjects of their freedom without even the semblance of a trial with complete impunity. Duke Karl Eugen of Württemberg, for example, by invoking this privilege, kept the jurist J. J. Moser (one of the staunchest champions of the Estates' constitutional claims) and the poet C. F. D. Schubart in jail for years.[4] Not a few, amongst them Schiller, for example, were forced to flee from his state to evade imprisonment.

Before the Thirty Years War, the existence of provincial diets constituted at least some financial check on the extravagance of the princes' court expenditure. By the eighteenth century most of these assemblies had virtually disappeared. Where they did survive, they no longer exercised any effective power. Even in the state of Württemberg, where the diet succeeded in maintaining some semblance of power in the first decades of the eighteenth century, its civic spirit was eventually broken by the intolerance and the unscrupulous autocracy of Karl Eugen during his long reign.

Where the economic resources were severely limited, as in Württemberg and in some of the smaller states of central Germany, the lavish spending of some of their rulers led to the raising of money by the most despicable means, such as the sale of their subjects to foreign powers for

---

[4] Karl Biedermann, *Deutschland im Achtzehnten Jahrhundert*, second edition, 3 vol., Leipzig, 1880, vol. I, pp. 106–7; see also Adrien Fauchier-Magnan, *The Small German Courts in the Eighteenth Century*, trans. by Mervyn Savill, London, 1958, pp. 22, 210, 218, 223–5; and G. P. Gooch, *Germany and the French Revolution*, London, 1927, pp. 10–11.

military service or the putting up to auction of positions in their state
administrations, once the customary sources of revenue, taxation and
heavy borrowing, had become insufficient or exhausted.[5] The position
in some of the larger states, such as Saxony under the electors Augustus
II and III, or Bavaria under Karl Theodor, was little better.[6] Prussia,
on the other hand, under Frederick II, in whom many of the exponents
of 'enlightened government' saw the ideal ruler, was undoubtedly one
of the best governed of the larger German states. In the second half of
the eighteenth century, a number of German states, including Austria
under Joseph II, impressed by the economic success of Prussia's
administrative methods, attempted to emulate the example set by
Frederick the Great. Karl Wilhelm Ferdinand of Brunswick, Karl
Friedrich of Baden, Anna Amalia and Karl August of Saxe-Weimar
were outstanding examples of enlightened rulers anxious to improve
the material welfare and educational facilities of their subjects. By
pursuing policies of religious toleration and by granting virtual freedom
of the press, they greatly helped to create more favourable conditions
for the development of a more active intellectual and political life.

A ruler's treatment of the Jews gave some indication of his standard
of enlightenment.[7] In most German states where Jews were allowed to
reside at all, their numbers were carefully regulated; so also was the
'living space' allocated to them, usually in one street of the town, the
ghetto, which they were only permitted to leave at specified times of the
day. Jewish children were not, as a rule, admitted to public schools, and
the universities, where they were open to Jews, as in Göttingen, were
required by law to warn Jewish undergraduates that the attainment of
academic qualifications would not entitle them to enter the professions.[8]
These, like most productive occupations as well as the ownership of
land, were barred to Jews until they were granted full citizenship.[9]

---

[5] Karl Eugen, for example, sold troops to France, Holland and England. He received
15,000 livres from Louis XV per thousand equipped men, a subsidy which in case of war
was to be increased to 79,000 livres. Between 1752 and 1756 the Württemberg soldiery cost
France a million and a half livres. (Fauchier-Magnan, op. cit., pp. 208-9. See also
Biedermann, op. cit., vol. I, pp. 200-5.)

[6] F. Rörig, *Ursachen und Auswirkungen des deutschen Partikularismus*, Berlin, 1937,
pp. 28-9.

[7] It is of interest that Herder already stressed this correlation: 'All those laws that treat
the Jew worse than a beast', he wrote, 'indicate the barbaric constitution of a state.'
(XXIV, 71.)

[8] Götz v. Selle, *Die Georg August Universität zu Göttingen*, Göttingen, 1937, p. 352.

[9] Goethe's reminiscences in *Dichtung und Wahrheit* give a vivid insight into the
eighteenth-century Frankfurt ghetto and the precarious situation of the Jews. See also
W. H. Bruford, op. cit., p. 201, and William Rose's study 'Goethe and the Jews', in his
Men, Myths, and Movements in German Literature, London, 1931, pp. 157-80. Biedermann

Austria under Joseph II was the first German state to undertake measures for their emancipation. Under the Patent of Toleration (1781) Jews were given the same rights as other religious minorities; they were permitted to avail themselves of public educational facilities and encouraged to enter productive occupations. For the first time, too, Jews became liable for military service. It is doubtful whether these measures, however revolutionary at the time (most states in Germany did not accord full citizenship to the Jews until the second half of the nineteenth century), could have been effected under any but the most autocratic of absolutist systems, for they were highly unpopular. It is not surprising, therefore, that leading political thinkers of the eighteenth century put their faith in the progressive enlightenment of absolutist rulers rather than in the 'sovereignty of the people'.[10]

The prevailing class structure was another factor that induced many intellectuals to place their political hopes in reform from above. Unlike England and France, Germany had no *bourgeoisie* strong enough, and independent enough, to exert any political influence of its own. A considerable section of this stratum of society was absorbed into the multifarious petty bureaucracies and wholly subservient to the princely employer. 'Germany', wrote F. K. von Moser, 'was inundated with councillors. Had these people really given counsel, there would have been a dreadful chaos; but the councillors were so privy that no one ever heard them speak. All of them kept their secrets to themselves.'[11] The rest of the *bourgeoisie*, consisting of shopkeepers, small merchants and manufacturers, artisans, intellectuals, and peasant-farmers, had very little, if any, sense of common purpose. There were divisions of rank and class within this group no less sharp than those existing between members of the middle class and those of the nobility. 'In no period of German history', Biedermann records, 'was the separation of classes so striking and its effect so tragic.'[12] The only section of the population which was relatively homogeneous was that of the peasant labourer; invariably illiterate and living at mere subsistence level, he

---

also discusses in some detail the position of the Jews in the eighteenth century (op. cit., vol. III, pp. 1113–27).

[10] Among the German States that followed the Austrian example was the city of Mainz. Schlözer published in his *Stats Anzeigen* (vol. VI, 1784, p. 502) a decree of the Elector of Mainz, according to which Jews were to enjoy practically the same rights as Christians. This decree, too, met with much hostility.

[11] Quoted in A. Fauchier-Magnan, op. cit., p. 55. The tiny principality of Zweibrücken, for example, possessed no less than 500 officials. (Perthes, *Das deutsche Staatsleben vor der Revolution*, cited by Fauchier-Magnan, op. cit., p. 55.)

[12] Biedermann, op. cit., vol. II, p. 4.

had no political say whatsoever. Indeed, east of the Elbe, where feudal conditions still predominated, the peasants were wholly subject also to the jurisdiction of their masters.[13]

Neither the peasantry, then (amounting to over two-thirds of the total population), nor the urban middle class, could be counted upon as an effective political breakwater against the powers of the nobility.[14] Germany, throughout the major part of the eighteenth century, remained essentially a *terra obedientiae* (as Herder called it), with no political parties or societies, where, indeed, it was generally 'forbidden to talk politics'.[15] Discontent, more often than not, was, therefore, forced to simmer under the surface.

In view of these conditions it is hardly surprising that political consciousness and political thinking were at a low ebb in Germany, particularly in the first half of the century, and that most political ideas that gained currency in Herder's time, apart from the native theories of natural law, were of either French or English origin. Nevertheless it would be wrong to dismiss all German intellectual endeavour of this period as being of no political significance. A good deal of the religious controversies, for example, contained elements that increasingly came to have relevance to political thinking. Similarly the writings of poets and dramatists succeeded in drawing attention—under more or less ingenious disguises—to some of the most acute problems of absolutist government. By contrast, the political theories of the jurists and professional administrators—they were frequently both—made a lesser impact on the public mind, concerned as they mostly were with problems of fiscal policy and techniques of administration.[16]

The main centres of intellectual life as also of political theorizing—such as it was—were university towns, Imperial Cities, or state capitals in the domains of the more tolerant of absolutist rulers. These centres frequently became the refuge for those persecuted for their religious or political views, and it was in these centres that the middle class began to revive again.[17] But there was no Paris, no London;

---

[13] G. F. Knapp, *Die Bauernbefreiung und der Ursprung der Landarbeiter*, Leipzig, 1887, pp. 28 ff.; also K. Th. Heigel, *Deutsche Geschichte vom Tode Friedrich des Großen bis zur Auflösung des alten Reiches*, Leipzig, 1889, vol. I, p. 106.

[14] The nobility was, of course, divided too, and the *nuances* of social rank were most religiously observed. (See G. P. Gooch, op. cit., p. 17.)

[15] XVIII, pp. 356, 535; see also Herder's letter to F. Jacobi (11 November 1792), H. Dünther, *Aus Herders Nachlaß*, Frankfurt a. M., 1856, vol. II, p. 301.

[16] For an interesting study of these administrative theories see Geraint Parry, 'Enlightened Government and its Critics in Eighteenth-century Germany', *The Historical Journal*, vol. VI, 2 (1963), pp. 178–92.

[17] Ralph Flenley, *Modern German History*, London, 1953, p. 80.

Germany had no single dominant cultural and intellectual centre any more than it possessed a political capital.[18]

Whilst the English and French brand of the Enlightenment inclined towards a more positivist, empirical and utilitarian attitude, the leaders of the German Enlightenment continued to build on the natural law tradition of Pufendorf and Thomasius and on the rationalist philosophy of Leibniz.

Sir Ernest Barker has drawn attention to the close relationship that existed between the writers on Natural Law and the philosophers during the seventeenth and eighteenth century. He attributed this circumstance to the predominantly academic nature of most speculation on Natural Law, moving in the field of thought rather than in that of political action. 'Just as the writers of Natural Law go to the philosophers for their principles', he wrote, 'so the philosophers have recourse to Natural Law for their political terminology and many of their political ideas.'[19] Barker mentions Hobbes and Spinoza, Locke and Rousseau, Leibniz and Wolff to illustrate this point. It is an important point. It suggests strongly that the much abused 'eclecticism' of the Enlightenment was much more the result of an organic development, of a continual process of cross-fertilization of ideas and method, than the outcome of sheer mechanical fusion.

What is more, it was this combination of juristic and critical thinking which constituted a major and decisive challenge to much that hitherto had been accepted or simply taken for granted. The most outstanding representative of this new critical temper of thought in Germany was Christian Thomasius.[20] However more profoundly Leibniz was to determine the intellectual orientation of the German Enlightenment, it was to Thomasius that it owed its very existence from the outset.[21]

[18] Goethe said to Eckermann in 1830: 'Paris is France. All the main interests of that great country are concentrated in the capital. . . . It is quite different here in Germany. We have no city, we have not even a region of which one could say: "Here is Germany!" If we put the question in Vienna, we should get the reply: "Here is Austria!" If we asked it in Berlin, the reply would be: "Here is Prussia!" ' (Quoted by Fauchier-Magnan, op. cit., p. 23.)

[19] Ernest Barker, *O. Gierke's Natural Law and the Theory of Society*, Cambridge, 1934. (Introduction), p. xlii.

[20] Herder made many appreciative references to Thomasius throughout his works. See, for example, V, 413; VIII, 234; IX, 425; XIV, 323; XVI, 594; XVII, 205, 274; XVIII, 128; and XXIII, 70, 466, 493.

[21] Fritz Brüggemann calls Thomasius the 'father of the *Aufklärung*'. See his *Das Weltbild der deutschen Aufklärung*, Leipzig, 1930, p. 17, and his *Aus der Frühzeit der deutschen Aufklärung*, Leipzig, second edition, 1938, p. 5. See also Paul Hazard, *The European Mind*,

Free enquiry was his first demand. The search for truth must not be restricted by reverence for authority or by established beliefs and prejudice.

Challenge prejudice as the prime source of all errors and mistakes. Never rely in the discovery of truth upon the authority of any one person, whosoever he may be, if you yourself lack the inner conviction that what has hitherto been generally believed is founded upon principles of undoubted validity.[22]

Do not, therefore, Thomasius insists, trust authority; do not accept uncritically the words of your superiors, not even those of your parents and teachers. For no one is infallible except God. You must seek the sanction for your beliefs within you and not place reliance on external authority.[23]

The individual mind must be free to accept or reject ideas irrespective of their source or sanction; it must be free to follow its own light, its own reason. Even theology must accept the challenge of free enquiry in the light of human reason: 'The mysteries of God do indeed surpass the human understanding, but they are not incompatible with it.'[24]

Thomasius's second main aspiration was to break down the barriers that separated the world of learning from practical everyday life. Learning, he maintained, must serve the needs of society; it must become associated with all sections of the community, even with women, and cease to be regarded as the exclusive property of a distinct profession. Above all, no one should deem himself educated if he cannot succeed in putting his education to some practical use.[25] The universities, Thomasius argued, must turn out men who will make their mark 'in *vita civili*'.[26] To this end Thomasius put forward some radical proposals for the reform of the universities.[27] He also decided, against accepted academic custom, to use German instead of Latin in most of his writings and lectures, thus removing the last vestige of medieval scholasticism. He justified his decision in those words: 'Everybody uses his mother-tongue. After all, the Greek philosophers did not write in Hebrew, nor did the Roman philosophers write in Greek.'[28]

---

trans. by J. Lewis May, London, 1953, p. 176. Hazard sees in Thomasius the 'glorious inaugurator of the German *Aufklärung*', the 'hero in the great struggle for enlightenment'.

[22] Christian Thomasius, *Außübung der Vernunfft-Lehre*, Halle, 1705, p. 16.

[23] Thomasius, ibid., p. 50; for the passage as a whole, see ibid., pp. 43–50.

[24] Thomasius, *Einleitung zu der Vernunfft-Lehre*, Halle, 1691, p. 82.

[25] ibid., pp. 84–8.   [26] ibid., 'Vorrede', p. 2.

[27] Thomasius, *Historie der Weiszheit und Thorheit*, Halle, 1693, pp. 1–59. In particular he urges the teaching of Economics as a separate discipline.

[28] Thomasius, *Einleitung zu der Vernunfft-Lehre*, op. cit., 'Vorrede', pp. 13, 16.

Undoubtedly his decision to use German helped his ideas to gain wider currency. But the chief reason for his success in disseminating a spirit of intellectual adventure and in arousing a greater interest in current affairs lay in the man himself. For Thomasius was first and foremost an 'intrepid man of action'.[29] To use his pen as a weapon in the battle for social and legal reforms was to him a self-evident civic duty. With complete disregard for his personal prestige and safety, Thomasius attacked common beliefs and prejudices and criticized established legal practices. In the name of 'common sense' he pleaded for religious tolerance and for a more humane and enlightened attitude towards legal offenders. His chief campaign was against witch trials and the use of torture.[30]

His efforts were not in vain. In 1728, the year of his death, Prussia witnessed the last witch trial, and just over a decade later Frederick the Great, publicly acknowledging Thomasius's services to the cause of Enlightenment,[31] abolished the practice of torture.

No less impressive was his achievement as a university professor. Within a decade of his teaching, Halle rose to become one of the leading German universities, renowned for its legal faculty, a circumstance of some relevance to the political development of Prussia.[32] For it was mainly from Halle that the Prussian administration drew its recruits in those decisive years of transition from the semi-feudal Estates to enlightened absolutism.[33]

Thomasius anticipated in several important respects the direction which subsequent thinking on Natural Law was to assume. Whilst he upheld most of the principles of Grotius and Pufendorf, his immediate forerunners, he broke the link which they still tried to maintain between natural law and divine law, by insisting on the complete autonomy of the former.[34] Following Hobbes, Thomasius demanded the supremacy of secular over ecclesiastical law in all matters affecting the external relations of citizens within the State. Whilst the 'inner peace' of the

---

[29] Max Fleischmann, *Christian Thomasius, Leben und Lebenswerk*, Halle, 1931, p. 48.

[30] Thomasius, *Ernsthaffte, aber doch Muntere und Vernünfftige Thomasische Gedancken und Erinnerungen über allerhand auserlesene Juristische Händel*, Halle, 1720–1, 4 vols.; see particularly vol. I, 105–18 (on superstition and libel), 125 ff. (on torture), 223–5 (on suspecting Jews of ritual murder), and 197–206; as also vol. II, 300–39 and vol. III, 221–33 (on witch trials).

[31] *Oeuvres de Frederic II*, Berlin, 1789, vol. I, p. 376.

[32] Dernburg, *Thomasius und die Stiftung der Universität Halle*, Halle, 1865, p. 4. (Cited by Fleischmann, op. cit., p. 39.)

[33] Schmoller, 'Preußischer Beamtenstand unter Friedrich Wilhelm I', *Preußische Jahrbücher*, vol. 26 (1870), p. 148 f. (Cited by Fleischmann, op. cit., p. 124.)

[34] Thomasius, *Institutiones Iurisprudentiae Divinae*, Halle, 1694, lib. I, cap. 4, § 22, and lib. I, cap. 3, § 5.

individual was legitimately his own concern, regarding which he may or may not wish to seek the guidance of theologians, his 'outer peace' was the responsibility, and the sole responsibility, of a body specifically instituted for that purpose and subject to no other law than that which common sense recognized as a valid precept for the ordering of social relations.[35] Thomasius's stress upon a more empirical approach to Natural Law (which owed much—as he readily acknowledged—to his reading of Locke), also marked a significant departure from the prevalent Rationalist conception, and heralded the increasingly positivist and historical-minded approach to law and politics of men such as Möser, Schlözer, Herder and the Romanticists.

In so far as the eighteenth century can be said to have given the most vigorous expression to the twin objectives of the preceding Humanist tradition, namely the secularization of knowledge and the recognition of the primacy of the individual, Thomasius can in a sense be regarded in Germany as the living link between the Renaissance and the Enlightenment. His work, moreover, demonstrated the feasibility of effecting a synthesis between ideas from diverse intellectual disciplines such as philosophy, law, and politics, and thereby lent point to the intellectual endeavour of the *Aufklärung* to maintain the unity of knowledge.

Yet the danger of missing the unifying element, of failing to effect the fusion, of being forced instead to make do with a mere mechanical piecing together, was ever present, none the less. That it was averted, that the fusion, in fact, came to embody a creative organic synthesis, pregnant with ideas transcending even the confines of the Enlightenment, was due chiefly to one man: Gottfried Wilhelm Leibniz. Even if the wider implications of his intellectual contribution were barely realized at first, his philosophy nevertheless succeeded in steering the course of thinking in a direction in which it had only been groping so far.

Though rooted in the heritage of Descartes and Spinoza, Leibniz's metaphysics differs from both. In place of Descartes's dualism and Spinoza's monism, Leibniz postulates pluralism or multiplicity. This multiplicity is said to be inherent in the monads, each of which is different, and is due to the monad's constantly changing state. There is, Leibniz suggests, a constant 'becoming', a ceaseless development of inner forces or energies, an uninterrupted continuity. Every present state of the monad is naturally resulting from its preceding state, so that

---

[35] Thomasius, *Der Politische Philosophus*, Frankfurt and Leipzig, 1724 (*Vorrede*). See also *Institutiones Iurisprudentiae Divinae*, op. cit., lib. II, cap. 2, § 7, and *Versuch vom Wesen des Geistes*, Halle, 1699, p. 8.

its present is big with its future.[36] In his posthumously published *New Essays Concerning Human Understanding* (1765), Leibniz speaks of *petites perceptions*, meaning by these unconscious perceptions and obscure intimations and sensations, which he distinguishes from those which are both clear and distinct, to which he applies the term 'apperceptions', retaining here Descartes's terminology, though applying it in a modified form. Leibniz hints here at a view of psychological experience which goes beyond the Rationalist outlook of his age. Similarly his conception of nature only acquires a fuller understanding towards the end of the *Aufklärung*. Whilst Descartes, Hobbes and Spinoza, in their different ways, had developed a strictly mechanical interpretation of nature, Leibniz, by substituting the monad for the atom, gave birth to an organic conception of the universe in which it is no longer regarded as the sum of its parts but as a whole unfolding its multiple aspects, where the parts are not merely constituent elements but individual entities existing in their own right. The relevance of this conception to Herder's own concept of Organism is undeniable, as will be evident from the next chapter. Similarly, Leibniz's interpretation of history as a continuous process of development, energized by human striving, the evaluation of which entails considerations of motivating purposes projecting into the future as much as investigations into external antecedents, profoundly affected Herder's historical thinking.

It is not surprising that Leibniz is commonly acknowledged as the founder of modern German philosophy, nor really that Herder speaks of him as 'the greatest man Germany ever possessed',[37] bearing in mind the wealth and versatility of his ideas and discoveries both within and beyond the field of philosophy. Indeed, it may be true to say that his total achievement cannot be adequately appraised even now. Yet few could better the words in which Ernst Cassirer sums up Leibniz's creative synthesis of the intellectual antecedents of the Enlightenment with his own philosophy.

The classical Cartesian form of analysis and the new form of philosophical synthesis which originates in Leibniz are now integrated. From the logic of 'clear and distinct ideas' the way leads to the logic of 'origin' and to the logic of individuality; it leads from mere geometry to a dynamic philosophy of nature, from mechanism to organism, from the principle of identity to that of infinity, from continuity to harmony.[38]

---

[36] Leibniz, *Monadology*, §§ 15, 22. Leibniz describes the monads thus: 'they have no openings (windows) through which anything could either enter or depart' (§ 7). 'No monad is exactly like any other; no two things are perfectly homogeneous in nature' (§ 9).

[37] XXX, 135.

[38] Ernst Cassirer, *Die Philosophie der Aufklärung*, Tübingen, 1932, pp. 46–7 (pp. 35–6 in

That the ideas of reason and 'reasonableness' gained so strong a hold over the minds of educated people in Germany was, after Thomasius and Leibniz, partly due to the increasing influence of Deistic thought (mainly from England), but chiefly it was the result of the teaching of Christian Wolff.

Like Thomasius, Wolff chose to write his most important works in German, reaching thus a wider reading public, to which he set himself to transmit what he considered to be the main principles of Leibniz's philosophy. He has, for that reason, commonly been described as Leibniz's 'popularizer'. This has tended to detract from Wolff's own intellectual contribution. Though his philosophical ideas owed much to Leibniz, the method that he adopted in his philosophical, legal, and political works was very much his own.

Wolff held that by modifying some of Leibniz's philosophical tenets he could evolve a coherent system which would embrace all knowledge on the basis of 'sufficient reason'. It was his aim to show that although all empirical facts could not be reduced to formal logic, they were nevertheless subject to rational principles. Thus he held that man's moral conduct, for example, was solely determined by his rational cognition of good and evil. This rational cognition consisted essentially, Wolff argued, in man's capacity to know the extent to which he was capable of augmenting happiness in this world.[39] It must be noted, however, that in Wolff's ethics 'happiness' was not the end, but rather the natural by-product of moral conduct. It was this feature which distinguished ethical thought of the earlier from the later phase of the German Enlightenment. Gottsched, for example, who was one of the first of Wolff's followers to spread Wolffian ideas at Leipzig, declared that since the desire for happiness was innate in man, all speculation and philosophy must chiefly concern itself with its promotion.[40] Philosophy must become, as it were, a prescription for the attainment of happiness. It was Gottsched, therefore, rather than Wolff, who gave

---

the English translation). See also, for a more detailed and extremely penetrating analysis of Leibniz's philosophy, Cassirer's *Leibniz' System in seinen wissenschaftlichen Grundlagen*, Marburg, 1902.

[39] Christian Wolff, *Vernünfftige Gedancken von der Menschen Thun und Lassen*, Halle, 1720, part I, ch. 1.

[40] It was largely as a result of J. C. Gottsched's *Erste Gründe der Weltweisheit*, Leipzig, 1733-4, that Wolff's philosophy became widely known. Eight editions appeared in German apart from translations in French, Danish and Polish. Carl Philipp Moritz's autobiography *Anton Reiser* (1785) vividly illustrates the impact of Gottsched's work on his contemporaries. (C.Ph. Moritz, *Anton Reiser*, trans. by P. E. Matheson, London, 1926, pp. 224 ff.)

the German Enlightenment its eudaemonist character and its optimistic faith in human perfectibility.

But this emergent belief in man's capacity to augment his worldly happiness by no means sought to replace or invalidate his religious convictions. Indeed, it is the hallmark of the German Enlightenment that it strove to deepen man's religious faith by a thorough re-appraisal of the origin and nature of religion as such. A failure to realize this point may lead to an utter misconception of the *Aufklärung* in its diverse manifestations. For whilst undoubtedly one of its manifestations was the affirmation of the right to doubt established truths, including those that derived their sanction from religious orthodoxy, this affirmation was not the expression of religious hostility or the outcome of sceptical dis-belief. Once this is recognized, it no longer seems paradoxical that some of the most passionately religious thinkers of the era were engaged in the quest for a religious re-orientation.

The process of religious re-orientation assumed various forms in eighteenth-century Germany involving much acrimonious polemic. It never quite reached, however, the degree of bitterness that it attained in France, perhaps because the Leibnizian notion of 'harmony' was never entirely abandoned. The philosophical origins of the religious re-thinking could be traced chiefly to the Wolffian system, whilst on the practical side it was characterized by its stress on 'activity' rather than mere receptivity, in accordance with the teachings of Pietist leaders such as P. J. Spener and A. H. Francke.

Wolff did not oppose revelation to reason. Both, he maintained, had their proper function in religious belief. But revelation, he insisted, must not contain logical contradictions; it must be clearly distinguished from mere imagination and dissociated from false pretence. In so far as it was miraculous, it was contrary to contingent truth (i.e. to truth of fact), but not to necessary truth. Wolff was here aiming at a compromise with orthodox theology. That did not, however, save him from being violently attacked by his theological adversaries at Halle. They still considered his rationalism too dangerous and eventually forced him to leave Halle.

The persecution of Wolff helped, however, more than it harmed the propagation of his views and those of his more radical followers, such as Semler, Spalding and Jerusalem, who, though also retaining the concept of revelation, subjected it to a still more rigorous rational examination. All those aspects of theological dogma which could not be logically comprehended were dismissed as later accretions to the original faith. Recourse was also increasingly had to experience. 'My experience is my proof,' exclaimed Jerusalem.[41] The appeal to individual, subjective judgment, to 'conscience' as the final arbiter of true religion, brought these writers quite close to the ideas of English deism, the basic aim of which, in spite of the variety of individual presentations, was to banish 'Mysteries, Miracles and Secrets' from religion.[42] 'What is revealed in Religion, as it is most useful and necessary, so it must and may be as easily comprehended, and found as consistent with our common Notions, as what we know of Wood or Stone, of Air, or Water or the like.'[43]

At a time when English deism was gradually being replaced by outspoken scepticism, it became a dominating influence in Germany.[44] Spalding translated Shaftesbury's writings in 1745, Bergmann Bolingbroke's in 1758, and Resewitz translated Hume's *Natural History of Religion* in 1768. Locke, who was regarded as the philosophical leader of the deistic movement, enjoyed high admiration among writers such as Baumgarten, Semler, Ernesti and Michaelis. The support of Frederick II, too, did much to further the cause of deism in Germany.[45]

The *Aufklärer* of the Berlin circle, represented chiefly by Friedrich Nicolai, Moses Mendelssohn, G. E. Lessing, Thomas Abbt and J. J. Spalding, all shared in varying degrees Wolffian ideas, fused as they had become by now with the natural theology of the English deists. Mendelssohn was perhaps the most outspoken advocate of natural religion, finding, apparently, nothing in its principles that would run counter to Judaism as he saw it. Nicolai, though his own writings were of minor value, was nevertheless instrumental in providing a forum for the airing of these new ideas by his enterprising editorship of a number of journals. It was through a publication in one of these (*Briefe die neueste Litteratur betreffend*, 1759–65) that Herder made his entry into the world of letters. He thus came in contact, at the beginning of his literary career, with ideas which helped to colour his own religious outlook.[46]

The intellectual as also the political climate of opinion, such as it was,

---

[41] Quoted by Cassirer, *Die Philosophie der Aufklärung*, op. cit., p. 236; see also Aner, *Theologie der Lessingzeit*, Halle, 1929, for a detailed account of these neo-religious trends in Germany.

[42] John Toland, *Christianity Not Mysterious*, third edition, London, 1702, p. 79.

[43] Toland, op. cit., p. 79.

[44] G. V. Lechler, *Geschichte des Englischen Deismus*, Stuttgart and Tübingen, 1841, p. 436.

[45] Lechler, op. cit., pp. 447 ff.

[46] R. Haym, *Herder nach seinem Leben und seinen Werken*, 2 vols., Berlin, 1880, vol. I, p. 280.

owed much to the literary activities of the Berlin *Aufklärer*. They demonstrated to their countrymen the value of discussion, driving home the lesson that a free exchange of opinion required mutual respect and tolerance. The correspondence *Concerning the Destiny of Man* (*Ueber die Bestimmung des Menschen*) between Spalding, Mendelssohn and Abbt was widely read and had to be reprinted four times.[47] The attitude of these writers epitomized not only the critical element which is usually associated with the Enlightenment, but also its positive, nay, missionary character. One, perhaps the greatest of them all, was Gotthold Ephraim Lessing; an unfettered spirit if ever there was one; a great critic and, in his own way, a firm believer. But 'religion' means different things to different people at different times. This much is evident from his *Education of the Human Race* (Die Erziehung des Menschengeschlechts) (1780), an analysis of the religious development of mankind. Lessing's work, however, was more than an historical treatise on comparative religion. And the 'more' was nothing short of a *credo*, of an almost messianic faith in the power of education to effect a transformation of society in which there will be no social barriers and in which men will strive towards the attainment of the highest level of morality of which they are capable. Lessing's message found an echo in Herder's own faith in 'education' and in many a reformer's creed ever since.

The starting point with Lessing—as a true representative of Enlightenment thought—was the individual. To help the individual to attain the highest possible realization of his potentialities was the primary function of education, though Lessing recognized that 'education as such cannot give man anything which it is not in him to become; it only gives it to him more speedily and with greater ease.'[48] Education, moreover, must have a conscious goal to aim at, 'a goal towards which to strive and this applies to mankind no less than to the single individual.'[49] Lessing saw in moral striving, in moral 'becoming', as he put it, the essence of all education. Man could only be truly himself by consciously realizing his humanity. *Humanität*, then, was the goal of education, the true aim of enlightenment. This implied, however, Lessing maintained, the cultivation of a rational conviction that such a goal was eventually attainable. For only if man felt convinced of the possibility of its realization would he cease to weigh up the purely

---

[47] Robert T. Clark Jr., *Herder*, Berkeley and Los Angeles, 1955, p. 25.
[48] G. E. Lessing, *Die Erziehung des Menschengeschlechts*, § 4. (*Gesammelte Werke*, ed. by Paul Rilla, Berlin, 1956, vol. VIII, p. 591.)
[49] Lessing, op. cit., § 82 (*Werke*, op. cit., p. 611).

immediate advantages of his actions and would do good for its own sake.[50] The idea that 'humanity' was not a state into which man was born but rather a *task* demanding fulfilment by the conscious development of his potentialities, whilst inherent already in Wolff's philosophy, received here its most eloquent expression. It was this conception which dominated henceforth the *Humanität* philosophy of all subsequent writers from Herder and Goethe to Humboldt and Fichte.

Though the Wolffian interpretation of nature, religion, and morals was the main current of thought in the philosophy of the German Enlightenment, by the middle of the century it found itself confronted, if not already permeated, by a parallel ethico-religious movement that drew its chief inspiration from Pietist sources. J. G. Hamann, F. G. Klopstock, J. K. Lavater, Matthias Claudius and Friedrich Jacobi were, in their different ways, the chief exponents of this emotional and frequently mystical religiosity. And yet, whilst these men were decidedly at variance with their Rationalist rivals, rejecting the superior claims of reason in favour of the primacy of the human heart, they fully shared the rationalists' subjective conception of religion. This common agreement about the intrinsic worth of the individual judgment, implying as it did the rejection of external authority as the ultimate sanction in religious and moral questions, was a significant factor, the import of which was not confined for long to ethico-religious thought. 'The challenge to tradition', as G. P. Gooch put it, 'could not draw rein at the frontiers of religion; and, though the theological rebels lacked interest in politics, the habit of questioning authority and seeking grounds for beliefs spread through the educated *bourgeoisie* and encouraged it to bring secular ideas and institutions before the tribunal of the individual judgment.'[51]

It took some time, however, before the critical spirit of the *Aufklärung* turned its attention towards political questions. The transition towards a more specifically political awareness derived, if not its original impetus, at least its accelerating momentum, from primarily foreign sources. Three names stand out particularly: Shaftesbury, Rousseau, and Montesquieu.

In the dawn of the eighteenth century there were few writers whose works enjoyed a wider reading public than those of the third Earl of Shaftesbury. His *Characteristicks* ran to no fewer than five editions

---

[50] Lessing, op. cit., § 85 (*Werke*, op. cit., p. 612).
[51] G. P. Gooch, op. cit., p. 20.

within just over twenty years.[52] Moreover, his writings had an immediate European impact. 'He profoundly influenced the best brains of our age', Herder wrote towards the end of the century.[53] A more recent writer, describing Shaftesbury's influence in Germany, put it thus: 'Shaftesbury's apostrophes to nature exerted a decisive influence; they gave expression to those fundamental forces which shaped the philosophy of nature of Herder and the young Goethe.'[54] That this was the case was undoubtedly due to the emotional gap left by the predominantly Rationalist temper of mind that prevailed in early eighteenth-century Germany. Shaftesbury's *Gefühlsphilosophie* satisfied a long-felt emotional need.

The greater part of Shaftesbury's works consisted of letters, dialogues, reflexions and similar literary fragments, which he later (1711) published in collected form in three volumes under the title of *Characteristicks of Men, Manners, Opinions, Times*. Shaftesbury was critical of both Cartesian rationalism and Hobbesian utilitarianism. He defended the importance of spontaneous impulses and stressed the primacy of feeling in opposition to discursive reason. In particular he voiced sharp disagreement with Hobbes's psychological assumptions about human nature; man's social instinct, he argued, was just as natural as his sexual impulse; hence, he concluded, it was a mistake to oppose the state of nature to the state of society.[55] His emphasis on inner feelings, on the need for an internal sanction for morality, and primarily his belief in human goodness and in the natural harmony between self-interest and benevolence, helped to provide the psychological presuppositions for the eighteenth-century faith in progress and human perfectibility.

Next to Shaftesbury, no single writer so dominated the German intellectual scene as J. J. Rousseau. His ideas invaded all fields of cultural endeavour. The intensity and manysidedness of this impact were not, however, solely the work of his 'genius'. Rousseau's insistence on the pre-eminence of feeling was not a novel idea to the Pietists, nor to men like Mendelssohn and J. G. Sulzer who, in their investigations

---

[52] See Irvin Clifton Hatch, 'Der Einfluß Shaftesburys auf Herder', *Studien zur vergleichenden Literaturgeschichte*, ed. by Max Koch, Berlin, 1901, p. 78.

[53] XVII, 158.

[54] E. Cassirer, *Die Philosophie der Aufklärung*, op. cit., pp. 113–14; see also Cassirer, *The Platonic Renaissance in England*, trans. by James P. Pettergrove, London, 1953, pp. 198–9. Shaftesbury's concept of 'disinterested pleasure', together with his other concept of 'inward form', laid, in Cassirer's view, the foundation of eighteenth-century German aesthetics. (See ibid., pp. 186–96.)

[55] Shaftesbury, *Characteristicks of Men, Manners, Opinions, Times*, third edition, London, 1723, vol. II, p. 319.

into aesthetic experience, had enthusiastically welcomed the *Gefühls-philosophie* of Shaftesbury. Rousseau's religious ideas, too, contained little that was new. The 'natural theology' which he advocated had for some time been the subject of reviews and articles in learned journals in Germany.[56] In political theory, however, Rousseau broke new ground although here, too, it has been suggested that the soil had not been entirely unprepared.[57] But what primarily distinguished Rousseau from all that went before, was his vision, which transcended formal political principles. This vision combined a moral and social message with a new concept of education. It was this combination which fired the imagination of the young intelligentsia. Romanticism drew its initial propulsion from this source. It led to a search for the original force and simplicity of 'nature', for spontaneity, and found expression in an emotional fermentation, the *Sturm und Drang*, through which many of the literary figures of Herder's day were passing.[58] Herder himself played a vital rôle in this stage of the Enlightenment, a fact which has earned him the title of 'German Rousseau'.[59] This description, however, is apt to mislead, if it is not suitably qualified. For Herder, though he fully acknowledged the inspiration which he derived from Rousseau, especially during his studies under Kant,[60] never hesitated to question some of the most basic assumptions of Rousseau's social philosophy, as will be shown in subsequent chapters.

In an age of despotism—albeit occasionally more enlightened and

[56] See Hans M. Wolff, 'Der junge Herder und die Entwicklungsidee Rousseaus', *Publications of the Modern Language Association of America*, vol. LVII (1942), pp. 753–819.

[57] Ernest Barker, op. cit., Introduction, vol. I, p. xliv, and ibid., Gierke's text, pp. 74, 75.

[58] See Roy Pascal, *The German Sturm und Drang*, Manchester, 1953, especially chapters 1 and 2. The history of the *Sturm und Drang* movement and that of the Göttinger *Hainbund* in particular undoubtedly bear witness to a growing social and national consciousness among the young intellectuals of Germany. Most of them vigorously revolted against foreign influences in art and literature and against the social conventions of their times. But one must guard against reading too much political content into their literary efforts. For, whilst it is evident enough what these young poets were fighting against, it is less obvious what they were fighting for. To take two outstanding examples: Goethe's 'Götz' and Schiller's '*Die Räuber*': both were products of the *Sturm und Drang*, yet at the same time they contradicted the 'creed' of the 'movement'. Although they rebel against princely immorality and social artificiality, they also condemn their heroes' revolutionary methods of combating these social evils. Even the more outspoken 'social revolutionaries', such as Schubart, Bürger, Lenz and Klinger did not so much as hint at a new political order, and even their interest in social reforms was frequently short-lived. This almost complete absence of a coherent social philosophy or political ideology was not, however, chiefly attributable to personal characteristics of the writers concerned. It was rather a reflection of the social and political conditions in eighteenth-century Germany.

[59] See H. A. Korff, *Geist der Goethezeit*, Leipzig, 1923, vol. I, p. 74; and A. Gillies, *Herder*, Oxford, 1945, pp. 53–4.

[60] See Haym, op. cit., vol. I, p. 48.

liberal than one might assume[61]—the problem of controlling the controllers had decidedly become the most pressing issue demanding attention. The greatness of Montesquieu's *L'Esprit des lois* (1748) lay in attempting to deal with this very problem. It had other merits, but it was above all its timeliness which made it *the* political classic of the century. Montesquieu's emphasis on moderation—'political liberty is to be found only in moderate governments'[62]—eminently appealed to many a German intellectual who, like Montesquieu himself, saw in the British Constitution the ideal pattern of gradual and peaceful political development. Even the most sanguine harangues hurled against despotism by some of the poets and dramatists were aimed not so much at the abolition of dynastic rule as at its reform, its purging from the more flagrant excesses. Another reason for Montesquieu's popularity was the vogue which the classics enjoyed. For Montesquieu—no less than Rousseau—in his desire to extol the virtues of republican Greece and Rome drew heavily from classical sources.[63]

However, it was not until the outbreak of the American War of Independence had aroused a more widespread interest in political questions, that the full impact of the ideas of Rousseau and Montesquieu (as also of Helvetius, Holbach and D'Alembert—though to a lesser degree) made itself felt on German political thought. By that time the influx of political ideas from England and Scotland, in particular those of Burke, Hume, Adam Smith, and the Scottish Historical School (Ferguson, Robertson, and Millar) also helped to colour political speculations. In this respect the young university of Göttingen played a significant rôle.[64]

Throughout the first decades of the eighteenth century German political writers aroused little general interest. They were, as a rule, university professors, such as Gasser (1676–1745) and Dithmar (1678–1737), or professional administrators, such as Hornigke (1638–1712) and F. K. Moser (1723–98), or both, such as Seckendorff (1626–92) and Justi (1720–71). They were interested in methods of administration and in questions of public finance rather than in political philosophy, possibly because they felt it more prudent to

[61] Herder's own relationship to his princely employers bears this out. The affair over the candidate Stockes is of interest in this connection. (See XXXI, 741 ff.)

[62] Montesquieu, *De l'esprit des lois*, XI. 4, quoted from the translation by Franz Neumann, New York, 1949, p. 150.

[63] See Kingsley Martin, *French Liberal Thought in the Eighteenth Century*, second edition, London, 1954, p. 147.

[64] See G. v. Selle, op. cit., p. 190; and Roy Pascal, 'Herder and the Scottish Historical School', *English Goethe Society*, vol. XIV (1939), pp. 25 ff.

confine themselves to means rather than ends under the conditions of
absolutist régimes. But they were not mere apologists of absolutist rule,
attempting to provide a rationale for the political *status quo*, as Gierke
has suggested.[65] Nor were their administrative theories entirely devoid
of philosophical content. The conception underlying most of their
theories was an essentially mechanistic and manipulative one. Government was seen as an administrative machine, geared to achieve limited
and clearly defined ends. The 'Cameralists', as these writers came to be
known, favoured highly centralized absolutism because it afforded, in
their view, the best chance of constructing a scientific apparatus of
government without the risk of interference by the non-professional
outsider. They adopted Pufendorf's theory of absolute sovereignty,
but they ignored—as Gierke correctly observed[66]—its underlying
assumption of popular consent precisely because 'popular consent'
appeared to them as a threat to their scientific system. At the same time
they were convinced that a well-constructed bureaucratic organization,
operating within a framework of fixed rules, could not but further the
well-being of the subjects. A number of them also believed that by
perfecting the administrative machine as a system of strictly specialized
functions they were minimizing the risk of arbitrariness due to personal
forces, and thus ensuring fair and impersonal government.

Whilst it would be going too far to say that these writers were thinking of the administrative apparatus as a device for restraining the
absolute power of the ruler—for usually the ruler was envisaged as a
power outside and above the governmental 'machine'—they were
certainly far more interested in strengthening the power of the
bureaucracy than in buttressing the position of the monarch. Their
monolithic and mechanistic conception of government was undoubtedly
inadequate as a political theory in that it failed to take account of the
complexity and manysidedness of social and political life. But in their
emphasis upon administrative organization the Cameralists correctly
foresaw the growing rôle which bureaucracy was to play in the modern
State.

By the second half of the century, however, the principle of absolute
sovereignty itself began to be seriously questioned by German political
thinkers. Undoubtedly Christian Wolff was the most outstanding of
them, but he took good care to pursue his questioning with due
circumspection. After all, his most active teaching period was spent in
Halle, the chief training ground for the bureaucratic élite of the

---

[65] See O. Gierke, *Natural Law and the Theory of Society*, op. cit., vol. I, p. 144.
[66] ibid.

Prussian civil service at that time. Quite content, then, to leave the frontal attack against absolutism to others, he chose the medium in which he felt most at home: scientific method. If there was ground for questioning Pufendorf's principle of absolute sovereignty—as he believed there was[67]—it had best be done by establishing one's methodological credentials first. This he proceeded to do by invoking the Leibnizian antithesis between 'logically necessary truths' and 'truths of fact'. The 'necessary truths' are absolutely necessary in the sense that their opposite is held to be impossible since this would involve a contradiction. They are also axiomatic in so far as the primary ideas on which they rest cannot and need not be further defined. For the same reason they are not capable of, or contingent upon, further proof. The truths of fact, on the other hand, are contingent and their opposite is possible. With the former Wolff identified what he termed an *obligatio connata*, i.e. an innate duty, inherent in human nature and therefore, assuming human nature to be a universal constant, common to all humanity irrespective of varying empirical circumstances. According to Wolff, every right is derived from a corresponding or, more precisely, a prior duty, that is, from certain moral compulsions assumed to be inherent in every human being. These inborn obligations are contrasted with those that have been acquired or entered upon in the course of social and political developments to serve specific and changing circumstances. Such an acquired duty Wolff termed an *obligatio contracta* and classified it as a contingent 'truth of fact' in his logical system.[68] Only the contractual rights and duties are held to be amenable to political and legal adaption to suit particular circumstances. All political and legal distinctions, too, that are drawn between one subject and another belong to this category. The inborn rights and duties, on the other hand, such as the right and duty of preserving one's life, are held to be the same for all subjects and are, therefore, fundamental and inalienable.

It is important to note in this context, that Wolff interprets the concept of 'self-preservation' in terms of 'becoming' i.e. as a goal-directed activity and not in terms of mere 'being' or the avoidance of death. Self-preservation is in effect an unceasing process of human striving towards ends which are deemed to be worthy of pursuit. Thus conceived it is both a *conscious* act and a *value-pervaded* act as distinct

---

[67] Christian Wolff, *Jus Naturae Methodo Scientifica Pertractum*, Francofurti et Lipsiae, 1740-50, vol. VIII, §§ 29-36; see also his *Grundsätze des Natur- und Völkerrechts*, Halle, 1754, § 989.
[68] Wolff, *Jus Naturae*, op. cit., vol. I, §§ 17, 18.

from a purely physical propensity or an unchanging, *wert-frei* state. As a necessary condition for this value-directed activity, Wolff stipulates the existence of both security *and* liberty. Security and liberty, however, do not constitute final ends in the Wolffian conception of Natural Law, but antecedent requirements, without which man cannot become fully human; in their absence man has nothing to gain from being a member of a State. It follows that the function of the State is to provide security and liberty to enable man to give expression to what constitutes the essence of his humanity: the tendency (*habitus*) to aim at perfection in the light of worthwhile ends and the conscious effort (*conatus*) involved in realizing this tendency.[69] A State's ability to fulfil this function provides the criterion of, and determines the right to, its legitimate political authority.[70]

Wolff's argument in support of constitutional restraints merits interest not only, nor even primarily, for the methodological procedure which it employs—although it was what chiefly earned him the fame among his contemporaries—but rather for the conceptual ingenuity with which he applied the Leibnizian notion of 'becoming' to the field of politics. For by applying this notion Wolff brought back into the orbit of political discussion the problem of ends as a problem of multiple and changing values. It is here that Wolff clearly transcends the conventional limits of the Natural Law theorists and parts ways with the absolutist theories of 'mechanistic' Rationalism.

Unlike Wolff, J. J. Moser and his son F. K. Moser—two outstanding jurists and political writers of this period—did not shrink from openly challenging the misrule of the petty princes, the elder Moser in a last desperate attempt to maintain the ancient constitutional rights of the Estates, the son by drawing attention to the manifold abuses of despotic rule, the servility of public servants to the whims of the princes, and the wastefulness of their courts.[71] His contemporary, A. L. Schlözer, saw in F. K. Moser 'one of the most important of German political writers',[72] and Herder, too, commended him for his part in the struggle against the abuse of power by the petty rulers.[73] Yet Moser, although he is rightly regarded as a great patriot and 'one of the first to raise the voice of political liberty in Germany',[74] did not go beyond

[69] Wolff, *Jus Naturae*, op. cit., vol. I, §§ 17, 18, 26, 29, 31, 81, 85, 94; see also his *Institutiones Juris Naturae et Gentium*, Halae et Magdeb., 1750, §§ 74, 77, 95.

[70] Wolff, *Institutiones*, op. cit., § 106.

[71] F. K. Moser's *Der Herr und der Diener*, Frankfurt, 1759, of which ten thousand copies were sold when it was published, was undoubtedly the most widely known political treatise in Germany at that time.

[72] A. L. Schlözer, *Stats Gelartheit*, Göttingen, 1793, p. 173.

[73] XVIII, 258.   [74] G. P. Gooch, op. cit., p. 24.

advocating a better education of the princes as the main political remedy.

It was Nettelbladt at Halle, and Achenwall and A. L. Schlözer at Göttingen, who adopted and further expanded the constitutional theories of Christian Wolff.[75] Of these Schlözer was undoubtedly the most outstanding. His influence upon contemporary political thought was truly immense. His Journal, the *Stats Anzeigen* (*sic*), had a circulation of 4,000 copies, an astonishing figure for those days. Never before had a paper enjoyed so great a publicity. It was an achievement that remained unsurpassed for many decades to come. Hermann Wesendonck, writing nearly a century later, had this to say about Schlözer's feat:

Schlözer brought the standard of publicity to a level such as the German Press had not been able to attain again, even in our own days. No wonder, therefore, that Schlözer appeared to his contemporaries in the sphere of politics what Luther had been in the religious field. He lit the torch of political enlightenment in Germany by facilitating the expression of freer opinions, by uncovering appalling conditions in their stark nakedness, but chiefly by arousing and nurturing a sense of civic spirit.[76]

It was Schlözer's ambition to develop in Germany an interest in public life, to foster the creation of 'public opinion' so as to make it an effective guardian of justice and fair-dealing. There was no ill, he believed, that public opinion could not cure. He opened his Journal to all who, he thought, had a legitimate grievance to air 'provided it was supported by detailed evidence'.[77] He himself wrote little; 'twenty-two twenty-thirds (of what was written) is not written by myself', he pointed out in the *Stats Anzeigen* in 1783.[78]

Schlözer abhorred both absolutism and revolutions and favoured reforms on educational and constitutional lines. 'We ought to preach it from the roof-tops', he wrote, 'that the ruler is instituted for the benefit of the people and not vice versa; he is, as a ruler, the creation

---

[75] D. Nettelbladt (1719–91), professor of law at Halle and one of the outstanding German jurists of the second half of the century. He was a pupil of Wolff at Marburg and followed him to Halle later. G. Achenwall (1719–72) was also a professor of law, but like the publicist, political scientist and historian A. L. Schlözer (1735–1809), taught at Göttingen.

[76] Hermann Wesendonck, *Die Begründung der neueren Geschichtsschreibung durch Gatterer und Schlözer*, Leipzig, 1876, pp. 118–19.

[77] A. L. Schlözer, *Stats Anzeigen*, Göttingen, 1786, vol. IX, p. 294.

[78] A. L. Schlözer, ibid., Göttingen, 1783, vol. V, p. 516. Schlözer would probably hardly have achieved what in fact he did, had he been situated at any German university other than Göttingen. For here the professors enjoyed complete freedom from censorship, a privilege unknown in the rest of Germany. The close association of Hanover with England was undoubtedly an important political factor; as a result of this association Germans for the first time learned to experience the concrete meaning of political freedom.

of the people, and not of the Almighty; hence he owes to his people *comptes rendus*, and that before the Day of Judgment. All citizens of a state, the professor, the landowner, the peasant, must carry equal burdens since they all enjoy the same protection. I say, let us preach this loudly and we need fear no revolutions.'[79] His ideal was that of constitutional monarchy headed by an enlightened ruler. Like F. K. Moser, Schlözer cherished the hope of a resuscitated German Empire headed by a 'good king such as Frederick II (of Prussia) or Joseph II (of Austria)'.[80]

Yet, for all his courageous work in disseminating his and other people's ideas of reform, it must be admitted that Schlözer's views hardly ever transcended the level of contemporary political thinking. Though he detested absolutism as 'degrading to mankind',[81] he never went so far as to suggest ways and means whereby political power could be effectively diffused. Indeed one cannot help wondering whether Schlözer really came to grips with the problem of constitutional or representative government as a method of exercising political power. Neither the concept of popular sovereignty nor the concept of *Volk* appears to have been of much interest to him, if by *Volk* one means the political community of a nation and not merely the aggregate of subjects as distinct from the ruler.[82] Hence, likewise, the concept of the nation state had little meaning for him. But all this does not alter the fact that Schlözer was one of the most outstanding political teachers of his time. He rightly stressed the need of political awareness as the necessary condition of political participation and the importance of the principle of accountability. He was content to do just this and he did it well.

We must make mention here of one eminent contributor to Schlözer's *Stats Anzeigen*: Justus Möser. That Möser was invited to voice his opinions in Schlözer's Journal reflects credit on Schlözer's political broadmindedness. For Möser's views were very much at variance with those of his own.[83] Möser was a lawyer and high official

---

[79] Schlözer, ibid., Göttingen, 1792, vol. XVII, p. 253.
[80] G. v. Selle, quoting Schlözer, op. cit., p. 132.
[81] A. L. Schlözer, *Stats Gelartheit*, op. cit., pp. 142–4.
[82] Schlözer regarded the concept of the 'Sovereignty of the People' as one of the most pernicious words in the vocabulary of politics. (See his *Stats Gelartheit*, op. cit., p. 157.)
[83] In this respect Schlözer differed from his great predecessor at Göttingen, the jurist J. S. Pütter (who established Göttingen's reputation for its School of Public Administration) who strongly recommended Möser's views to his readers in support of his own arguments. (See J. S. Pütter, *Handbuch der teutschen Reichshistorie*, Göttingen, 1772, p. 38; and his *Vorläufige Uebersicht des teutschen Staatsrechts*, Göttingen, 1788, p. 13.) Schlözer's senior colleague, the historian J. C. Gatterer, was already more critical towards Möser's views. (See J. C. Gatterer, *Allgemeine Historische Bibliothek*, Göttingen, 1769, vol. I, p. 74.)

in the small state and bishopric of Osnabrück and is best known as the author of the *Osnabrückische Geschichte* (1768). His political views found expression in various articles, *pièces de circonstance*, thrown off in odd moments of leisure in a life devoted to public service, and later collected and published by his daughter under the title of *Patriotische Phantasien* (1775–8).

Möser was not exactly a 'reactionary', nor was he a 'conservative' in the nineteenth-century sense of the word. On the other hand, he was certainly no 'reformer' in the Enlightenment tradition, although he carried out a number of reforms aiming at improving the position of the peasant labourer in his own State. It would not, perhaps, be incorrect to describe him as a kind of German Burke, and that, moreover, some time before Burke had decided to write his *Reflections on the Revolution in France*. Möser was thus preparing, in a sense, the ground for Burke's own influence on German political thought in the wake of the French Revolution. Care must be taken, however, not to over-estimate Möser's influence as a political writer. For as such, the immediate impact of his ideas was limited. That they eventually gained wider currency was due largely to their appeal to such men as Abbt, Goethe, Herder and the Romanticists.[84]

Möser had no time for constitutional 'schemes' and nothing but contempt for political theories; he lumped them together under the terms of 'abstract ideas' and 'general principles', 'with no experience to support them'.[85] Thus his outlook differed fundamentally from the prevailing Enlightenment view, which sought a rational pattern in social and political life in the belief that the complex world of human endeavour could be reduced to clear and universally valid concepts and postulates in order to derive from these equally simple regulative maxims for practical conduct.[86] To Möser political life was essentially an historical growth rooted in ancient customs and traditions. These, he felt, were continuously threatened by political 'rules' and 'general

[84] Goethe in particular gave prominence to Möser's views. In a letter to Möser's daughter he wrote: 'I take them (Möser's writings) wherever I go. . . . And how often do I ask myself, when writing: "what would Möser have thought or said on this or that?" ' (Cited in the Abeken edition of Möser's collected works, Berlin, 1842–3, vol. X, pp. 233, 243.) On Möser's influence, see Ernst Hempel, *Justus Mösers Wirkung auf seine Zeitgenossen*, Inaug. Dissertation, Freiburg, 1931.

[85] Justus Möser, *Werke*, op. cit., vol. II, p. 165.

[86] Möser anticipates in this important respect Herder's own departure from the *Aufklärung*, that is to say, from an age in which, as Dilthey has put it, 'discursive thought was the means whereby everything was to be comprehended and regulated'. (Wilhelm Dilthey, 'Das achtzehnte Jahrhundert und die geschichtliche Welt', *Deutsche Rundschau*, Juli 1901, p. 359.)

laws'. 'It is the general malaise of the present century', he wrote, 'that so many general laws are made and so few observed. The root cause of this malaise lies in our trying to bring too many things under One Rule. We rather deprive Nature of her wealth than agree to alter our System.'[87] Only what has endured over centuries could claim an historical and hence, in Möser's view, a legitimate *raison d'être* worthy of socio-political recognition. In having 'history' to support it, an event gains its own justification which is beyond the reach of 'rational' criticism. In the light of this theory Möser rejected as absurd Rousseau's assumption of original equality and his belief in a universally valid social contract. There was nothing in history, Möser maintained, to support such presuppositions. 'It is idle', he argued, 'to invent social contracts for imagined people whose existence is wholly abstracted by the theorists from all concrete circumstances. A society of hunters or shepherds will unite under entirely different conditions from an agrarian society.'[88]

Schlözer's ideal of a politically united German Empire under a strong but enlightened ruler held out some attraction for Möser too. At the same time, however, he viewed the prospect of a centralized State under a powerful crown with considerable misgivings. He feared that this would inevitably involve uniformity and thus tend to destroy what, he felt, was most valuable in social and political life: the peculiar customs and distinct local traditions of the diverse parts of the Empire. This danger he regarded as a far greater threat to the civic pride and native patriotism of his fellow-countrymen than the existing political divisions. Consequently, *Kleinstaaterei* seemed to him the lesser evil; it was more in accord with his political realism. Who knows, he speculated, 'particularism', pruned of its major abuses, may yet prove to be the best of all possible realities. Why should not every forest have its own particular rules, each townlet its own police system, each village its own special laws, according to local requirements and individual historical traditions? Why bring all these different entities under one general political ordinance? Why indeed, if, in order to succeed force will more likely than not have to be resorted to?[89] The possibility that political loyalties would be extracted by means of sheer physical power filled Möser with fear and anguish; it profoundly offended his political sensibilities. If, therefore, Möser supported Schlözer's campaign against petty absolutism, he did so for

[87] Justus Möser, *Werke*, op. cit., vol. II, p. 26.
[88] Möser, *Werke*, op. cit., vol. IX, p. 174.
[89] Möser, *Werke*, op. cit., vol. II, p. 25, and vol. III, p. 67.

somewhat different reasons. Möser's objection to absolutism arose from his conviction that absolutism tended to disrupt the traditional pattern of society. This traditional pattern Möser identified with a social and political framework in which the nobility found itself confronted with a socially self-confident and politically articulate middle class of property-owners, be they merchants in the towns or farmers in the countryside.

It is significant that property-ownership constituted for Möser the necessary prerequisite of every political right. A person without property had no stake in the body politic and hence could lay no claim to political participation.[90] The thought of attempting to alter the existing property structure with a view to creating greater equality was utterly alien to him. 'It is manifest violence', he exclaimed, 'if members of the lower class unite and attempt to claim the same property-rights as members of the higher class by simply declaring their common human origin.'[91] He even defended serfdom as an 'historical fact', though he deplored the excessive economic exploitation and social degradation of the serfs as being inimical to the long-term interests of the State.[92]

Möser's political ideas, which Treitschke described as 'strong and original',[93] were, it is obvious enough, rather out of tune with the prevailing tenor of thought. At a time of rational universalism and cosmopolitan *Weltbürgertum*, Justus Möser stood out as the lone fighter for traditionalism and local patriotism.[94] It is true, there were others, though not many, who sang and preached the theme of patriotism, men such as Abbt, Gleim, Klopstock and Sonnenfels, for example, but none of them conceived it in so narrow a sense as Möser, to whom the Greek city-State was the only political model worth emulating. Möser's political gospel of *Kleinstaaterei*, however, attracted few disciples. Perhaps this was so because, as a modern writer has put it, 'the patient was sick of the very particularism and traditionalism'

---

[90] Möser, *Werke*, op. cit., vol. III, pp. 291–308, and vol. V, pp. 195, 203.

[91] Möser, *Werke*, op. cit., vol. V, p. 182.

[92] Möser, *Werke*, op. cit., vol. IX, p. 241; see also ibid., p. 173.

[93] Treitschke refers to Möser as 'the only strong and original political thinker among the younger German writers'. (Heinrich v. Treitschke, *Deutsche Geschichte*, op. cit., vol. I, p. 140.)

[94] The French Revolution left him quite cold. 'The concept of the rights of man: has it not caused confusion enough in criminal law!' he commented in 1790 (*Werke*, vol. V, p. 194). Likewise, he had nothing but scorn for the prevalent cosmopolitanism: ' "Love of humanity" has become fashionable at the expense of one's local loyalties' (*Werke*, vol. II, p. 164).

which Möser exalted.[95] But partly it was no doubt also due to the circumstance that Möser, unlike Schlözer, was not a very bold and enterprising publicist. None the less, his empirical and historical approach to politics as well as his veneration for the medieval past found a resounding echo in the political and historical thinking of the subsequent century, whilst his emphasis on the organic or 'growth' element in socio-political development appreciably affected Herder's own organic conception of politics and history.

We have attempted in this chapter to survey the political scene in eighteenth-century Germany with particular reference to the social conditions and political currents of thought prevalent in Herder's lifetime. Against a general background of political apathy, one can witness the emergence of a certain degree of political consciousness, mainly as a result of the influx of foreign ideas and the impact of political events abroad, although the ground was not entirely unprepared by writers of the Natural Law School, by the Pietists, by the *Aufklärer*, and by a number of poets and dramatists.[96]

It could be objected that we have not made any mention of the political writings of one of the greatest thinkers of the century, Immanuel Kant. This omission, however, was deliberate. It is not easy to assess correctly Kant's general influence on Herder, but in the sphere of political thought it is doubtful whether Herder was at all affected by Kant's political works, most of which were not published until after the French Revolution, by which time Herder had almost completed those works that contain his chief political ideas.[97] During Herder's formative years, Kant was interested in philosophical, theological and

[95] G. P. Gooch, op. cit., p. 29.

[96] Perhaps mention should also be made of the so-called 'philanthropists' and the freemasons. In their zeal for educational reforms the philanthropists most strikingly exemplify the faith of the age in education as *the* remedy for its social and political ills. Some of them, such as Basedow, for example, were chiefly concerned with spreading the light of learning among the upper classes by concentrating their efforts on improving teaching methods in schools for the gentry. But there were others, such as Campe and Trapp, for example, who espoused also social reforms aimed at strengthening the ranks of the aristocracy of merit as distinct from that of natural birth. The freemasons, too, urged the lowering, if not the removal, of social barriers, but only too frequently the gap that separated their professed ideals from actual performance gave rise to the sort of criticism which we find voiced in Lessing's 'Ernst and Falk'.

[97] Admittedly, Herder's maxim in the *Ideen* that man, unlike the animal, did not require a master, may have been prompted by a polemical urge to reverse Kant's dictum that man was an animal that needs a lord, put forward in his Essay 'Idee zu einer allgemeinen Geschichte in weltbürgerlicher Absicht' (1784). At the same time Herder's maxim is so much in keeping with his general political philosophy that it would probably have found expression even without this 'provocation'.

mathematical rather than political questions. This is not to say, however, that Kant's philosophical writings were devoid of political implications. His definition of moral freedom and his doctrine of the autonomy of the will, in particular, were undoubtedly instrumental in helping to establish the principle of self-determination as the political *summum bonum* of nationalist doctrine. But this was evident in the nineteenth rather than the eighteenth century, as it was also in the nineteenth century that Kant's more specifically political writings, such as the *Idea for a Universal History* (1784) and his more elaborate *Thoughts on Perpetual Peace* (1795), began to affect German political thinking.[98]

In Herder's Germany we find, as yet, in spite of the emergence of a more articulate political consciousness, little evidence of a collective sense of national identity. Developments were astir, however, mainly during the period of the *Sturm und Drang*, which were to prove of some import in the unfolding of nationalist thinking. The most characteristic feature of these developments was the growing emphasis upon the German language as a medium capable and worthy of expressing man's highest achievements in art, philosophy, poetry and science in as good a fashion as the medieval Latin or the contemporary French. This 'linguistic' self-assertion which had been gathering force ever since the days of Martin Luther and Christian Thomasius was now reaching its climax, with Klopstock and Gottsched demanding the creation of an all-German Academy of the Arts and Sciences, and with Herder actually drawing up a plan in 1787 for an 'Institute of German National Enlightenment' (*Patriotisches Institut für den Allgemeingeist Deutschlands*).[99] The members of the Berlin circle, too, as also most of the universities, devoted much thought and activity towards the fostering of the German language and the engendering of a German cultural consciousness. This deliberate cultivation of the German language may also be viewed, no doubt, as a political device employed by the rising *bourgeoisie* against the 'Frenchified courtiers and nobles' composing high society.[100] But, admittedly, all these strivings towards a sense of national identity were, as yet, a far cry from the conception of nationalism that was to stir the heart of a Kossuth or Mazzini, and with which the French Revolution was to usher in a new period of

[98] See Franz Schnabel, *Deutsche Geschichte im Neunzehnten Jahrhundert*, 4 vols., second edition, Freiburg, 1948–51, vol. I, p. 188.

[99] R. Haym, op. cit., vol. II, pp. 487–8.

[100] Max v. Boehn, *Modes and Manners*, trans. by Joan Joshua, London, 1935, vol. IV (The Eighteenth Century), p. 38.

political consciousness. It was Herder who was to play a vital rôle in forging the link. For it was he who firmly established the principle that language was the most natural and hence indispensable basis of socio-political association; that language *created* a *Volk*.

In identifying the fundamental or basic unit of socio-political association with a community possessing a common language, Herder has, in the words of an American writer, 'struck the rock from which has gushed forth ever since a prolific stream of national speculation'.[101] What is more, in applying the term *Volk* to such a language community, investing it with the indestructible force of nature (*Kraft*) *and* with the political concept of *Nation*, he laid the ideological foundations of a new dogma in the dialectic of political argumentation.

[101] Carleton J. H. Hayes, 'Contribution of Herder to the doctrine of Nationalism', *American Historical Review*, vol. XXXII (No. 4, July 1927), p. 720.

II

ORGANISM: HERDER'S CONCEPTUAL FRAMEWORK

THE foregoing account makes it evident that there was as yet no agreement as to what factors should determine the territorial limits of any given State. That this question should have engaged Herder's mind is in itself not so very startling. Already as a young man Herder, feeling in himself the desire to be the equal of a Lycurgus or a Solon, resolved to make his mark in the active life of politics.[1] What, however, did prove significant and highly seminal for subsequent political theorizing was the fact that Herder's interest in politics was but an aspect of a much wider interest which encompassed not only art and literature but also a distinct cosmology and philosophy of history. For it was this close association of political, historical, poetical and religio-cosmological thinking which was to characterize the comprehensive, 'ideological' style of political thought from the Romanticists to the Marxists.

The keynote of Herder's synoptic approach to politics was the concept of organism. Herder was intent on discovering forces of social and political cohesion, in view of which he could formulate a theory of community which would decisively scotch the notion of the State as a mere artefact instituted to serve closely limited ends. Once it could be shown that lasting political associations, as distinct from transient political bodies, were products not of manufacture but of growth, once it became evident that political activity was not something conforming to set procedural rules, geared to achieve fixed and limited ends, but a natural process in history directed towards a multiplicity of ends, then, surely, theories which treated of the State as if it were a timeless and lifeless machine will be judged to be utterly out of touch with the reality of social and political life and the natural design of the universal order. This undertaking presupposed, of course, that there was such a thing as a 'natural order' in which political communities

[1] IV, 401. In this as in other important respects the diary (*Journal meiner Reise*) which Herder kept on his sea journey to France in 1769 is most revealing. (See especially IV, 353–64, 401–74.)

persisted in time as natural entities in response to intrinsic and spontaneous forces. But what warranted such a supposition? Was it not conceivable that diversity in the natural no less than in the social realm was nothing but chaos, that change was not tantamount to growth or 'development', but simply the succession of fortuitous accidents? And if this was not conceivable on grounds of introspection and/or empirical observation, what was the principle of unity in the one, and the principle of continuity in the other? To seek answers to these questions Herder regarded as the necessary prerequisite for postulating an organistic as opposed to a mechanistic theory of politics. It is the purpose of this chapter to trace the thought pattern in terms of which Herder sought to satisfy this prerequisite, and to elicit the epistemological and metaphysical assumptions on which it rested.

I. THE PROBLEM OF UNITY

Epistemological assumptions

Herder set out on his quest adopting the attitude of the 'ordinary man' who is distrustful of metaphysical abstractions and *a priori* theorems and hence tries hard to be a thoroughgoing empiricist.[2] But he came to realize before long that sense perception by itself could not furnish man with knowledge (*Erkenntnis*) of the external world. He recognized, that is, that the stuff of our experience of nature was not something coming to us direct from the external world and revealing the external world as it was, but a composite stuff, which had already in the process of becoming our experience been worked up by the conceiving mind. Experience, therefore, which Herder defined as any datum of perception which had attained to some degree of consciousness,[3] was an active function of the individual mind by which it transformed sensations in its own image. It was a creative process. Similarly, Herder came to recognize that man is so complex a creature that despite all his endeavours to single out the data of perception he is incapable of a wholly simple condition. At the moment he sees, he also hears, and imperceptibly he also absorbs from without influences which, though they largely remain obscure sensations, nevertheless incessantly take part in secretly fashioning the sum of his mental state (*Zustand*). He floats in a sea of impressions, in which each wave, touching him now more, now less perceptibly, represents a modification of his inner

[2] II, 326; VI, 83, 183; VIII, 267; IX, 413.   [3] XV, 525.

condition through the *stimuli* of his environment. Considered in this sense, each man is in himself a microcosm. Among his senses, eye and ear, drawing upon the ocean of obscure sensations, bring before his mind in the clearest and most tangible manner the objects of his environment. And, as he has the gift to retain and designate these by means of words, he finds in language a means whereby he can create for himself an orderly world of perception and ideas. Even the most abstract ideas of the mind can be traced to eye and ear, as is evident in such terms as 'viewpoint', 'ideas', 'fancy', 'images', 'notions', 'objects' and many more. After eye and ear, touch, especially the tactile function of the hand, furnishes the mind with ideas, whereas taste and smell contribute less.[4]

Herder's mode of expression in the above passage may suggest an affinity between his theory of experience and Locke's Representationalism. But this similarity conceals an important difference. Admittedly, Herder shares Locke's conviction that all our ideas are derived from experience and revealed to us through the senses. But whilst Locke distinguishes two stages in the process of perception, treating the ideas of sensation as the raw materials of experience upon which the ideas of reflection can then set to work, Herder makes no such distinction. The act of experience, complex though it is, is nevertheless held to be a single, creative process. Creative, because, Herder insists, we do not merely see but also create our images.[5]

That the difference between Locke's and Herder's approach to the problem of experience is fundamental will also be evident when we come to consider Herder's arguments in support of the postulate of unity, in particular his principle of inter-relations, his concept of *Kraft*, and his theory of the mind. But before we turn to this task we have to enquire a little further into Herder's concept of knowledge.

The preceding account would indicate that the only knowledge we can be said to have of the outer world is that which the mind constructs in the process of perception, which, though empirical in its mode of operation, involves also the integrating and creative function of the mind. If this is the case we can, however, never be sure that things really are what we think them to be. Herder does not dispute this. He agrees that what we call knowledge is wholly contingent on, and relative to, the conceiving mind. What we perceive and think to be true of the external world is dependent on the psycho-physical determinants of each individual.[6] Therefore, Herder argues against

---

[4] XV, 523–4.   [5] XV, 526.   [6] VIII, 190.

Locke, it is not the external object as such which is the determinent of what we perceive, but the perceiving mind.[7]

This conclusion would point to Herder's taking up a position not unlike that of Berkeley. This would also entail the acceptance of its logical implication that we cannot be sure that external objects really exist at all. Herder's initial arguments in the *Metakritik* (1799) appear to lend support to such a view. He stipulates there different degrees of knowledge according to the nature of that which constitutes the object of consciousness. In relating what appears as cause and effect, for example, we are merely observing—and here Herder follows Hume—regularities in the occurrence of events of the necessary connexion of which we can never have demonstrable knowledge, though we may link them in our imagination and thus *presume* their causal relation.[8] Similarly, when talking about the characteristics of things, about their similarities and differences, we are far from certain about their real nature or even their real existence. Only when the individual self is the object of our consciousness can we say with assurance that we *know* of its existence.[9]

Now the significance of this conclusion lies in the inference which Herder draws from it. For it is this inference which represents the point of departure between Herder's position and that of subjective idealism. Herder's inference is that if self-consciousness is certain knowledge, and hence by implication the presupposition of all human knowledge, it cannot be wholly subjective. For self-consciousness contains an objective as well as a subjective element, in that the self is both the object which is known and the subject that knows.[10] It follows also that the self is not the product of consciousness, for as 'knower' it is logically prior to it.[11]

Herder's treatment of self-consciousness is of direct relevance to his theory of organism for the light it throws upon one of its central issues: the subject-object relationship. Herder defines self-consciousness in terms of an 'inner experience', or an 'inner discerning sense'.[12] At the same time he is most anxious to ensure that it is not confused with an innate, intuitive 'faculty', or conceived in a purely *a priori* sense.[13] Self-consciousness, Herder declares, cannot be intuitive or *a priori*

---

[7] XV, 528.　　　　[8] XXI, 150–7; see also XVI, 522.

[9] We shall see below that by 'self' Herder does not mean a static entity which endures through change, but the existence of an individual force or *Kraft* which, though subject to continuous change, or rather, *implying* change, is more than the aggregate of its changing states, owing to its 'continuity' or relational unity.

[10] XXI, 292.　　　　[11] XXI, 152.

[12] XXI, 158; see also XV, 527–8 and XXIV, 383.　　　　[13] IV, 5.

because it cannot be divorced from the self's experience of the outer world. 'This inner sense is neither a mystical *a priori* category nor something wholly apart from our awareness of the objects of the external world.'[14] This statement brings us to the heart of the matter. For if self-consciousness is not conceived as a separate entity or process, divorced from, or unrelated to, the objects of the knowing self, if, that is, the knowing self and the known object are not really separate things which are somehow brought together by the relationship of knowing, then we cannot but conclude that self-consciousness is an integral part of nature or reality. But this conclusion obviously raises the problem of the relationship that is said to exist between the knowing self and the known object. It also raises the problem of the nature of that which is said to be inter-related.

To take the second problem first. If we think of the self's consciousness as something fundamentally different from the physical objects which constitute its environment, if, for example, we regard the one as being immaterial and the other as being composed of material substances, then it is difficult to conceive how they can be inter-related at all. Indeed the problem would seem strictly insoluble (as Descartes clearly recognized) unless it can be shown that the dualism between an immaterial self-consciousness and a material environment arises from a false presupposition. In order to see how Herder strove to deny the existence of such a dualism we shall have to turn now to the ontological and broadly 'metaphysical' assumptions which underlie his theory of cosmic unity.

Ontological assumptions

Herder's basic premise is the axiom that existence ('Sein') implies *active* being ('*Dasein*'), since passive being is held to be not only inconceivable but also contradictory.[15] And if 'being' implies activity, it necessarily presupposes a medium through which this activity can assume physical reality. This medium we style 'matter' without, however, realizing that it is always activated matter that we are talking about and not a dead mass. Matter itself, then, must be conceived as an organically structured entity since it is only through organs that activity can manifest in nature.[16] What we call reality, therefore, is a universe pervaded by organic activity, or, in other words, a living universe, since life and organic activity are synonymous terms. It follows from this that matter as such cannot exist in isolation. It can only exist in so far as it is fused with activity and, hence, with life. The concept of

[14] XXI, 87.   [15] XVIII, 340.   [16] XVI, 452.

'mere extension', therefore, is a complete myth. The more we know about matter the more we realize the vacuity of this concept. Life and matter, in short, are not two distinct entities; nature has not put 'iron boards' between that which is 'material' and that which is 'immaterial'.[17] The apparent difference between what in common parlance is termed 'immaterial' and 'material' is a difference of degree only. The fundamental antithesis which is assumed to exist between them is wholly unfounded.[18]

Herder, then, disposes of this problem by treating it as a spurious problem. The 'stuff' of reality is presented as fundamentally homogeneous, namely as organic activity in which biological and physical phenomena are inseparably interwoven. The universe is seen in terms of an organism, or perhaps more precisely, as a complex of interrelated organisms and envisaged as a whole or unity in the sense in which we think of the human organism as a whole or unity.

By speaking of the universe as a whole Herder is anxious to distinguish it from a mere aggregate, which is simply the sum total of its parts, where the parts are separate and unrelated entities, the number of which can be increased or reduced without this having any effect on the *nature* of the total but merely on its *size*. A whole, on the other hand, is something more than the sum of its constituent parts. This 'more' is not contained in the parts considered in isolation, but rather arises from their mutual inter-relation, whilst the nature of the parts and their relationship is in turn determined by the whole to which they belong since the whole is logically prior to its parts. The whole constitutes, as it were, a system of functions which condition each other. One cannot, therefore, manipulate the parts without at the same time fundamentally affecting the structure and nature of the whole. The nature of the whole, in brief, is that of an organic unity, whilst the nature of an aggregate, even if it forms a unit, is that of a mechanical assembly. In the former the parts are functionally integrated by virtue of internal relations, in the latter they are brought into relation by an external source. Changes in the former are the result of *growth* taking place from within, whilst changes in the latter are the result of external manipulation. Activity in organic wholes is self-generated; in mechanical assemblies it is not. The most distinguishing characteristic, therefore, of organic wholes is the *intrinsic* nature of their functional relations.

Herder stipulates, however, a further characteristic of organic wholes, in that he insists on the uniqueness and diversity of the constituent

[17] VIII, 193.   [18] XIII, 172; see also VIII, 178.

parts. No two grains of sand are identical, let alone more complex organic structures such as plants, animals or human beings.[19] Indeed, diversity is posited as the necessary corollary of intrinsic inter-relation since the latter is envisaged as a process of reciprocal interaction.[20] The notion that the world consists in nature, no less than in society, of inter-related and interacting organisms, each of which is necessary to the whole in its most determinate individuality is the principal notion of Herder's theory of organism and one of the central theses of his philosophy of history in the *Ideen zur Philosophie der Geschichte der Menschheit* (1784-91), the work for which he is best known.[21]

Herder links with this notion the epistemological principle that no one thing can be known in abstraction from its inter-relationships.[22] This brings us back to the problem of the nature of the relationship between the knowing self and the known object. Although the individual organism in Herder's theory can be compared to the Leibnizian monad, there is one important difference: the Herderian 'monad' *has* 'windows'. The individual units, though internally energized, are not conceived as being self-contained and somehow related by an external link. Rather they are thought of as embodying *in themselves* a propensity towards inter-connexion and interaction with other units.[23] By analogy, self-consciousness—in the sense of the self's awareness of itself—is presented as a process which, though it occurs within the self, is at the same time inconceivable in abstraction of external experience. The self's awareness of its environment as of its inner states is seen as a function of the continuous interaction that is taking place between the self's 'inside' and 'outside'. The individual, far from being enclosed within himself, *derives* the awareness of himself, from outside, from his contact with the world around him, in the absence of which it could probably never awaken in the first place.[24]

It follows that the relation between the knowing self and known object is not something that lies outside either but rather something that is inherent in the nature of each. And since the manner of inter-relation is that of interaction, the picture which emerges is that of a universe in which the constituent parts are all actively inter-linked within a dynamic network of reciprocity. If this picture is correct, it means in effect that no single thing in the universe can exist independently of, or be properly known and understood outside, the context of its inter-relationships.

[19] VIII, 226; see also XIV, 83.   [20] XXI, 182.   [21] XIV, 83-4.
[22] XXI, 179.   [23] XXI, 182.   [24] XXI, 152.

The picture is, however, incomplete unless we introduce the concept of '*Kraft*'. For *Kraft*—the connotation of which in Herder's use is that of a vital energy or life force, conditioning 'being' as such[25]—is posited as the inter-connecting link of all natural phenomena.

Herder reluctantly admits that the concept of *Kraft* is wholly metaphysical in origin.[26] It is intended to replace the traditional metaphysical 'support' of Substance in order to avoid the 'fatal dualism' which Herder attributes to the Cartesian system.[27] And as a substitute for Substance *Kraft* is also at times equated with God.[28] Herder makes no attempt to define it any further. To contrive to do so, he explains, would mean going beyond the knowable. Hence philosophy can only presuppose this primary source of being, it cannot explain it.[29] But on what grounds should it be presupposed? What evidence is there for its existence? Herder's reply is that we cannot but believe in this primary force because a 'hundred thousand' phenomena provide evidence of its existence.[30] *Kraft*, although it cannot be explained in terms of its origins, can nevertheless be observed and described by virtue of the manifestations which embody the process of its functioning. The effects of *Kraft*, therefore, can and should be studied with a view to increasing human understanding. These effects take the form of organic activity, for it is only through organs and organisms that *Kraft* can manifest itself. And in so doing, Herder concludes, they provide the most perfect evidence of psycho-physical fusion.[31]

Herder's treatment of *Kraft* is of interest also in that it illustrates one of the first attempts to apply considerations derived from the then new science of biology to philosophical speculations. Since in Herder's case these speculations are not confined to metaphysics, but invade also the regions of history and politics, it may not be out of place to mention briefly the history of the concept.

According to Professor R. T. Clark, *Kraft* is a Middle High German translation of the medieval concept of *vis*.[32] In keeping with their general 'faculty' approach, the scholastic philosophers confined the term *vis* largely to the meaning of 'faculty' or 'power'. *Vis* came to mean that by virtue of which an action took place. *Potestas* was another term frequently used to express the same idea. Not uncommonly these

---

[25] XXI, 228: 'What exists, exists through *Kraft*.'   [26] VIII, 178.
[27] XVI, 458, 549.   [28] XIII, 273–6; see also VIII, 197 and XVI, 453.
[29] VIII, 177; see also XV, 533 and XVI, 441, 522.   [30] VIII, 175.
[31] VIII, 175, 193; also XVI, 452.
[32] Robert T. Clark Jr., 'Herder's Conception of "Kraft" ' *Publications of the Modern Language Association of America*, vol. LVII, 1942, p. 740.

terms were used interchangeably.[33] But there was no suggestion yet of a single underlying *vis*. The tendency was to think in terms of a plurality of *vires* and of classifying these into superior and inferior categories. Leibniz was the first to introduce the concept of *vis viva* which, with mass, were treated by him as the original physical notions. It was not until Boerhaave applied the Leibnizian term to muscular action, however, that it came to assume a biological meaning. Albrecht von Haller further developed Boerhaave's physiological theories in his *Elementa physiologicae corporis humani* (1757) and it was from Haller that Herder 'borrowed' the idea of a life force.[34] But whilst Haller modestly refrained from stipulating a fundamental *vis vitalis* for which he could find no demonstrable evidence, and hence preferred to speak of a plurality of biological *vires*, Herder was not restrained by such inhibitions. He subsumed all *vires* under one prime *Kraft* as their original and common source. Herder's 'borrowing', therefore, entailed a metaphysical jump which went far beyond the biological knowledge of his time.

But Herder was not really concerned with making a biological discovery. His principal aim appears to have been two-fold. In the first place he was determined to dislodge the 'faculty' philosophers from their position of authority. In the second place he was anxious to deny the tenability of the Lockean doctrine of power. To succeed in the former seemed to him the essential prerequisite for postulating his own theory of the mind; to succeed in the latter was rendered necessary by his theory of development.

Psychological assumptions

The arguments which Herder adduces in support of his theory of the organic unity of the mind are, as one would expect, a corollary of his epistemological and metaphysical presuppositions which we attempted to trace so far. His treatment of the human mind is virtually that of a microcosmos within the larger whole which is the universe. Just as the universe, conceived as an organic unity, is more than an aggregate of its constituent parts, so the human mind is said to be more than an assembly of human organs or the sum total of sensations perceived through these organs. For the mind does not merely receive stimuli through the nerves which are the organs of sensations. It continuously

---

[33] Ludwig Schütz, *Thomas-Lexicon*, Paderborn, 1895, p. 865, cited by Clark, loc. cit., p. 740.
[34] Herder, it is evident, had studied Haller's *Elementa* in some detail; see especially Part IV of his *Aelteste Urkunde des Menschengeschlechts* (1774–6) where Haller's work is frequently mentioned, often with volume and page references.

reacts to these stimuli and the reaction of the mind is greater than the aggregate of the perceived stimuli owing to its activity.[35] This activity, Herder maintains, is not a mechanical operation, comparable to the working of a clock, but a creative process. In combining sensation the mind creates something which is new and richer than the sensations which have occasioned its activity.[36]

But what precisely *is* the mind? Herder's answer to this question is singularly clear and well-defined. 'Mind' is not part of a human being; it is *the* human being.

The mind, whether it is perceiving, or thinking, or judging, or building conceptual images, is always *one* single vital power, one active unity amidst the diversity of its operations . . . and, as such, no less than the whole sentient being of man; indeed it *is* man.[37]

Thus the mind is not a 'place'. Herder rejects the Cartesian conception of mind as something separate, as a particular part of man. The mind has no *locus*, such as Descartes's pineal gland, but is the combination of all the nerves, the interaction of all human organs. It is more than the brain. Indeed, what goes on 'in the mind', Herder points out, is more often than not the result of causes that one wrongly searches for in the head, but which in reality may lie under the diaphragm.[38]

Herder's answer obviously rests on his assumption of the inter-relation and interaction between what is commonly distinguished as life and matter and, in the present context, as mind and body. The arguments which lead him to this assumption have engaged us earlier and there is no need, therefore, to repeat them here at length. Herder, we may recall, makes no fundamental distinction between physical and biological phenomena. Similarly, in the present context, he refuses to treat physiological and psychological characteristics as distinct entities. Already in the *Journal* he observes to this effect: 'Mind cannot function without a body'.[39] In his psychological treatise *Vom Erkennen und Empfinden der menschlichen Seele in ihrem Ursprunge und den Gesetzen ihrer Wirkung* (1778) we find a fuller exposition of this point, the conclusion of which is contained in the following quotation: 'In my humble opinion, psychology that is not joined at every step with physiology is a sheer impossibility.'[40] Accordingly, there can be no theory of the human mind divorced from a theory of the human body; there can be no psychology which is not at the same time physiology. Here Herder is again 'borrowing' from Haller more than Haller was

---

[35] VIII, 291.   [36] VIII, 249 and ibid., 291.   [37] XXI, 19, 83 and IV, 28.
[38] VIII, 179.   [39] IV, 454.   [40] VIII, 180.

able to lend. For Haller still conceived physiological and psychological *vires* as entirely separate entities.[41] And he did so, in Herder's view, because he could not free himself from the prevailing habit of thinking in terms of compartmentalized faculties.

It is precisely this habit of thought and the concomitant practice of classifying faculties into superior and inferior categories which, Herder feels, has to be discarded, if one wishes to cease speaking in terms of verbal abstractions and to replace a mechanistic by an organic conception of the mind. To quote his own words: 'One is wont to attribute to the mind a number of subordinate faculties; . . . but to treat of these (mental) energies as if they were "ideas" is merely to scratch at the surface. In this way one shall never penetrate to the bottom of things. What is even worse is to view each of these "faculties" in isolation as if they were separable into water-tight compartments.'[42] Herder is particularly anxious to dethrone 'reason' from its position of dominance as *the* supreme faculty of the mind.[43] He pours scorn and irony on all philosophers, however great, who treated reason in this way. Philosophical nonsense, he calls it.

Human reason has been conceived as a novel and quite distinct faculty of the mind, as something that had been added to man to distinguish him from the animal; a kind of fourth rung of a ladder over and above the three lower ones, destined to be singled out for special consideration. But to speak of reason in this manner is to talk philosophical nonsense, even if the greatest philosophers do the talking.[44]

But he is equally critical of those who, like Rousseau, speak of reason as a mere capacity or potentiality. To talk in this fashion, he decrees, is to make an empty sound.[45]

For Herder 'reason' approximates to 'reasoning'; it is a *process*, not a faculty. Reason, thus conceived, cannot, however, be divorced from the other activities of the mind. Herder elaborates this view in his *Metakritik* as follows:

When in our thoughts and words we single out reason from among the other (mental) energies (*Kräfte*) of our nature we do so for a specific (conceptual) purpose; but in doing so we must never forget that in actual fact it cannot subsist in isolation apart from the other mental energies. It is one and the same mind that thinks and wills, that understands and perceives, that seeks reason and applies it. All these tendencies or energies of the mind are so

---

[41] Albrecht v. Haller, *Elementa*, op. cit., vol. IV, p. 464, cited by Clark, loc. cit., p. 746.
[42] VIII, 195-6.
[43] In this endeavour Herder is a true follower of Hamann and, of course, of Hume, to whose writings Hamann frequently drew Herder's attention.
[44] V, 29.   [45] V, 32.

close to one another, so intertwined and interacting, not only in practical application, but even in their origin and development, that we must never presume that in naming any one operation of these energies we are actually naming a distinct faculty in a substantive sense. For by the act of naming we do not erect compartments in our mind; we do not sub-divide it. All we are doing is to classify its operations, the application of its energies.[46]

This passage merits being quoted in full not only because it sums up succinctly Herder's position on this issue, but also because it epitomizes rather well his attitude towards Kant's *Critique of Pure Reason*, as a criticism of which the *Metakritik* was written.

Reason, then, is neither a separate, nor a superior, nor a prior faculty of the mind, but rather an integral element in the processes of the mind with which it is related and interacting. All this is consistent enough with, and, indeed, logically derivable from, what we have learned hitherto about Herder's theory of organic interaction. What is more, his treatment of reason and the organic unity of the mind is exceptionally free from ambiguity.

Not quite the same can, however, be said about the concept of *Besonnenheit* which is clearly intended to play a pivotal part in Herder's theory of the mind.

It would, I think, be misleading, to translate this term as 'reflexion'. For 'reflexion' has too close an association with the Moral Sense School (which Herder rejected) as it is also too reminiscent of Locke's dualism (which Herder wished to avoid). Moreover, Locke's 'reflexion' signifies a particular operation of thinking,[47] whilst *Besonnenheit*, which Herder defines as 'the entire economy' of man's perceptive, cognitive and volitional nature, is presented as the essential *condition* of thinking. It is held to constitute, that is, the 'totality' within which the process of thinking can operate.[48] In effect this means that Herder thinks of *Besonnenheit* as the *power* of thinking. This is deducible also from his theory of language, in which he contends (1) that human language is co-terminous with *Besonnenheit*, and (2) that the process of thinking is inconceivable without language.[49]

By using the term 'power of thinking' we may appear to come perilously close to the terminology of Rousseau which, as we observed, Herder finds unacceptable. This impression will be avoided, however, if it is remembered that by 'power' Herder does not mean a mere

[46] XXI, 18–19.
[47] Locke, *An Essay concerning Human Understanding*, Book II, ch. 1, sect. 4, 10, 24.
[48] V, 28–9.
[49] V, 124. Herder's *Abhandlung über den Ursprung der Sprache* (1770) was his first major raid into the territory of philosophy and psychology. See also I, 417; and ibid., 420.

potentiality, but an actual creative energy or *Kraft*.[50] What is less easy
to account for, however, is Herder's apparent distinction between his
concept of mind and his concept of *Besonnenheit*. For although all that
he has to say about the latter concept would be equally applicable to the
former, Herder nowhere suggests that these concepts are in fact interchangeable.

Somewhat less perplexing, if not altogether free from ambiguity, is
the closely associated concept of *Besinnung*, which could be best
rendered perhaps as conscious discernment or awareness. Herder is
presumably making use here of the Leibnizian distinction between
'apperception' and the *petites perceptions*. For the reason for introducing
this additional term appears to be the desire to draw attention to
activities of the mind, such as dreaming for example, which do not
entail *Besinnung*, but which still presuppose *Besonnenheit*, since we are
still thinking even though not so coherently or distinctly as when we
are awake.[51]

But Herder suggests a further, and quite different distinction between
Besinnung and *Besonnenheit* when he says: 'Man is from the very first
moment of his existence a human being and not an animal because he is
right from the start a creature of *Besonnenheit* (i.e. a thinking being)
even though he is not yet a creature endowed with *Besinnung* (i.e.
conscious awareness).'[52] Now, although this further distinction
introduces an element of ambiguity into the meaning of *Besinnung*, it
lends at the same time an added interest to the concept. For it implies
that the self is not only logically but also temporally prior to its consciousness and hence reinforces Herder's contention that knowledge
can never be *a priori* nor wholly subjective. Consciousness, that is to
say, is not innate, but rather a function of *development*. It is the result
of the peculiar manner in which the growing self receives, and reacts to,
the *stimuli* of its environment. The significance of this implication is a
matter which will receive attention in the subsequent section in which
we propose to turn to Herder's second main reason for postulating his
concept of *Kraft*. Before doing so, however, let us briefly sum up the
main arguments by means of which Herder sought to refute the
traditional doctrine of faculties or mental powers.

Applying his principle of active inter-relation to the activities of the
mind, Herder comes to the conclusion that the diverse organs of the
mind and the activities which they perform are not separate entities
existing in isolation from one another. Reason, for example, which
hitherto has been treated as a distinct and dominant faculty of the

[50] V, 32–3.   [51] V, 99.   [52] V, 93.

mind, is presented as a process of thinking which cannot be divorced from other processes such as feeling or willing. The mind, therefore, is not to be thought of as an assembly of separate faculties but rather as an integrated whole. And since the mode of operation of the interlinked processes is not to be envisaged in terms of the working of a mechanism, but as a creative activity, Herder postulates the existence of a vital power which constitutes the *internal* energizing source of this activity. As such it represents the principle of unity within the diversity of the inter-related processes through which it manifests itself. Herder's theory of the organic unity of the mind, then, which is advanced in place of the doctrine of faculties, no less than his notion of the unity of the universe conceived as an organic whole, is directly derivative from his metaphysical concept of *Kraft*.

2. THE PROBLEM OF CONTINUITY

Change as 'growth'

To deny the tenability of Locke's theory of power was, we suggested, Herder's second aim in postulating his basic concept of *Kraft*. When Locke used the term 'power', he understood by it a capacity for producing change *and* a capacity for receiving change. 'Thus we say', Locke explained, 'fire has a power to melt gold . . . ; and gold has a power to be melted . . . ; the one may be called "active" and the other "passive" power.'[53] In order to bring out the contrast between Locke's concept of power and Herder's concept of *Kraft* it may be convenient to make use of the concepts of *vis* and *potestas*. These, as we noted earlier, were frequently used interchangeably by the 'faculty' school. We propose to draw a distinction between them by identifying *vis* with an internal energy corresponding roughly to the Aristotelian concept of 'entelechy', and *potestas* with 'power' in the sense in which Locke employed the term, implying by it both an active and a passive connotation.

Now it is not difficult to realize from what has been said so far about Herder's concept of *Kraft* that he could hardly entertain a belief in the possibility of a passive power. If 'being' entails 'activity' then it also implies the existence of an energizing source. And to speak of such an energizing source as a passive power would, in Herder's view, constitute a contradiction in terms. What is more, the acceptance of the possibility of an active *and* a passive power would militate against the

[53] Locke, *Essay*, op. cit., Book II, ch. XXI, sect. 1 and 2.

monistic philosophy of organic unity which Herder wishes to advance in opposition to dualistic interpretations of reality. It is this consideration as much as the first which underlies Herder's determination to postulate a single creative power as his metaphysical support in place of the traditional Substance.

But, it may be objected at this point, in disposing of the dualism which the Lockean conception of power apparently implies, Herder is far from establishing his own case. For it remains to be explained how we can conceive of the universe or of reality as a whole or unity, if the 'stuff' of this reality is not an unchanging Substance but a creative power manifesting itself through continuous activity. How can we, that is to say, reconcile the universe's fundamental unity with the notion of continuous activity and *change*? For are we not by postulating the latter denying the former, since the universe as it is and the universe as it may become are not one but two? By raising these questions we are of course questioning the very legitimacy of Herder's undertaking in postulating an active *Kraft* in place of Substance. The latter, as Spinoza clearly saw, had to be conceived as unchanging, for if it were not so conceived, one state of Substance would be different from another and hence could no longer constitute a single all-embracing unity. Moreover, if Substance is the same as God, as Spinoza maintained, change is equally inconceivable. For there cannot be change other than movement from one state towards another. If, therefore, we mean by God that which is wholly perfect, we would, by postulating a changing Substance, either have to admit that God is other than Substance or that He is not wholly perfect. To admit the former would mean denying the postulate of unity on which Spinoza's theory of monism rests; whilst to admit the latter would render the concept of God meaningless.

Now Herder regarded himself as a Spinozist.[54] He even went so far as to identify *Kraft* with God, as we remarked earlier, in the belief that by substituting *Kraft* for Substance he succeeded in making the Spinozist system so much more coherent and intelligible.[55] Apart from the light this throws upon Herder's somewhat ambivalent theological thinking, it also suggests that Herder hardly seemed to realize how very different his metaphysical presuppositions were from those of Spinoza, and how profoundly, therefore, in spite of superficial similarities, his brand of monism differed from that of his 'precursor'.

---

[54] See Herder's letter to Gleim, dated 17 February 1786. (H. Düntzer and F. G. v. Herder, *Von und an Herder*, Leipzig, 1861-2, vol. I, p. 116.)

[55] XVI, 458, 549.

Indeed it would not be wrong to say that Herder's notion of 'unity' was as fundamentally at variance with that of Spinoza as his concept of *Kraft* was with the Lockean conception of power.

Let us explore now briefly how Herder came to replace the notion of static unity by that of a dynamic whole; how, that is to say, he attempted to reconcile the principle of one-ness with the principle of activity and change.

We may recall that Herder conceives of the universe in terms of an organism or, more precisely, in terms of a plurality of inter-related organisms, each of which is necessary to the existence of the other so that we must think of the totality of these connected organisms as constituting an integrated whole. We have noted, too, that the inter-relationship is held to be one of interaction rather than one of a passive 'being-in-relation'. Indeed, we have seen, it is the process of this inter-action which is presented as the core or 'stuff' of reality. The *nature* of interaction is that of organic activity and hence by implication fundamentally homogeneous. In order to maintain this claim, Herder denies the distinction between mind and matter or between material and immaterial 'substances', and stipulates instead a single psycho-physical force or energy (*Kraft*) as the common source of activity. This force, however, is not to be thought of as an external agency acting *upon* the universe but as an *internal* force acting *through* the universe. The universe, in other words, is the manifestation of *Kraft*. This being so, it cannot be a changeless universe. For *Kraft* entails activity and activity entails change. We arrive, therefore, at the conclusion that the universe as the embodiment of an immanent vital energy (*Kraft*) is a stream of continuous change.[56]

A corollary of this conclusion—and one which is of considerable relevance to Herder's philosophy of history—is the notion that 'time', far from being something imposed upon reality by the human understanding, is in fact a necessary function of reality. For if reality is a flux of change, time is of its very essence.[57] Phenomena, therefore, are not timeless in reality, but are instead 'agents of time'.[58] It follows also that time or duration (Herder uses both terms) must be conceived as an active and vital force and, as such, as the very principle of existence.[59] It is not surprising, therefore, that time or duration is treated by Herder as a notion which is implicit in his concept of *Kraft*.[60]

---

[56] IX, 371 and V, 512.   [57] IX, 371-2.   [58] XXII, 314.
[59] XVI, 566 and IX, 371.
[60] XXI, 64. Herder is not altogether consistent, however, in his treatment of time. (See, for example, XVII, 80, where time is defined as a 'thought-image'.)

Kraft, Herder's metaphysical support for his principle of interaction, is conceived, then, as a *process in time*. By identifying this process with 'becoming' or development, Herder hopes to succeed in presenting his concept of 'unity' as the relational unity of a process. At this point we may introduce the distinction between *potestas* and *vis* to which we made reference at the beginning of this section. Herder's treatment of *Kraft* does not make it difficult to decide to which conception of power his own concept more closely approximates. His theory of development finally settles the matter. If by *vis* we mean, as we have stipulated, an internal energy corresponding roughly to the Aristotelian 'entelechy' then the *direction* which the process of change assumes is inherent in the nature of the changing 'thing'. Development, accordingly, is a process in which that which is already latent becomes actual. This is precisely what Herder understands by development which he, therefore, identifies with 'growth': 'Within every grain of seed there lies the plant with all its parts; within every animal seed the creature with all its limbs.'[61] Even if environmental factors are recognized as having a modifying influence, it is primarily the innate, or, as Herder prefers to call it, the 'genetic' propensity towards the attainment of a thing's end which is said to constitute the determinate driving power of its growth.[62] For it is the genetic propensity that determines what manner interaction will assume and to what extent external influences will succeed in affecting the process of growth by means of which a thing will realize its full nature.[63]

Growth and human development

But if the end towards which things develop is implicit in the unfolding of the genetic propensity, then, surely, the result of the process is virtually pre-determined by the initial nature of that which undergoes the process of change. This Herder does not deny. At the same time he realizes that the application of this sort of blind teleological determinism or functionalism to human development would offer little scope for the exercise of choice. He carefully distinguishes, therefore, human and social development from other forms of growth. Whereas the latter develop in an unconscious or instinctive manner,[64] human beings, as creatures of *Besonnenheit*, are capable of realizing consciously the nature and direction of their development.[65] The extent to which they

---

[61] II, 62. In using the Aristotelian notion of 'entelechy' I do not wish to imply that the Aristotelian psychology as a whole admits of being reduced to biology.

[62] XIII, 273, 276, 277.　　　[63] ibid.　　　[64] V, 98; see also XIII, 102.

[65] V, 29.

do will differ, however, from individual to individual according to the degree to which *Besonnenheit* results in *Besinnung* or actual consciousness.[66] The process of human development is envisaged, therefore, as the unfolding of *Besonnenheit* into *Besinnung*, by virtue of which it ceases to be a 'blind force' and becomes instead the expression of a conscious self-determining mind. Environmental factors are again not overlooked but their significance is secondary in that their effective influence is dependent on the active apprehension by the individual mind. Thus while everything in the total environment (to which Herder applies the term *Klima*[67]) is of some relevance to the development of the self towards its fullest realization (to which Herder applies the term 'individuation'[68]), different things will be relevant in different degrees. Man's recognition of what is most relevant to his own development in the light of individually conceived purposes constitutes presumably what Herder means by conscious becoming.

The life of the individual, then, is seen as a process of activity in which internal and external factors are inter-related and blended according to their relevance to the individual's conscious aims or purposes and not merely in accordance with the functional requirements of his physical needs. The realization that life is not a mere succession of separate and random psycho-physical states, but rather the flow of connected purposive activities is one of the most distinguishing features of human existence.[69] Without this realization there could be no sense of *continuity* and hence no conception of human *history*. By the same token, there would be no point in speaking of man's capacity for self-determination and self-perfection unless he was in a position to grasp the inter-connexions and the directional determinants of his own development.[70]

Herder's theory of development and self-determination contains, however, in spite of its attractiveness, a very fundamental difficulty. I think Herder is right in distinguishing the self from an aggregate and in stipulating the relational unity of a process in place of a mere succession of psycho-physical states. We do not, as a matter of empirical fact, think of the self as 'nothing but a bundle or collection of different perceptions'.[71] We do, that is, envisage some sort of identity of the self within its changing states. And I suggest that we do so on grounds not unlike those advanced by Herder's theory. For what we generally

66 XXI, 152.   67 XIII, 272.
68 XVI, 574. See also XXI, 106 regarding this passage.   69 V, 98.
70 XVII, 115 and XVI, 574.
71 Hume, *A Treatise of Human Nature*, Book I, Part IV, sect. VI ('Of Personal Identity'); Everyman ed., p. 239.

regard as the identity or unity of the self is a measure of consistency in the purposive direction of its changing states. Nevertheless, it is somewhat of a mystery how we can account for that 'something' which 'recognizes' the purposive relationship of the changing states. For this presupposes that the 'something' is distinct from the self's states. In postulating the concepts of *Besonnenheit* and *Besinnung* as two *distinct* ideas, identifying the former with the power of thinking as such, and the latter with a capacity for conscious self-awareness, Herder seems to make an attempt to meet this difficulty. For 'conscious awareness' could conceivably apply to that state of the self in which it is aware of the purposive relationship of its other states, in view of which it recognizes the relational unity of the 'mind', i.e. (in Herder's terminology) the totality of the self as an individual personality. But the matter is not entirely clear.[72]

3. UNITY AND CONTINUITY

Continuity as the relational unity of a process
If the plurality of diverse parts is said to be a prerequisite for the existence of the whole, and if it is also maintained that the existence of the whole is inconceivable unless 'existence' is envisaged in the form of continuous activity or change, then it is the nature of the relation between the 'parts' and the 'whole' and between the 'now' and the 'later' which constitutes the decisive issue. The problem of unity and the problem of continuity, therefore, which we have singled out as the core problems in Herder's philosophy of organism, are, it would appear, in fact reducible to a single problem, the problem of relation. Herder's answer to this problem is, as we have seen, the principle of interaction. According to this principle all that exists does so in a state of continuous becoming, in which the 'now' and the 'later' are inseparably fused, the 'now' containing the 'later' in the manner in which an acorn 'contains' the oak. The relation characteristic of this process therefore, is one of growth, i.e. of continuous activity directed by an internal end or purpose.[73] At the same time the activity of any

---

[72] It may, of course, be argued that this 'difficulty' arises from asking an illegitimate question, i.e. a question to which one simply cannot expect to get an answer on any theory.

[73] I am using the words 'end' and 'purpose' as alternatives and not as synonyms, to distinguish teleological processes such as the growth of a plant or an animal, where the 'end' does not imply a conscious aim, from those where it does. In the former case *telos* implies simply a tendency towards biological completion; in the latter case *telos* implies conscious striving towards the attainment of envisaged goals. (For an extremely lucid treatment of this distinction, see Dorothy Emmet, *Function, Purpose and Powers*, London, 1958, pp. 46–51.)

individual unit is inseparably linked with that of every other in such a manner that the existence of one is indispensable to the existence of the other, even though no single unit is exactly like any other. The nature of the relationship, therefore, is also one of mutual inter-dependence. Growth and functional inter-dependence, accordingly, constitute the joint characteristics of Herder's principle of active inter-relation or 'interaction'. They are characteristics which are associated with organisms rather than with mechanical bodies, for they presuppose the existence of an *internal* source of activity. It follows, therefore, that growth and inter-dependence are but a function of an active energizing force or power which underlies the organic activities of which they are the relational characteristics. To this single force or power Herder applies his concept of *Kraft*. This concept, then, which Herder intended as a synthesis between Spinoza's monism and Leibniz's pluralism, represents the basic presupposition of what unquestionably constitutes the central idea of Herder's philosophy of organism: the principle of interaction. This principle implies, we have found, a state of continuous change or flux between inter-penetrating events. Accordingly, every event must itself be conceived as a continuous process within this flux. What we are confronted with, therefore, is not a series of separate events but a network of relations. Moreover, and this is highly important, the relations themselves are not distinct from the things they relate, but are held to be inherent in their very nature. This is implicit in the postulate of *organic* inter-relation from which Herder draws the consequence that no single thing can be studied or understood when treated in isolation, that is, in abstraction from the context in which it occurs.

In order to realize the methodological import of this consequence it must be remembered too, that the nature of the relationship is held to be teleological. For from this it follows that the 'meaning' or 'significance' of any one thing, said to be deducible only if it is studied within its context, is its end or purpose. Now both the postulate of continuous process and the concept of functional or purposive relation[74] raise the question of how far Herder's principle of interaction by-passes, if it does not supersede, the law of causation as it is ordinarily

[74] Again I wish to stress that the 'or' expresses a distinction, and not an identity, between functional and purposive relations. Both functional and purposive relations are inter-connecting links in a system or structural 'whole'. But the 'meaning' of the former will be interpreted in terms of their functional effects within a system, whilst the 'meaning' of the latter will be interpreted in terms of purposive intentions. This formulation is not wholly satisfactory, but I hope it is sufficiently clear to bring out the point I wish to make here, namely that the *nature* of the explanation in each case will be different.

understood. For if things are not really separate from one another, to speak of *a* cause and *an* effect would mean the arbitrary singling out of two events from what is in fact a continuous series. What is more, if an event is not an isolated occurrence in space or time, then, really, there would appear to be no need to invoke a causal law in the form in which it is commonly known.

Teleological causation

Herder's ideas on historical causation, to which we propose to return in a later chapter,[75] are undoubtedly the most difficult as also the most controversial aspect of his social philosophy. In the present context we merely wish to draw attention to the connexion between Herder's 'organic' conception of the universal order and his approach to the problem of causation.

The ordinary view of causation presupposes that an event, a cause, which is separate from another event, the effect, and earlier than the effect in point of time, brings about or determines the latter. When, therefore, we say that 'A causes B' we not only mean that B follows A, but also that B results from A, in that A is the sufficient condition for the occurrence of B. We mean, that is, that there is a determinate connexion between the two events. But what precisely is the nature of that which is said to link two separate events in this determinate manner? Surely, to have causal effect it must possess causal *power*. Now the action of this power constitutes, as it were, if it is something external to A and B, an additional event, the separate existence of which is causally inexplicable unless we resort to an infinite regression. But if it is not something separate, then A and B cannot be separate either for we have no way of distinguishing their separate existence. The alternative is to stipulate the existence of causal characteristics as something inherent in the events themselves. In the former case, where A and B cease to represent separate events, the law of causation in the customary sense is rendered inapplicable, whilst in the latter case the postulate of an internal power is necessitated. Hume, rejecting the second alternative, could not, therefore, but conclude that the law of causation was either unnecessary or unfounded. By postulating it we are not talking about something which is inherent in, or derivable from, reality. All we do and can do is to link in our imagination events which past observation has shown to occur regularly together as if they were necessarily related. Accordingly, all we *should* mean when we say that A is the cause of B is that A is regularly followed by B.[76]

[75] Ch. VI.   [76] Hume, op. cit., Book I, Part III, sect. VI; Everyman ed., p. 163.

At first sight Herder's own view on causation appears to coincide
with that of Hume. We merely assume, he says, the existence of a causal
relation with the aid of mental constructions based on analogy and
observation.[77] Yet on further examination it becomes evident that what
Herder questions is not the reality of causation as such but the
acceptance of causation as something simple and readily intelligible.
When he agrees, therefore, with Hume that finite minds may only be
able to construct causal hypotheses based on the observation of 'outside' relationships, that is, of sequences which appear to reveal
regularity, he does so for different reasons. For Herder, it will be
remembered, *does* presuppose the existence of an internal causal power
and hence the causal relation which he stipulates is that of an *internal*
relation. Furthermore, since he only denies the separateness but not the
individuality of phenomena, the mode of causation which he puts
forward in place of 'simple causation' is that of pluralistic causation of
an exceedingly complex and varied pattern. It is this complexity which
occasions Herder's doubt of the possibility of gaining a true or complete
knowledge of causal relations. For to gain such complete knowledge
we would have to be able to penetrate into the inner being of things.
To succeed in this, however, is clearly beyond our ken. In the natural
sciences all we can do is to stand outside and observe from the
outside.[78]

It is not difficult to see why, if 'internal causality' is something
essentially unknowable, Hume found himself unable to accept such a
postulate. But the same cannot be said of Herder. Two related reasons
account for this. The first is that Herder invokes his metaphysical
concept of *Kraft* to support his 'empiricism' and the second is the
teleological element in his theory of causation.

In spite of his desire to think as an empiricist and his declared
distrust of metaphysics, Herder could not dispense with his metaphysical 'support' of *Kraft*. It was not only the unifying principle of his
philosophy of organism; it was also the basic concept in his theological
cosmology. In *Kraft* he saw both the First Cause and the continuous
energizing power of 'becoming', which he identified with existence.
Kraft, therefore, embodied for Herder the continuous manifestation
of God.[79] The principle of internal relation, similarly, entailed for
Herder the existence of an inherent harmony in the universe;[80]
but he advanced no argument in support of this belief. Presumably
he regarded the internal harmony of the universe as the necessary
corollary of the postulate of *Kraft*—the divine source of all existence.

[77] XVI, 522.   [78] XVI, 551.   [79] XXXII, 228.   [80] XVI, 547-51.

Herder, in short, unlike Hume, was not a thoroughgoing empiricist at all. At heart, whether he knew it or not, he was not only a metaphysician, but a religious metaphysician at that. This fact needs stressing, for it is exceedingly relevant to Herder's approach to politics and history.

Closely allied with the metaphysical element in Herder's theory of causation was the teleological element. Herder's model of causation was that of an organism, the operation of which he held to be activated by a directional power. 'Cause', according to this view was, therefore, not wholly, or not even necessarily, explicable in terms of the origins of an event, but rather in terms of its end or purpose. That Herder wished to emphasize the causal efficacy of the end was not surprising in view of his theory of becoming, in which the end or purpose of a process was held to be implicit in the process of its development. To explain a process we must, in other words, not only look backwards to that which occasioned its existence, but also forwards to the end towards which it is tending. For 'becoming' not only reflects its past, but also foreshadows its future.

Natural scientists in particular and empiricists in general may (and on the whole do) share Hume's doubts about the methodological value of teleological approaches. Yet in the field of human study it may well be asked whether it is not the Humean, that is, the so-called 'scientific' pattern of causation which gives equal cause for doubt. And I would venture to submit that in this sphere Herder revealed a truer insight into the nature of historical and sociological explanations than the great Scotsman whom he so deeply admired. But this is not the place to enlarge on the relevance of Herder's teleological approach to the study of man and society and, in particular, to the interpretation of history. Our main concern in this chapter was to elicit the epistemological and metaphysical strands in Herder's philosophy of organism and, more specifically, to show how, by combining the Aristotelian notion of teleological development with his own conception of *Kraft*, Herder arrived at a position which enabled him to identify the idea of unity with that of the unity of a process, and thus to demonstrate the essential one-ness of the principle of unity and the principle of continuity.

III

ORGANIC POLITICS

THAT in spite of the plurality and diversity of its constituent parts the world forms a single integrated whole, is, we have found, central to Herder's 'organic' interpretation of the universal order. Applied to the human realm, this doctrine attempts to reconcile the uniqueness of man as an individual with his dependence upon other individuals within the larger whole of his social setting: he is a microcosm in himself and yet he cannot exist by himself alone. Diversity *and* relatedness, these are the basic features, therefore, that confront the social philosopher no less than the student of nature.[1] The problem is to discover a manner in which men can associate and co-operate without sacrificing their distinct individualities.

Herder is not the first to perceive the challenge of this problem. Of this he is perfectly aware. Rousseau is uppermost in his mind: 'His great theme is most closely akin to mine', he remarks in one of his early notebooks.[2] But although he shares with him the basic premise asserting man to be a social animal, born in and for society,[3] he differs from him in significant details.

When Herder asserts man to be born into society, he means by 'society'—and here he echoes Justus Möser—an already integrated social unit such as the family, the clan, the *Volk*—a kind of 'family writ large', as he terms it[4]—or one which is in the process of social integration.[5] In either case it is a social setting arising out of human interdependence, i.e. out of a natural need. There is no cause, therefore, Herder feels, to postulate a 'social contract', conceived historically or, as with Rousseau, hypothetically.[6] We cannot but regard social life as something that is given: the state of society *is* man's state of nature. To think of the individual as something outside society is to think in terms of an abstraction. It deludes one into treating him as a repository of

[1] On the passage as a whole see: IV, 37; VIII, 210, 226, 314; XIV, 227.
[2] XXXII, 41.
[3] IX, 313. These are not, of course, original ideas; they recall those of the thinkers of antiquity; nearer home, they are not so very different from those of Shaftesbury, the continental idol of the eighteenth century.
[4] XIII, 384.   [5] IV, 369.   [6] VII, 294.

natural inalienable rights to be maintained against the encroachments of 'society'. It is this misconception which, Herder believes, underlies the doctrine of natural rights. But there is no ground for positing a fundamental antithesis between the individual and society. The two are inseparable; they are complementaries, not opposites. This view does not, in Herder's opinion (as we shall see later), rule out the possibility of social conflict. What it does preclude is the supposition of an *a priori* antagonism between an isolated unit—the individual—on the one hand, and a collective body—society—on the other.[7]

But Herder goes further. Man is not only a social animal but also of necessity a political creature.[8] For his life in society necessitates some form of organization, some regulative device for the ordering of his relations. Government, conceived in this sense, is therefore an integral part of man's social existence: 'Man has never existed without political organization; it is as natural to him as his origin.'[9] Hence it is nonsense, Herder declares, to speak of a non-political state of nature.[10]

The ordering of social relations and the accommodation of wants and interests by rules and regulations, essential though they are, represent for Herder, however, only the outer forms of political activity. He searches for the inward springs of socio-political life, for its inner *Kraft*. For, like Shaftesbury, Herder sees in the inwardness of a thing the source of its strength and staying power. And—rather paradoxically perhaps—he comes to identify this inner sustaining force of socio-political association with what most strikingly reflects the individuality of a human being: his native language.

I. LANGUAGE AND POLITICAL ASSOCIATION: '*VOLK*'

Herder's prize essay *Ueber den Ursprung der Sprache* (1770, published in 1772) has rightly been acclaimed as an outstanding contribution to the study of language.[11] But it was more than that. The issues which it raised transcend the confines of philology.

The subject of the *Essay* (the origin of language) had long fascinated

---

[7] IX, 538; see also V, 509 and XIV, 227.   [8] XVI, 48, 119; see also IX, 311–19.
[9] IX, 313.   [10] V, 44.
[11] It has been variously described as 'the first psychological and philosophical beginning of a theory of language' (Ernst Cassirer, *Freiheit und Form*, op. cit., p. 199); as the 'foundation of a true philosophy of language' (R. Haym, op. cit., vol. I, p. 408); as the 'basis of the science of philology and the comparative study of languages' (R. R. Ergang, *Herder and the Foundations of German Nationalism*, New York, 1931, p. 106); and as Herder's 'most ingenious creative work' (H. A. Korff, op. cit., vol. I, p. 115).

Herder. The heated polemics which the subject aroused in the 'fifties and 'sixties of the century could not, therefore, escape his attention. He decided to join battle, for he felt that neither of the two contending theories was tenable.

Herder dismissed the hypothesis of the divine origin of language as 'humanly inconceivable' and as 'historically and philosophically insupportable'.[12] At the same time, he denied that language could be attributed to human invention. Reason no more than God had 'devised' language. For the emergence of language was not consequent upon, but simultaneous with, the power of reason; reason and language were co-terminous: 'Each nation speaks in the manner it thinks and thinks in the manner it speaks. . . . We cannot think without words.'[13] Herder had already made these points quite clear in the *Fragmente* (1767), which in several important respects foreshadowed the major themes of the *Essay*.

Man, then, was *naturally* endowed with the capacity to speak and the ability to reason. The one implied the other. Whilst Herder did not dispute that man expressed his strongest emotions in sounds and inarticulate cries in a manner indistinguishable from that of an animal, he failed to see what relevance this had to the origin of human language.[14] Were not language and sounds two totally different phenomena?[15] To agree about the animalistic elements in language was one thing; to trace its origin, however, to these elements was quite another. For how was the transition from primitive animalistic 'speech' towards the emergence of intelligible human language to be explained?[16]

That neither Condillac nor Rousseau could convincingly account for the 'jump' from primitive sounds to intelligible language did not surprise Herder since he saw no justification for postulating such a jump.[17] There was no transition from an animalistic to a human stage of language. Man *fundamentally* differed from animals. In place of the animals' instincts, he was endowed with *Besonnenheit*. In view of this, man was not simply an animal with reason superimposed, but a being *sui generis*, whose energies were developed in a wholly different direction.[18] Human language did not evolve from animal sounds. It was not the mere result of a peculiar formation of the mouth and throat, not simply the imitation of the cries of birds and beasts, but rather the corollary of a reflective mind. With the very first sign of consciousness man was a creature of language.[19] The idea, therefore, of an in-between

[12] II, 67.   [13] II,18 and I, 420.   [14] V, 5.   [15] V, 20.
[16] V, 9.   [17] V, 20.   [18] V, 29.   [19] V, 35.

or semi-human state of language, a kind of 'gibberish', as Blackwell had suggested,[20] preceding man's entry into political society, was wholly unfounded, apart from invoking again the 'phantom' of 'natural man'.[21]

Herder approaches the problem of language in terms of three of the dominant conceptual categories which have engaged us in the previous chapter: the principle of interaction, the concept of self-consciousness, and the doctrine of diversity. What is significant, too, is that by viewing language in its widest context Herder succeeds in fusing the epistemological and socio-political implications of *Kraft*, the basic concept of his philosophy of organism.

Herder not only stresses the closest inter-relationship between a community's language and its habits of thought and modes of life; he even draws attention to the interacting influences of such factors as climate and food: 'Climate, water and air, food and drink, they all affect language. . . . Viewed in this way, language is indeed a magnificent treasure store, a collection of thoughts and activities of the mind of the most diverse nature.'[22]

Language is the medium through which man becomes conscious of his inner self, and at the same time it is the key to the understanding of his outer relationships. It unites him with, but it also differentiates him from, others. Imperceptibly it also links him with the past by revealing to him the thoughts, feelings and prejudices of past generations, which thus become deeply ingrained in his own consciousness. He, in turn, again by means of language, perpetuates and enriches these for the benefit of posterity. In this way language embodies the living manifestation of historical growth and the psychological matrix in which man's awareness of his distinctive social heritage is aroused and deepened.[23] Those sharing a particular historical tradition grounded in language Herder identifies with a *Volk* or nationality, and it is in this essentially spiritual quality that he sees the most natural and organic basis for political association.

A language, then, is the criterion by means of which a group's identity as a homogeneous unit can be established. Without its own language, a *Volk* is an absurdity (*Unding*), a contradiction in terms.[24] For neither blood and soil, nor conquest and political fiat can engender that unique

---

[20] Thomas Blackwell, *Enquiry into the Life and Writings of Homer*, 1735. (Page references are to the second edition, London, 1736.) In the third chapter of the *Enquiry*, Blackwell describes the beginnings of language as 'broken, unequal and boisterous', a kind of 'gibberish' (p. 42). Only in the course of political development, during the 'infancy of states' is there a beginning of language properly so called (p. 43). Herder's references to Blackwell: I, 78, 289; V, 330, 341, 398.

[21] V, 44.   [22] V, 125, 136.   [23] V, 135.   [24] I, 147.

consciousness which alone sustains the existence and continuity of a social entity. Even if a *Volk*'s State perishes, the nation remains intact provided it maintains its distinctive linguistic traditions.[25]

Herder's faith in the sustaining and integrating power of language even led him to expect a higher measure of social cohesion to result from the conscious fostering of a common linguistic medium. Thus when he was asked in 1787 to draw up a plan for an 'Institute of German National Enlightenment', he thought of it not merely as an association for the promotion of the German language, but also as a kind of cultural parliament which, by developing and propagating German, would tend to reduce the gulf separating the diverse social classes and thus help to promote the expression of a 'general will'.

Germany has only one interest: the life and wellbeing of the whole; not the sectional interests of the princes or the Estates, not the interest of this or that class. All these divisions only give rise to oppressive restrictions. We Germans still do not understand the importance of a national language. The bulk of our people still think of it as something that only concerns the grammarian. To consider it as the *organ of social activity and co-operation*, as the bond of social classes and a means for their integration: this is something of which most of us have only the remotest notion.[26]

But if language is capable of arousing a sense of identity within a community, it will, in doing so, simultaneously give rise to the community's consciousness of difference from those speaking another language. This, Herder feels, is as it should be. For diversity is the fundamental characteristic of the universal order. The world must be a world of many nationalities.[27] Diversity, not uniformity, is the design of the Almighty. Emperor Joseph II is taken to task for ignoring what patently is a law of Nature and a decree of God: 'Truly, just as God tolerates all languages of this world, so too should a ruler tolerate, nay, treasure, the diverse languages of his subject nations.'[28]

A *Volk*, on this theory, then, is a natural division of the human race, endowed with its own language, which it must preserve as its most distinctive and sacred possession. Language is as much the embodiment of a *Volk*'s 'soul' or character, as it is the expression of an individual's unique personality. By forsaking it, a *Volk* destroys its 'self' for language and the national consciousness to which it gives rise are inseparably joined. Intermixture with other nationalities, therefore, is to be avoided. The situation most congenial to the preservation of the natural order of things is that analogous to the growth of a plant rooted in the soil.[29]

[25] XIV, 87.
[26] XVI, 607 and XVIII, 384; see also R. Haym, op. cit., vol. II, p. 486.
[27] XIV, 67, 84.   [28] XVII, 59.   [29] IV, 212.

If all nations remained where they were originally 'planted', one could look upon the world as a garden of diverse national plants, each flowering according to its own nature and development.

Joseph II's failure to respect the susceptibilities of the diverse linguistic groups of Austria convinced Herder that even an enlightened monarch could not be relied upon to tolerate the existence of national diversity within his State. Henceforth his still essentially 'cultural' nationalism took on a decidedly political complexion. The only natural State was to be the nation-State: 'The most natural State is a community with its own national character.'[30] States which comprised a multitude of nations were no more than mechanical contrivances, lacking in inner life. They were doomed from the very outset: 'These patched up fragile contraptions known as State-machines are wholly devoid of inner life. There is no sentiment, no sympathy of any kind linking their component parts. Just like Trojan horses they move together or against each other. Without national character they are just life-less monsters.'[31]

As a result of this close association between language and politics the most commonly accepted idea of 'nation' underwent a drastic change. A nation no longer simply meant a group of citizens united under a common political sovereign. It was now regarded as a separate natural entity whose claim to political recognition rested on the possession of a common language. But this change in meaning involved difficulties as great as those which it aimed to overcome.[32]

First of all, what is a language? Is it the spoken tongue or vernacular of possibly uneducated or even illiterate people, or is it the written language of law, politics, and literature? The former may be a strictly local vernacular, used only by a small but distinct ethnic group, or it may be a patois or local dialect of some greater tongue; in either case it may or may not contain a poetical tradition. The written language, on the other hand, may have a wider application, but only amongst the educated and literate section of the population. It may also in the process of its development as an instrument of more general usage have

---

[30] XIII, 384.   [31] XIII, 384-5; see also XVI, 48.

[32] This became only too evident when, after the 1914–18 War, linguistic considerations dominated the application of the principle of national self-determination. Yet already during the War there were some who quite clearly foresaw the difficulties involved in the application of this principle. The sociologist Robert Michels, writing in 1915, had few illusions about the alleged coincidence of nationalism and democracy, or that of 'one language—one nation' states and natural frontiers. 'Not one of these solutions is as far-reaching in its effects', he observed, 'as the respective discoverers imagined in the days of their first enthusiasm.' (Robert Michels, *Political Parties*, trans. by Eden and Cedar Paul, London, 1915, p. vii.)

acquired foreign words and hence lost its original purity. Which, then, is the natural language worthy of a *Volk*?

Considerable philological labour would be involved in attempting to find answers to these questions in any particular case.[33] Even if answers would present themselves, they would hardly provide solutions if linguistic considerations violently conflicted with geographical, strategic or economic considerations as regards the most satisfactory and 'natural' territorial frontiers of any one State.[34]

The identification of a territorial State with a language community or *Volk* can easily meet with two further difficulties. There may well be people outside the State's boundaries speaking the same language whose loyalty to their own State may be severely tried in deciding which of the two, the *Volk*, or their State, have prior claim to their allegiance. Secondly, if States must be formed of linguistically homogeneous nations, then in areas of mixed speech the unity of the national State may be seriously threatened by those ethnic minority groups who failed to attain political recognition for their territorial claims. The continued existence of such minorities will require a degree of toleration on the part of the dominant nationality which is not likely to be forthcoming. Hence their lot may turn out to be far more unfavourable under the changed circumstances than it was within a political framework which was not based on the nationality principle.[35]

Finally, there are peoples who regard themselves as nations without possessing a distinct language of their own (such as the Austrians or Argentinians); or there are those who, in spite of comprising several distinct languages, still consider themselves as one nation (such as the Swiss or Indians, for example); or again there are ethnic groups (such as the Irish or Welsh), claiming distinct nationhood, although only a small minority of their members speak their original tongue. All these cases would seem anomalies in the light of linguistic nationalism.

In view of these observations it is, to say the least, debatable whether language can provide a satisfactory method whereby nations may be

[33] Thus, for example, Pan-Slavist philologists may be able to 'prove' that all Slavonic tongues derive from Russian; German nationalists may claim that the Dutch and Flemish peoples are really speaking a dialect of German and hence ought to be part of the German nation. On the other hand, there are Ukrainians, Croats and Slovaks, demanding their own States, claiming that their languages are really distinct from Russian, Serb and Czech respectively.

[34] Czech nationalists invoked at one and the same time the linguistic principle to justify the creation of the Czech nation-State, and topographical and historic considerations in order to include strategically and economically valuable parts of the original kingdom of Bohemia, even though these were heavily populated by Germans.

[35] See Eugen Lemberg, *Nationalismus*, 2 vols., Hamburg, 1964. Vol. I, pp. 182-4.

distinguished from one another and constituted into sovereign States. Even if it is granted that linguistic considerations may conceivably perform an auxiliary function in settling conflicting territorial claims, they can hardly be regarded as the sole or even chief political criterion for determining a State's frontiers. States which result from the application of such a principle may be as full of anomalies as the heterogeneous empires which they replace.

It is understandable that to the philosopher and man of letters, with no experience in the exercise of political power, the thought of political frontiers being purely the result of physical power, skilful diplomacy, or historical accident, is a disagreeable thought. It pains his sensibility. A State based on force or dynastic arrangements is a sheer mechanical artifice. Lacking the consciousness of a common spiritual bond, it is like a body without a soul. Yet even if it is admitted that there can be no spontaneous community life in a State devoid of a spiritual bond, it does not follow that language constitutes the exclusive prerequisite for its existence. Similarly, it is one thing to invoke the principle of diversity to justify the preservation of the identity of different communities, and yet quite another to confine the mark of distinction to the possession of a common language.

Herder, to be sure, does not always think of *Volk* and national character—the two operative terms in his philosophy of nationalism—in this narrow linguistic sense. There are passages which reveal him to be fully alive to the complexities involved, passages in which he castigates those who indulge in glib talk and oversimplifications, and in which he warns against the dangers of rash generalizations: 'Each nation must be considered on its own merits, with regard to its situation and its own distinctive features; arbitrary selection or rejection of this or that characteristic, of this or that custom, do not render its history.'[36] His account of the Hebrews (in whom he sees the oldest and 'most excellent example' of a *Volk* with a genuine national character), in particular, illustrates his awareness of the manifold facets that constitute national character.[37] Thus, in an attempt to elicit the mainsprings of Jewish nationhood, Herder lays stress on four factors apart from language:

---

[36] XVIII, 248; see also III, 432 and XVIII, 56.
[37] X, 139. Herder's *Vom Geist der Ebräischen Poesie*, published in two volumes in 1782–3 can be regarded as one of his most mature works after the *Ideen*. For a fuller treatment of Herder's political interpretation of the people of the Bible, see my 'The Hebrews and Herder's Political Creed', *The Modern Language Review*, vol. LIV, October 1959, pp. 533–46.

(i) the land as the *Volk*'s common heritage;
(ii) the law of the constitution, as a covenant freely entered upon;
(iii) the family or clan origin, fostered and perpetuated by
(iv) reverence for the forefathers.

But even then it is not any one of these factors taken by itself which is held to be of decisive importance. For Herder views them as inextricably interwoven elements, constituting in a conceptual sense an organic whole. And it is in the literary traditions and in the language of a people that he finds both the source and the expression of this conceptual unity. The extraordinary fascination, for example, which the land of their origin has for the Jews, Herder attributes to the way in which the land and the law are inseparably linked in their holy literature.[38] Similarly, their sense of historical continuity as a *Volk* is held to be derived from, and reflected in, the emotive significance of the word 'father' in Hebrew. The Hebrew language, Herder writes, knows no higher term of distinction and endearment, and the esteem in which the word is held indicates the reverence which the Jews have for their forefathers, a reverence which is at once a family *and* a national manifestation.[39]

In the final analysis, then, it can be seen that even when Herder did recognize that factors other than language partook in fashioning national character, he never ceased to regard the linguistic element as the decisive determinant.[40] This had immense political consequences. The view that only those who share (or at least did once share) a common language and literary tradition were worthy of recognition as a nation, and as such should constitute a State, not only laid the ideological foundation of nationalist doctrine; it also led to the prodigious philological research which accompanied nationalist agitation. Henceforth the belief gained ground that political boundaries should be the result of linguistic enquiries and that, therefore, the assistance of professors of philology and collectors of folklore ought to be enlisted to aid, if not to replace, the modern statesman.

2. POLITICAL ASSOCIATION AND SOCIAL STRUCTURE: THE MODEL *VOLK*-STATE

Herder's interpretation of the history and literary traditions of the

---

[38] XII, 115, 335.   [39] XII, 107; see also VI, 60 and XIV, 84.
[40] This is also demonstrated by Herder's treatment of folk-song and folk-poetry. He once went so far as to deny the possibility of national character in the absence of a folk-song tradition (XXVII, 180).

Hebrews is of interest not only for the light it throws on his theory of nationalism; it is also indicative of his views on the socio-political structure of the envisaged *Volk*-State.[41]

It seems to have been Herder's innermost conviction that a healthy or natural community such as the *Volk*-State had no need for a sovereign authority wielding supreme political power. The *Volk*-State embodied for him a pattern of communal life, rooted in history and tradition, where the citizens were imbued with a sense of common purpose and conscious of their mutual inter-dependence. Admittedly, self-preservation, Herder agreed with Hobbes, remained a vital considera-tion. But self-preservation did not, in Herder's view, necessitate the institution of central political authority, for he denied that self-preservation implied a state of perpetual antagonism. Not war, but peace, Herder maintained, was the natural disposition of unoppressed humanity. War was the result of oppression, the corollary of the rule of force. The institution of a central political power, therefore, was not the beginning but the collapse of politics; it was the symptom of social decay and political bankruptcy.[42]

Herder's theory of government was essentially a teleological argu-ment grounded in his metaphysical and religious beliefs about the destiny of man. Its two basic postulates were:

(i) that man could only fully realize himself as a member of a *Volk*,[43] and

(ii) that it was not man's lot to rule or to obey.[44]

The first postulate is intended to imply that the *Volk* constitutes a sort of organic whole or unity of which the individual citizen forms a con-stitutent part. The second postulate presupposes a state of affairs in which the law rather than man governs. But to see more clearly what Herder actually had in mind, it may be worth while to examine briefly what he had to say on the Hebrew State and, in particular, on the Legal Code of Moses.

Herder looked upon Moses as one of the wisest legislators not only of

---

[41] Herder may well have found it more prudent to express his political views under this literary and theological disguise. For when he was reiterating them in the *Ideen*, he was advised to withhold them from publication. (See XVIII, 356; I, 528; and H. Düntzer and F. G. v. Herder, *Aus Herders Nachlaß*, Frankfurt a.M., 1856, vol. II, p. 268.)

[42] XIII, 319–22.   [43] XVIII, 309.

[44] XIII, 383: 'Man is an animal as long as he needs a master; as soon as he attains the status of a human being he no longer needs a master in any real sense.' Herder opposed this view to Kant's, that 'man is an animal that needs a lord when he lives with others of his species'. (*Idee zu einer allgemeinen Geschichte in weltbürgerlicher Absicht*, 1784; *Kant Schriften*, Preuss. Akademie der Wissenschaften edition, Berlin, 1923, vol. VIII, p. 23.)

the Jews but also of mankind as a whole.[45] The Mosaic Law, Herder further urged, should be studied not merely for its ethical content but also for its political significance.[46] Indeed, Herder went so far as to suggest that in case Moses had only pretended his laws to be of divine origin, he did so, if he did, out of political wisdom.[47]

But whilst Herder believed that laws to be truly efficacious should enjoy almost divine reverence, he rejected that conception of Natural Law which postulated a fundamental covenant in the manner in which Althusius and Pufendorf spoke of the agreed basis of the *corpus symbioticum*. Thus, although Herder saw in the Mosaic Law the oldest example of a written constitution, he did not regard it as a rigid contract.[48] On the contrary, he held it to have been intended as a flexible constitutional document, amendable to suit changing circumstances. Moses himself, Herder observed, never hesitated to alter the constitution when the situation required it.[49] For example, Moses found it necessary to confine the exercise of some public duties to one tribe, the Levites, whereas the original constitution had stipulated that the first-born of all tribes should have equal participation in public affairs, including the administration of law and justice.[50] To the prophets Moses assigned the right and the duty not only of protecting the constitution, but also of preventing it ever becoming a 'dead letter'. The prophets were to be the shield against tyranny.[51] They were to be the guardians, the sages of the people, who were to arouse it if it, or its priests, remained passive in the face of political oppression of any kind.[52]

Herder also repudiated the notion of inalienable individual rights that are alleged to be prior to, and beyond the reach of, political or positive legislation. There is not a shred of evidence, Herder declared, that Moses thought in terms of innate and inalienable rights which the individual could be said to have possessed before the constitution came into being. Indeed, the individual as such was not the major concern at all. The purpose of the Mosaic constitution, according to Herder, was the creation of a free people, subject to none other than its laws. It was

---

[45] XI, 450.
[46] Herder writes to this effect in a significant footnote: 'The reasons for his legislation were not only moral and philosophical but also national' (XI, 462).
[47] XII, 122.   [48] XI, 452.   [49] XI, 453.
[50] Moses was however careful, Herder adds, to curtail his people's political freedom as little as possible even then by ensuring that the Levites had no executive or legislative powers. 'The tribe of Levi was the most *learned, but not the* ruling tribe; every *political* decision', Herder points out, 'depended on the tribal elders of the whole people' (XII, 120).
[51] XII, 114.   [52] XI, 458.

the *Volk* which Moses is said to have had in mind, chiefly, *its* right to national existence and national freedom.

This did not necessarily mean, Herder adds, that the liberties of the individual were overlooked. The very fact that the constitution provided for a republican system, the essence of which was 'nomocracy', i.e. the rule of law, wholly precluded, in Herder's view, any form of arbitrariness. As long as the law remained the supreme arbiter, the citizen had no ground for fear: 'That law should rule and not the Legislator, that a free nation should freely accept and honour it, that invisible, reasonable and benevolent forces should guide us and not chains enslave us: this was the idea of Moses.'[53] Under such a system men would not submit to the power exercised by other men under the name of government. For its sole 'government' would be the rule of law.

Good government, then, means invisible government. As long as a political system can dispense with personal rulers, as long as it succeeds in operating without having recourse to physical power as a sanction of authority, so long will it remain compatible with the dignity of the human spirit. The gentler, the more invisible the political bonds which link a community, the greater, Herder feels, will be the degree of its permanence.[54] In a republican system, presumably, it is laws and institutions that matter, not personalities or superior physical power. This at least seems to be the implication. For Herder regards the republican form of the Mosaic constitution as its most vital characteristic. God alone is king. With the institution of kings Herder considers the constitution to have become invalidated.[55]

Four main points emerge from Herder's interpretation of the Mosaic Law:

(i) Herder visualizes a written, republican form of constitution; flexible in theory, but less so in practice. For the main emphasis is not on the flexibility of, but rather on the reverence for, law. By stipulating that the written constitution is to enjoy almost divine esteem as the supreme political institution, changes are not really encouraged. Although Herder explicitly rejects Pufendorf's concept of natural law, his insistence on regarding the republican form of the constitution as vital (without which he deems the constitution to be suspended) suggests that at least in this respect there is an element of contractual rigidity in the manner of an original and basic covenant.

By invoking an almost divine reverence for the constitution and laws of his model *Volk*-State, Herder may be said to be encouraging or

[53] XII, 117.   [54] XII, 117.   [55] XII, 121; see also XII, 82, 115.

condoning another form of servility. For the reverence for the Law may become, or at least entail, the tyranny of custom. It is probable that Herder, if thus challenged, would retort that to liberate a community from what is called the tyranny of custom, is to enslave it wholly to the tyranny of man. In his model State Herder clearly looks upon the conservative forces within the community as the surest safeguard against any encroachment on the liberties of its members.[56]

(ii) Herder conceived the organization of Hebrew society on what may be termed *quasi*-pluralistic lines; a many-centred as distinct from a monolithic structure. There is no single focus of power. Within the apparently undifferentiated social and economic framework of the entire *Volk* (undifferentiated in a vertical sense), a number of sectional groups (the Levites, the priests, the prophets, the elders, and presumably other associations and semi-corporate bodies) co-exist.[57] It is true, legislative power is confined to one group, the elders of each tribe. But their effective power is not intended to be very substantial. Custom and tradition, maintaining the 'reverence for the Law', will act as a brake on their legislative freedom, especially if the 'reverence' is backed by any of the various co-existing sections and *foci* of influence.

(iii) Political government is not vested in any one permanent administrative body. It is identified with a 'representative' body of the people, the elders, who meet as circumstances require. In this sense the elders are, no doubt, sovereign. But their sovereignty is, for reasons indicated above, only a shadow, only a caricature of what a Hobbes or Rousseau meant by that term.

The political structure envisaged by Herder may seem, on the other hand, vaguely similar to Locke's separation of powers, or to its more developed form, Montesquieu's system of checks and balances. But the resemblance is deceptive. There is no suggestion in Herder's account of a division into, or a separation between, legislative, executive, judiciary or federative powers. The very concept of *power* has no place in it.[58] Again, Montesquieu's phraseology, if not necessarily the conception underlying it, is distinctly 'mechanical'. His State appears like a vast piece of intricate machinery. Each cog is kept in operation by an exact calculation of the impact of counteracting forces. It is a matter of

[56] In this respect there is a marked affinity between Herder and Rousseau. (See the latter's *Considérations sur le Gouvernement de Pologne*, ch. XI, where Rousseau is urging the preservation of ancient customs as a vital political safeguard.)

[57] Herder's insistence on the co-existence of sectional bodies is in marked contrast to Rousseau's hostility to any form of pluralism.

[58] Indeed, one could say that in Herder's political system the legitimacy of the political framework is made contingent on the absence of physical power.

political engineering based on Newtonian physics. Herder, on the other hand, wishes to dispense with political 'machinery'. His is an 'organic' State. The *Volk*-State is conceived as a territorial community with its own language, laws and customs. It is the 'natural' social framework within which various sectional bodies and associations operate and co-operate, and not an administrative machine. Indeed government is virtually reduced (or elevated) to 'co-operation'. There are no 'rulers'. Their existence is regarded as a denial of the rule of law. Government must be impersonal, non-physical; otherwise it will, Herder fears, constitute a burden upon a healthy community.

(iv) The right of the nation rather than that of the individual engages Herder's main attention. This shift of emphasis foreshadows what was to differentiate the 'liberal' outlook of the Enlightenment from that of the nineteenth century, at least in continental Europe. The 'individual' is conceived as an integral part of a whole which is the language community or *Volk*. At the same time it must be remembered that the 'whole' is only meaningful for Herder if it is thought of as the integration of a great variety of smaller wholes which are self-regulating units in themselves and do not originate from, or depend on the existence of a central power. What Herder advocates in his model *Volk*-State is not centralized collectivism, but a kind of partnership between a variety of social, economic, cultural, religious, and legal bodies and associations within a political framework free from any one determinate pressure-centre. No separate political body, apparently, is required to co-ordinate and control these heterogeneous institutions.

This may seem odd. But Herder, it will be recalled, denies the existence of a natural antagonism between the members of a *Volk*. In place of the notion of continuous tension between the centrifugal and the centralizing forces within a State, which underlies the concept of social contract and the theories of Natural Law, Herder puts the notion of partnership between self-regulating, yet inter-dependent, social bodies. On this notion there is little point in formulating specific individual rights as a safeguard against the encroachments of non-existing central governments.

3. POLITICAL ASSOCIATION AND CENTRAL AUTHORITY

Herder's hostility towards vesting supreme political power in a central government was in a sense the obverse of his cherished belief in diversity. He feared that a central authority could not but threaten the free unfolding of, and the harmonious co-operation between, the diverse centres of activity. Believing, as he did, that diversity united by creating the conditions of reciprocal service, he felt that only by providing the fullest scope for diversity could a genuine and lasting feeling of social unity be engendered and maintained. Since he suspected that a central sovereign body would inevitably be resented by some, it would, in order to preserve its authority, sooner or later have to resort to compulsion. But in such an attempt it would impose 'unity' at the price of diversity and thereby destroy the natural and spontaneous forces that make for unity in a healthy, diversified social order. It would create uniformity and not true unity which can only function amidst diversity.[59]

The other chief reason for Herder's opposition to the idea of a determinate political body stemmed from his belief that man's authority over man was an affront to human dignity. Governmental authority, exercised by one man or a body of men, implied the citizen's willingness to obey the commands of such an authority. This, in Herder's view, was an unnecessary humiliation. The existence of such a body, moreover, also ran counter to Herder's notion of law as something binding on all members of the State, since it meant the issuing of laws and commands by an authority which was not subject to them. Such a state of affairs, Herder feared, could not but result in arbitrariness.

Herder thought of law essentially in medieval terms, as a declaration of custom and time-honoured usage, to be discovered rather than made. Law was something inherent in the traditional mode of life of a natural society of men, such as the *Volk*, and, provided it was correctly discerned, legislation had no need of coercive sanction. For it was then the expression of a people's moral consciousness and therefore exercised *inner* compelling power. A law, on the other hand, which had not grown out of communal traditions, which was simply a rule promulgated by an authority backed by coercive power, was but a lifeless shadow.[60]

That Herder's main grounds for opposing the institution of central government are not beyond challenge is obvious enough. Both his belief in diversity as the *sine qua non* of harmonious social co-operation and his credal affirmation of folk-law can be questioned on empirical and logical grounds. Diversity may be the natural order of things, but it may have disintegrating as well as unifying characteristics. Folk-law may be time-honoured but also archaic and ambiguous. Laws in harmony with a people's moral consciousness may be good laws, but they may also be thoroughly bad laws. It is not diversity as such, or law

[59] Herder, we shall see below, argued on similar lines against absolutist rule and political censorship (IX, 354–62).
[60] IV, 466–9.

based on custom, which can be looked upon as an infallible safeguard against social and political ills. For there is no necessary connexion between diversity and co-operation or between folk-laws and just laws.

Nevertheless, Herder's fundamental purpose in the matter is not difficult to see. By stressing the *inward* forces of socio-political cohesion Herder hoped to render external coercive power superfluous and, at the same time, to define the nature and area of individual freedom. Like Kant, Herder believed that man was only free when obeying the laws which he found within himself; 'self-determination', he felt, was the highest moral and political good, the chief remedy for the ills of society. That this idea posed more problems than it set out to settle may well be said today. At the time, however, it not only profoundly changed the mode of political theorizing, it also palpably affected the trend of political action.[61]

By drawing so close an analogy between the collective unit of *Volk* or nation and the individual person (for self-determination was held to be equally applicable to both), Herder suggests that he was thinking of the *Volk*-State in anthropomorphic terms, investing it with a body and soul, with a 'personality' of its own. His reference to the Hebrew people as a *'genetisches Individuum'* and his use of biological metaphors lend further support to such a view.[62] Yet it is of interest that in his choice of biological similes Herder nowhere stipulates a subordinate organic relationship such as that of a leaf to the tree, or of a limb to the human body. Instead he insists on functional co-ordination between units which, though mutually inter-dependent, are none the less unique and *active* wholes in themselves. It is in view of these internal energizing forces that Herder views the State as an organism rather than as a mechanical assembly. But his image of an organism is that of a complex of integrated organisms rather than that of a single human body in which the head could be identified with the central power of the State. In spite of the use of biological metaphors Herder seems to be in no doubt that being a member of a social whole or organism is quite a different relation from that of being part of a body.

In having recourse, therefore, to anthropomorphic and horticultural examples, Herder was not oblivious of the very fundamental differences between a social unit and a single individual, on the one hand, and between plants and human beings on the other. But there was one organic characteristic which he held to be common to social life no less

---

[61] We shall return to Herder's theory of self-determination in a subsequent chapter (ch. V).

[62] XVII, 285; see also I, 151; IV, 212; XIV, 67, 84; XX, 136.

than to plant life or the life of a single human being, namely, the element of *growth*. Herder, that is, wished to emphasize that for a State to be a natural political body that would endure in time, it had to be the result of spontaneous growth out of, and within, a specific cultural environment in which language and literary traditions were the determinate and distinctive characteristics. Although he applied biological terms like 'genetic' and 'organic' to this process of growth,[63] he did not think of it primarily in a biological sense. His main concern was the historical continuity of a *Volk*, and he identified this continuity with the conscious transmission of social cultures and not with physical characteristics that attend heredity. He held this transmission to be 'genetic' because language *via* education made it possible to effect a linking of a *Volk*'s social heritage between one generation and another, and 'organic' by virtue of the manner in which it was assimilated and creatively re-applied.[64] The *Volk*-State was, therefore, conceived as a partnership in a twofold sense: it was the sphere of co-operation between its members at any given time; but it was also a partnership of generations.

The question has sometimes been raised whether or not Herder's organic conception of *Volk*, with its emphasis on 'genetic' national characteristics has helped to inspire modern racialist doctrines.[65] Herder, it is true, did not favour the inter-mixing of communities of diverse ethnic origins. His scathing remarks about the 'wild mixing of entire nations', could possibly, especially when quoted out of their context, give rise to the view that Herder was advocating a kind of racial purity.[66] This view could be further reinforced if Herder's favourite word 'genetic' is interpreted in the terminology of modern biology. On the other hand, it must be remembered that it was not blood but language which Herder regarded as the essential criterion of a *Volk*. *Volk* was conceived as an ethnic and not as a racial community. Herder did not recognize any intermediate collective units between

---

[63] XIV, 84 and XIII, 348.

[64] Herder's theory of the transmission of social cultures will engage us further in chapter VI.

[65] See, for example, Benno v. Wiese, *Volk und Dichtung von Herder bis zur Romantik*, Erlangen, 1938, p. 18; or his 'Der Gedanke des Volkes in Herders Weltbild', *Die Erziehung*, 1939, pp. 121, 137; or Max Rouché, *La Philosophie de l'histoire de Herder*, Paris, 1940, p. 554; or R. G. Collingwood, *The Idea of History*, Oxford, 1946, pp. 86–92; or K. R. Popper, *The Open Society and its Enemies*, second edition, London, 1952, vol. II, p. 52; or finally, H. S. Reiss, *The Political Thought of the German Romantics*, Oxford, 1955, pp. 2, 8.

[66] XIII, 384. Herder is here not concerned with 'racial purity', but with the forcible inter-mixing of nationalities as a result of military subjugation.

Volk and mankind, and he thought of mankind as being biologically undifferentiated. Whilst he believed that mental habits may differ considerably between national groups, he nevertheless denied that these differences were attributable to differences of race. 'However diverse the forms may be in which mankind manifests itself; it is none the less everywhere one and the same human species', Herder declared in the *Ideen*, and concerning the concept of 'race', he remarked simply: 'I see no cause for employing this term.'[67] What is more, the idea of racial superiority, which is the key concept of modern racialism, was completely alien to Herder's mind. He firmly rejected the notion of 'superman' and the idea of master-nations or master-races.[68] Domination or persecution of any kind, whether of man by man, or of one nation by another was abhorrent to his very being.[69] There is no need to labour the point. Herder, the 'high priest' of *Humanität* was singularly ill-qualified for the part of a precursor of racialist doctrine.

It must be recognized, however, that Herder's paradigm of a political unit, the 'organically' integrated community—which he opposed to the 'mechanistic' model of the bureaucratic State, put forward by the political jurists—is, in spite of its sociologically significant positivist implications, an essentially normative model. As such it undoubtedly has its use as a heuristic device for judging the nature and degree of social cohesion in actual States. But it has its danger too. The concept of power may well be irrelevant to a theory which views society as the outcome of historical *growth* and as a network of spontaneous co-operative activities and shared cultural traditions. Yet when actual conditions fail to correspond to those envisaged in Herder's social theory, the application of his political terminology may help to disguise the realities of power-politics in a way that would make political matters indistinguishable from linguistic and metaphysical questions where power is not involved.

Although Herder was not always successful in keeping the real and the ideal apart, he was aware of the gap that separated them. We shall now have to enquire how Herder visualized the bridging of this gap in his proposed transformation from the 'mechanical' to the 'organic' State.

[67] XIII, 252, 257. In this respect, too, there is a significant divergence of views between Herder and Kant. The latter, in his review of the *Ideen* in the *Allgemeine Literaturzeitung* of 15 November 1785, makes a point in criticizing Herder for his 'inadequate and unsympathetic treatment of the concept of race'.

[68] XVII, 115; see also XVIII, 248: 'There must be no order of rank; . . . the negro is as much entitled to think the white man degenerate as the white man is in thinking of the negro as a black beast.'

[69] XVII, 273: 'From early childhood I have found nothing more abominable and detestable than persecutions.'

IV

FROM MECHANISM TO ORGANISM

MOST political thinkers of the Enlightenment were primarily interested in how men should be governed and not in who should do the governing. They were more concerned that men should be governed with benevolence and competent ability than that men should themselves participate in government. They had no serious objection to aristocratic privilege, nor even to absolutist rule, provided the rulers heeded their 'enlightened' demands for toleration, the abolition of torture, the emancipation of the serfs and the provision of greater welfare. Certainly men such as Leibniz, Thomasius, Wolff and the *Aufklärer*, Voltaire, Diderot and his fellow-Encyclopaedists thought on these lines. Even A. L. Schlözer never went further than that. The idea that ordinary men, men of the common people, could or should be expected to share in the responsibility of government seemed absurd or did not occur to them at all.

The young Herder shared this outlook too. He had unbounded faith in the enlightenment of capable rulers. It is true, he had no profound sympathies with Frederick the Great until after the latter's death. But he undoubtedly expected great things from Catherine II. He even published an enthusiastic poem on the occasion of her coronation in 1765.[1] He was to be disappointed. Similarly he looked forward with anticipation to the reign of Joseph II. Again his hopes were not fulfilled. This time he was not merely disappointed. He was disillusioned. 'He wanted the best for his subjects, but he wanted it as a despot.'[2] Joseph's failure at reform marked a turning point in Herder's political outlook. It is impossible, he now maintained, to combine the most progressive, the most enlightened ideas with personal absolutism.[3]

But this change of view was not a sudden and dramatic conversion. Herder's faith in the enlightenment of absolute rulers had been on the wane even before he had begun to realize that Catherine II, though she delighted in listening to Diderot, had not the slightest intention of

---

[1] XXIX, 24–7; see also Haym, op. cit., vol. I, p. 108.
[2] XVII, 61.   [3] ibid.

paying any heed to his political suggestions.[4] Between the days in Königsberg (1762–4) and his arrival at Weimar (1776), Herder had thought a great deal about politics as his notes and particularly his Travel Diary (1769) reveal. 'The State must be reformed from below', he decided in those years, though he kept it, as yet, to himself.[5] The first inkling we get from his published work of a fundamental change in his outlook is in his Essay *Auch eine Philosophie der Geschichte zur Bildung der Menschheit* (1774). For here he made it quite clear what his preference would be had he to choose between the efficient government of the enlightened despot and the possibly less efficient and less orderly political arrangement in which the people had a share in government: 'Even if institutions are not perfect; even if men are not always honest; even if there is some disorder and a good deal of disagreement—it is still preferable to a state of affairs in which men are forced to rot and decay during their lifetime.'[6]

Henceforth the conviction takes root that, to be natural, States had to be *both*: national and popular. It is this conviction which gives political direction to Herder's reforming zeal: *Volk* and *Nation* must be one.[7]

I. *VOLK* AND NATION

When Herder was speaking of the Hebrews as a *Volk*, he meant by it both: (1) a homogeneous *national* unit and (2) a virtually unstratified *social* unit. Contemporary States, on the other hand, were neither. Even where conditions approximated to the linguistic requirements which Herder deemed essential for the existence of a national State, the *Volk* was only a part of the political nation. Which part? Occasionally Herder identified it with all those who were being governed as distinct from the rulers. More commonly, however, he drew a distinction between *Volk* and *Pöbel* (rabble) on the one hand, and *Volk* and the intellectuals on the other. With each of these sectional groups he

[4] John Viscount Morley, *Diderot and the Encyclopaedists*, London, 1923, vol. II, pp. 112–14.
[5] XXXII, 56. The quotation is taken from his undated notes.
[6] V, 516.
[7] In this respect Ergang's observations on the political significance of Herder's folk-song movement are of interest (op. cit., pp. 198–211). Herder's insistence on building a national tradition upon the speech and songs of the common people was a revolutionary notion. The idea that the *Volk*, the lowest order of society was not simply an inarticulate mob but rather the creative source of a nation's culture, became the ideological armour of those who subsequently presented the case for democracy and nationalism as essentially one argument.

associated primarily certain mental and emotional characteristics. But whilst the line separating the 'learned' from the 'ordinary' people was somewhat fluid,[8] the 'rabble' was sharply marked off as a social substratum *apart* from the *Volk*.[9] Similarly, on the other end of the social scale, the aristocracy was excluded too.[10]

In effect, then, Herder distinguishes between two *Volk* elements, the majority, consisting of the *bourgeoisie* (*das Volk der Bürger*), and the minority, consisting of the intellectuals (*das Volk der Gelehrsamkeit*).[11] The *Bürger* are, however, not only the most numerous, but also, Herder insists, the most useful and venerable part of the *Volk*, if not, indeed, *the Volk* proper.[12] Herder associates with the term *Bürger* all those occupations that figure prominently in folk-song: the farmer, the fisherman, the craftsman and artisan, the small trader; all those, that is, who, he feels, are least affected by the influence of 'civilization' and, accordingly, embody most truly the original *Volk* characteristics of the nation. The qualities he has in mind are features such as spontaneity, 'earthiness', *Naturverbundenheit*; a kind of naturalness and simplicity found in children.[13]

It is not clear whether Herder thinks of the *Bürger* as forming a homogeneous group without significant economic and social distinctions, or whether he regards them as a group which, in spite of such distinctions, derives a certain degree of homogeneity from a similarity in mental habits. Similarly, it is not evident what part of the population is designated by the term 'rabble'. Herder nowhere suggests that he is applying the criterion of property-ownership, commonly employed by eighteenth-century political writers. 'Rabble' may, therefore, refer to a group of people of a somewhat lower mental outlook (*Denkart*) rather than to a specific economic class.

There is no indication, either, whether Herder considers serfdom to be a thing of the past or, if not, whether the serfs are also included in the term *Bürger*. He only says who is excluded: the aristocracy, the men of learning, and the 'rabble'. But since he refers to the *Bürger* as the labouring part of the nation which, though it is the most numerous, is nevertheless the most oppressed and exploited section of the population,[14] it is feasible to assume that Herder makes no distinction between *Bürger* and serfs.

---

[8] II. 25; see also V, 185.   [9] XXV, 323; see also III, 413.
[10] XVII, 391, 413.   [11] XXXII, 60.   [12] I, 392; see also VI, 104.
[13] V, 182; see also VII, 265. It may be of interest to note here that Herder, commenting critically on social and political conditions in Russia, observed in his *Travel Diary*: 'He (the Russian) has no word for *Bürger* in his language' (IV, 419).
[14] XXIII, 210; see also XXX, 200.

Certain overtones in the words which Herder used in this connexion have a familiar ring in our own time. It is, however, very much an open question whether Herder would have readily applied his favourite collective term *Volk* in the sense of *Bürger* to the modern industrial proletariat. For what impressed Herder most was not chiefly the size of the *Bürgertum*, nor its productive value, nor even the degree of economic exploitation and political oppression to which it was subjected, although all these circumstances did not leave him unconcerned. It was rather the conviction that the working folk were the 'national' salt of the earth, the most genuine expression of national character, that really fired his enthusiasm, his zeal for political reform. He saw in them the embodiment of all that was natural and original in a nation. It is a moot point whether he would have associated these characteristics with the modern factory worker.

What is beyond doubt is that Herder looked upon education, or rather its absence, as the chief cause of the *Bürger*'s social inferiority and political impotence. That the major part of the nation should be so uneducated, if not wholly illiterate, was not, Herder argued, attributable to natural circumstances such as differences in innate ability. It was rather the harvest of persistent and wilful neglect, for which, Herder declared, the ruling aristocracy must entirely shoulder the blame.

Where, in all the different parts of our country, do we find educational institutions for the most deserving and venerable part of our public, the part which we identify with 'the people' (*Volk*)? What a difference there is in the education and mentality of the multitude! But are the members of this multitude not human? Are they—who are the core of the nation—not capable of enlightenment, not worth educating? Is it the nobility only that needs enlightenment in order to enable it to exploit and dominate the former more effectively?[15]

Herder's aversion to hereditary rule and to the existence of an hereditary aristocracy was deep-seated. 'He is dreadfully hostile to the aristocracy; he regards it as the very embodiment of human stupidity, as something which conflicts with every principle of Christianity and, of course, with the very concept of human equality', Johann Georg Müller reported in his diary after a visit to Herder.[16] Herder never tired of questioning the principle of hereditary rule as a method of political

---

[15] VI, 104-5.
[16] J. G. Müller, *Aus dem Herderschen Hause* (1780–1782), ed. by J. Baechtold, Berlin, 1881, p. 109. See also Herder's letter to Johannes v. Müller (dated 10 October 1796): 'Alas, if the *Germans* mattered instead of their princes!' (Joh. v. Müller, *Briefwechsel mit J. G. Herder und Caroline v. Herder geb. Flachsland, 1782–1808*, ed. by K. E. Hoffmann, Schaffhausen, 1952, p. 44.)

government. It appeared to him not only senseless but also pernicious. Nature had not divided her best gifts in families: 'Why should one man, merely by virtue of his birth acquire the right to rule over thousands of his brethren?'[17] That those as yet unborn should be destined to rule over others not yet born, simply by virtue of their blood, seemed to Herder the most unintelligible of propositions that human language could devise and the most blatant example of unreason in the history of human reason.[18]

It was Herder's thesis that war had created the conditions conducive to the emergence of aristocratic rule.[19] But war was not only responsible, in his view, for the existence of an hereditary nobility; it was also, he held, the cause of serfdom which, unlike Justus Möser, he condemned on both moral and economic grounds.[20] These 'corollaries of conquest, subjugation and exploitation', Herder maintained, were kept alive and perpetuated by the continuance of the hereditary system and by the deliberate restriction of social mobility.[21]

2. REFORM FROM BELOW: 'HUMANIZATION' AND 'ARISTO-DEMOCRACY'

In view of this hostility to the existing form of political rule, it is not surprising that Herder showed little faith in the likelihood and efficacy of reform from above. Instead he pinned his hopes on the emergence of popular leaders, 'men of the people', who, imbued with missionary zeal, would preach and spread the gospel of education (*Bildung*) and guide the rest of the nation to a stage where it would no longer be in need of political rulers.

The phrase 'men of the people' is clearly defined by Herder. This is unusual. And, paradoxically enough, it is also confusing.

Although Herder opposed the division of society into classes that were sharply marked off from one another, he none the less attached considerable importance to the 'middle class', which he held to be the 'pillar' of a State.[22] And it was from this class that Herder visualized his 'men of the people' to originate: 'Intellectual and cultural activity has its source in the middle class; in order to re-vitalize the whole of the people it will need to become diffused in both the upward and the

---

[17] XIII, 332; see also ibid., 377 and XVII, 61.   [18] XIII, 377.
[19] ibid.   [20] XIII, 377–8.   [21] XIII, 378.
[22] XXIII, 429. Herder attributed, as Montesquieu had done, England's rise as a commercial power, and her possession of greater political freedom to the early participation in government by her middle class (XVIII, 108).

downward direction.'[23] But unless Herder was here widening his concept of Volk (as synonymous with Bürger) to include those associated with guiding intellectual and cultural activities, he could only mean by 'men of the people' men who would lead the people to a higher standard of cultural and political maturity, but who themselves did not originate from it. Leaders of, but not from, the people.

It was, presumably, to this period of transition in which all members of the nation were to attain better education and a more developed political consciousness that Herder's concept of 'aristo-democracy' was intended to apply.[24]

The ultimate aim of aristo-democracy Herder saw in the disappearance of the State as an administrative 'machine' of government, and its replacement by an 'organic' way of ordering social life, in which active co-operation would render all forms of sub-ordination obsolete and superfluous.[25] But the immediate task of the aristo-democrats was what Herder called the 'humanization' of the existing political order.[26]

By 'humanization' Herder chiefly meant the provision of education and social welfare under conditions of political freedom. This, Herder insisted, presupposed as the most basic requirement the absence of political censorship and the abolition of absolutist rule.

Herder's arguments against political censorship are comparable in their eloquence to those J. S. Mill was to advance in his essay On Liberty. Their main contention was that censorship harmed most those who imposed it. In suppressing the critically disposed in any society, it helped superstition and all kinds of obscure myths to gain ground. Being inimical to all progress, it stifled all that was new merely because it involved changes from the old. This was as senseless as it was impertinent, and could only result in blind conservatism and widespread dullness. (Herder actually uses the English term.) Under such circumstances neither science nor the arts could thrive and all efforts towards enlightenment and social improvement would come to a standstill. And who would be the greatest loser? The State itself. For cultural and economic stagnation could not but undermine its social and political fabric. Hence, Herder concluded: 'In the realm of truth, in the spiritual sphere and the domain of thought there can and should be no worldly power exercising any decisive influence. This is no task for governments, let alone their appointed censor.'[27] Governments should, therefore, if only in their own interests, tolerate and, indeed,

---

[23] XXIV, 174.   [24] XVIII, 331.   [25] XIV, 217.   [26] IX, 407.
[27] IX, 358; for the passage as a whole see IX, 354–62. Herder clearly goes here beyond Milton's plea for freedom of expression voiced in his *Areopagitica* (1644).

actively encourage the free exchange of opinions and further all branches of learning and human endeavour that may lead to the discovery of new truths.[28]

Herder realized that freedom might be abused, but he felt that this was a risk which had to be borne. Without freedom there was no life for the human spirit.[29]

Herder opposed absolutism for very much the same reasons. Admittedly, he did so also because he abhorred the cult and hero-worship of any single individual,[30] but his main argument against it was that absolutist rule demoralized the people, that it corroded its very soul.[31] It created slaves, cringing base creatures, and shameless flatterers.[32] Insisting on uniformity, on 'order and obedience', it turned men into one mass of pulp, or treated them as if they were lifeless cogs in a vast wooden machine.[33] Worst of all, absolutism reared arbitrariness and lawless force, and thus constituted the most serious threat to the very notion of morality: 'Lawless force is the most detestable thing under the sun; a disgrace to anyone wielding it, for in doing so he deprives his actions of every shred of morality, of every claim to rightful recognition.'[34]

Given, then, a suitable climate for 'humanization' to get under way, what is to be the content of the educational process of *Bildung* which Herder visualizes?[35]

In one of his *Schulreden*[36] and in a letter to his duke, outlining proposals for school reforms, [37] Herder makes a number of rather penetrating remarks on this question. Man, he says, is neither good nor bad by nature; he only has propensities (*Anlagen*) that await and require

[28] IX, 361; see also XVII, 233, where Herder also stresses that the only effective antidote to chimeras and error is the free unfettered enquiry into truth from every possible angle.
[29] XI, 202; see also XXXI, 776.   [30] XVIII, 310.   [31] XIII, 381.
[32] IX, 365.   [33] V, 516.
[34] XVIII, 309. Herder is, however, aware that arbitrariness and the rule of force can be disguised as legal actions. (See especially his remarks regarding so-called 'crimes against the State': XVII, 60.)
[35] I shall in subsequent pages frequently use the German word *Bildung* in preference to an English term, simply because there is no real equivalent in the English language. The word is practically untranslatable. In the sense Herder uses it, it is perhaps best rendered as 'conscious human development'. It is a process of education in the widest sense in which the individual becomes aware of his relationship to his environment and of what he can receive from, or add to, the cultural heritage that is transmitted to him.
[36] Herder's (unpublished) school addresses contain material of more than purely educational interest. Many an acute political observation is woven into the fabric of these speeches, most of which were made during one of the stormiest periods of German history since the Thirty Years War. The speech cited, of which a sketch has survived, was made in the year 1793 (XXXII, 518).
[37] The letter is dated 14 December 1785 (XXX, 429-52).

development. Herder distinguishes a threefold aspect in these propensities:

(a) Physical and emotional;
(b) Intellectual and aesthetic; and
(c) Moral and political.[38]

It is the function of the State, Herder maintains, to help each citizen to develop these propensities, not only for his own sake, but also in the interest of the State itself.[39] For by neglecting the *Bildung* of its citizens the State both deprives itself of its most valuable 'assets' and also endangers its very existence, since talents that are being thwarted easily become the most insidious source of political unrest.

To fail to make use of man's divine and noble gifts, to allow these to rust and thus to give rise to bitterness and frustration, is not only an act of treason against humanity, but also the greatest harm which a State can inflict upon itself; for what is lost with such 'dead' and 'buried' assets is not merely the capital including the interest. Since in actual fact these assets are life forces, they invariably defy burial and hence tend to create a great deal of confusion and disturbance in the body politic. An unemployed human being cannot rest, simply because he is alive, and in his frustration he is likely to use his gifts for destructive ends. Social and political chaos is the inevitable outcome of this human tragedy.[40]

The passage deserves to be quoted in full. It reveals Herder's grasp of the economic and political implications of *Bildung*, and his awareness of the close interaction between educational and economic opportunities on the one hand, and political developments on the other. That unused, undeveloped human resources—'dead capital assets that cannot help being alive', as Herder puts it—involve not only individual frustration, but also political consequences that can seriously threaten the social and political structure of a society, has become a truism in our own day. But this was not quite the case a few decades ago, and still less so when Herder wrote. It also draws attention to the connexion between a State's educational opportunities and the degree of social and economic equality that is being attained. Whilst Herder recognizes that absolute equality is neither realizable nor, indeed desirable,[41] he also feels certain that the degree of natural inequality is by no means as marked as the

[38] XXX, 517 and XXXII, 518.
[39] Herder expressed similar views in VI, 104; XIV, 209; and XXIV, 109.
[40] XXX, 234.
[41] Even if equality could be attained in one generation, it could not, Herder points out, be maintained for long. (See XVII, 127.)

inequality that actually prevails owing to differences in educational opportunity.[42]

Herder does not overlook, however, the importance of social and economic factors as such. His concept of 'humanization' incorporates not only education, but also social or national welfare. By this Herder means a certain standard of physical health and material well-being which all individuals composing the nation should be able to enjoy, and which it is the second main function of the State to provide.[43] Educational *Bildung* and material well-being, Herder insists, must go hand in hand: 'A country needs not only letters (*Buchstaben*) but also bread.'[44]

Herder believes that the process of 'humanization' will result in the development of the self not only as an individual but also as a *member* of a community. For it involves, in Herder's view, the individual's realization that he cannot exist by himself alone; that, in order to achieve his fullest possible human development, he must actively co-operate with other individuals. By means of such active co-operation both the individual *and* society achieve their highest possible 'maximum'.[45]

It is the fostering of co-operation, of joint activities, between individuals and groups of individuals within the State that Herder primarily has at heart. The actual form which government assumes in this period of transition between the 'mechanical' and the 'organic' State does not greatly concern him, provided it does not claim hereditary or despotic powers and provided it remains conscious of its eventual redundancy as a governing body *sui generis*.

I do not find sufficient evidence for the view (expressed by Haym, Kühnemann, Schierenberg and others) that Herder regarded constitutional monarchy as the 'ideal' political constitution during this transitional period. Herder certainly preferred constitutional to absolute monarchy as the lesser evil. He also greatly admired the 'British compromise', which, he held, succeeded in combining dynastic continuity with the principle of government accountability.[46] But he also viewed constitutional monarchy with a good deal of scepticism: 'Moderate monarchy?—an equivocal concept! . . . Only despotism or a republican system are the two extremes, the poles around which the ball revolves. Moderate monarchy is merely the irregular oscillation between one pole and another.'[47] On the other hand, there is no dearth of evidence that Herder found a republican system most compatible

[42] XIII, 381; see also ibid., 295 and XXIII, 414.   [43] IX, 401; see also XVI, 601.
[44] IX, 408.   [45] XIV, 227.   [46] XXIII, 155-8.   [47] XVIII, 317.

with his conception of political government. In its advocacy he went even further than Rousseau. Whilst Rousseau doubted the applicability of the republican form of government to large States,[48] Herder saw no reason why large republics should be any less viable than small ones.[49] But even republicanism represented for Herder only the 'relatively best' of constitutional systems, there being no such thing as the 'best form of government' for all times, peoples and areas of the globe: 'No form of government endures; for time brings change with every minute. . . . The so-called *best form of government* has, alas, not been invented yet; if it had, it would scarcely be of use to all nations in the same fashion at one and the same time.'[50]

Herder is also said to have favoured 'democracy'. This view needs to be qualified if it is not to mislead. Herder rejected 'direct democracy' for very much the same reasons as did most eighteenth-century political writers. Centuries of neglect, Herder argued, had left the *Volk* (in the sense of *Bürger*) educationally and politically unfit for government. For the time being, all one could wish for was not that the *Volk* should rule, but that it should undergo education.[51] Moreover, direct democracy as practised in the Greek city-State, was clearly, Herder agreed with Rousseau, inapplicable to the nations of the modern world.[52] It would be quite inconceivable that all members of the *Volk* could under these conditions have equal participation in government: 'Even if they all had a share in legislation, they could not have an equal share, at least not in the form of equal direct participation.'[53] Herder rejected majority rule on similar grounds. Also he could see no virtue or wisdom in majorities as such.[54] There remains the question of representative democracy. Herder does seem to visualize some kind of representative system during the transitional period of 'aristo-democracy'. The 'representatives' or political leaders, however, who are to guide the *Bürger* to a state of higher educational and political maturity, are not expected to originate themselves from the *Bürger*, as we noted earlier. If, therefore, representative democracy is taken to mean government by directly elected people's representatives, Herder's 'aristo-democracy' could hardly be subsumed under it, not, at least, in its initial stage.

It is of some interest, however, that Herder, in contrast to most contemporary political writers, Justus Möser in particular, regarded the ownership of property as neither a relevant nor even a desirable

[48] J. J. Rousseau, *Emile, or Education*, trans. by B. Foxlex, Everymans ed., London, n.d., pp. 427-30.
[49] XVIII, 317; see also XVIII, 523 and IX, 365, 376.
[50] IV, 467 and XVIII, 283.   [51] XVII, 96.   [52] XVIII, 331-2.
[53] XVII, 127.   [54] XVII, 96; see also XIII, 149.

qualification for political leadership. His aristo-democrats were 'men of learning', representatives of the intellectual section of society, a kind of philosopher-kings. Since the promotion of universal education was, in Herder's view, the principal purpose of government in the period of transition, it was best left, Herder felt, to scholars and professional educators.[55] Not being burdened by the cares of property-ownership, they were clearly, Herder argued, the most suitable to serve the public good, and least prone (being scholars as well as politicians) to derive enjoyment from the sheer possession of political power. Once the *Volk* had attained political maturity, the aristo-democrats would be only too glad to make themselves dispensable. They would, therefore, strive to hasten rather than retard the process of socio-political *Bildung*.

The function of political leadership, then, during the period of 'humanization' has a twofold significance: it is to enable the *Volk* to reach the desired goal *earlier*; but it is also to ensure that the desired goal is attained by the *Volk*'s *own* efforts: 'The leader is to shorten our path, but he must let us do our own walking; he must not, that is, attempt to carry us lest we should thereby become paralysed.'[56] The *Volk* must travel under its own steam. The political leader, therefore, must take care that he does not assume too much responsibility, lest this diminish the *Volk*'s own sense of political consciousness and thus defeat the very object at stake: self-determination.[57]

Self-determination, that is, the ability and willingness of individuals and groups of individuals to order their social and economic lives within a legal framework of their own making, conscious of their freedom *and* inter-dependence: this is the goal of the political transformation which Herder had in mind. It is to this final stage, if at all, that the term 'democracy', albeit in a rather diffused and almost anarchistic sense, could be applied.

This is as far as Herder would go. We search in vain for a more detailed treatment of the transition from the somewhat paternal system of 'aristo-democracy' to the 'pluralist' diffusion of government associated with his concept of 'nomocracy'. It is not manifest, either, how the 'aristo-democrats', the men of recognized ability, are to assume power in the first place. Herder makes it clear, however, that revolution

---

[55] Herder's faith in the political capability and moral integrity of the scholar-politician may have had some influence on the pattern of political leadership which many nationalist movements assumed in Europe, particularly in Central and South-East Europe, where professors have had considerable political prestige. Although Herder's conception of leadership during the transition from 'mechanism' to 'organism' differs in important respects from Weber's notion of charismatic leadership, it does seem to entail charismatic elements.

[56] IV, 454.   [57] XIII, 149 and XVIII, 339.

as a means of dislodging the hereditary holders of office is ruled out: 'My motto remains gradual, natural, reasonable evolution of things; not revolution.'[58]

3. NATURAL GROWTH AND NATURAL POLITICS

This axiomatic belief in a gradual evolution of the new order from the old, without breach of continuity or abrupt change of the social fabric during the process, obviously presupposes certain assumptions about the nature of the forces that are held to be operative in socio-political development. What these assumptions are is a matter to which we propose to return in subsequent chapters.[59] But the central idea underlying them has emerged already in an earlier chapter (ch. 2). Herder, we found, thinks of social development as an organic process, as 'growth', activated or energized by an inner force. But since this inner force is also held to be the expression of divine power, 'development' assumes a double denotation: it is both a way of describing the nature of physical change and the working out of a divine purpose: it is at once an empirical tendency investigable by science and a theodicy which is not thus investigable. Added to the difficulties inherent in such an identification of natural and divine forces is the problem of deciding to what extent, if at all, these forces are amenable to human control. Is 'development', in other words, the outcome of inexorable divine or physical powers, or is it, at least in some measure, the result of human endeavour? Herder never quite succeeded in disentangling these problems, perhaps mainly because he acknowledged no real dichotomy between the realm of natural philosophy and theology on the one hand, or, on the other, between a providential order and one in which man was destined to play an essential and active part.[60]

It is only fair to add, however, that Herder was grappling here with problems with which many a thinker before, during and after the eighteenth century has sought to come to terms. If he proved no more successful in supplying satisfactory answers, he nevertheless succeeded in establishing two credal principles that were appreciably to affect subsequent political thinking. One was the belief that once the imperfections due to non-national and non-popular governments were removed, closer harmony between the two spheres of nature—the

---

[58] XVIII, 332.   [59] See particularly chapter VI.

[60] It is idle to speculate whether Herder would have evolved a more consistent philosophy of nature and of history had he been unencumbered by theological considerations.

sphere of physical powers and the sphere of human endeavour—could be attained. The other was that the very removal of these imperfections was an evolutionary process inherent in the nature of man's development and in the unfolding of cosmic forces.[61]

Both of these credal principles derived much persuasive power from the use of biological analogies. If social regeneration was but an instance of a universal tendency towards biological change, could not the pattern of thinking applicable to the latter also apply to the former? If there was growth and decay in nature, why not in society? In the point at issue— the transformation from aristocratic to popular rule—could not the method of change, therefore, be envisaged in terms of an historical process entailing two complementary, yet opposed, tendencies of decay from above and growth from below? Contemporary events in Germany, of which Herder was acutely aware, seemed to support this hypothesis.[62] At the same time, these events demonstrated only too clearly that 'growth from below' was not a necessary corollary of 'decay from above', but rather a matter requiring fostering care. Herder was quick to realize this. It was in view of this realization that he emphasized the need for a transitional period of social and political education, in which the required national and social consciousness could be deliberately fostered.

Herder did not sufficiently appreciate, however, that 'consciousness' alone without procedural constitutional machinery was not enough. For, obviously, the very possibility of bringing about such a consciousness might be in question in the absence of a favourable institutional framework. This lack of political realism was no doubt in part a corollary of Herder's essentially cultural approach to politics. Partly, however, it was also the result of his inability to distinguish fully enough between the wider community of the State and the natural unit of the family from which it conceivably sprang. Having accepted Aristotle's account of natural man as a political creature and of the family as a natural community,[63] Herder could not resist invoking the image of a 'political family' both for his ultimate goal—the organic State—and for indicating the path that was to lead towards it. For in a sense Herder thought of the functions of the political leader during the transitional period in terms of the duties of a provident *pater familias*, whose principal concern was the education of his children to responsible

---

[61] But Herder did not think of 'evolution' in the sense in which Darwin was to apply it to biological development.
[62] See particularly Herder's school address of 1796.
[63] Aristotle, *Politics*, I, chs. 2 and 4.

manhood.[64] But the analogy does not really help Herder's argument. Far from shedding light on the most crucial aspects of the envisaged transformation—the problem of social control and the proper sphere of political authority—it merely helps to confuse the issue. Human beings must have fathers by nature; but this biological truism leaves wide open the question concerning the proper extent of parental authority. What is more, the notion of parental control with its corollary of infantile dependency is in direct conflict with Herder's vision of a society that can dispense with institutionalized direction.

Herder, it seems, failed to recognize that to say that members of a State *ought* to perceive a sentiment comparable to that shared by members of a family was quite a different sort of observation from that of saying—as he also did—that the nation State *was* but an extension of the family.[65] The first observation, that fear of coercive power ought to give way to the feeling of affection and devotion which members of a family may have for one another, is of a purely normative nature. We may wonder, on empirical grounds, whether the ethnic or national community of the *Volk* is too large a unit, and hence the feeling of national identity too remote, to command this kind of loyalty; but we do not thereby question its legitimacy as a recommendation. The second observation, on the other hand, is a statement of fact. As such it is not only of doubtful validity, but also of little relevance to Herder's notion of 'natural government'.[66] For under this system authority is wielded by *elected* bodies with powers limited to their sphere of competence, whose term of office is deemed to expire with the completion of the task for which they were constituted.[67] Moreover, the family is a model of an hierarchical pattern of authority with a vertical up-and-down structure of responsibility, a structure which Herder associated with the mechanical State.

Herder's failure to see that the difference between the family and the State was one of kind, and not merely one of degree, accounts no doubt for the lack of consideration given in his socio-political theory to procedural questions and in particular to the problem of delimiting and, if necessary, reconciling the spheres of authority of the diverse centres of control in his proposed pluralist scheme. On the other hand, had Herder been mainly concerned with the institutional aspects of

[64] See for passage as a whole XIII, 384, 456.   [65] XIII, 384.

[66] Herder calls the system applicable to the more ramified social structure of the *Volk*, 'natural government of the second order'; the family being the 'natural government of the first order' (XIII, 375-6).

[67] XIII, 375-6; see also XIV, 489.

social and political life, he would hardly have been the author of a vision in which government was to be transformed into something that in essence was no longer political. For it must be admitted that Herder's notion of the organic State as a spiritually integrated community engaged in shared co-operative activity, living under a system devoid of governmental direction and under a law which enshrines the social and moral consciousness of its members, has more in common with a religious creed than with a political doctrine. This admission does not imply, however, a denial of its political significance. Indeed, it may well be true that what lent Herder's organic conception of politics its inspirational power was its underlying faith in a secular redemption.

This faith, though it contained its share of utopianism, was none the less alive to the obstacles that lay in the path of establishing 'organic' social relationships. Herder may have underestimated the need for, and efficacy of, 'institutional' politics, but he spared no effort in impressing upon his readers the need for a spiritual regeneration through the cultivation of proper social and international 'attitudes'. To establish such attitudes, Herder realized, will make heavy demands on an individual's sense of social responsibility and national solidarity, no less than on a nation's sense of international morality.[68] But unless such national and international attitudes were successfully cultivated, the realization of the organic Volk-State as a viable political entity was utterly inconceivable. So long as States were like ships, surrounded by countless dangers and hostile forces, so long would they remain involuntary institutions extending to peoples in a given territory for the sole purpose of maintaining internal order and external defence.[69]

A world of 'organic' nation-States, in which political government in the orthodox sense was replaced by centrally unco-ordinated autonomous ad hoc institutions, presupposed, therefore, not only a highly developed sense of social co-operation within individual States, but also an unusual degree of international harmony in the relations between States. Herder visualized the attainment of such national and international conditions as the outcome of a tendency which he held to be inherent in human society no less than in nature: the tendency of diversity towards unity.[70]

For Herder, then, it would appear, nationalism and internationalism were not currents that ran in opposite directions but rather successive stages of historical development. The particularist tendencies of nationalism and the universal tendencies characterizing international-ism were seen by him as complementary and not as contradictory

[68] XVI, 601.   [69] IV, 354-5.   [70] XVIII, 300.

forces. National and international 'humanization' was *one* single process. This belief in the natural harmony between the particular and the universal, between diversity and unity was, in a sense, the logical corollary of Herder's organic conception of the cosmic order. Basically, however, it was an act of faith, a moral and religious conviction about man's social destiny. The doctrinal and emotional source—for it was both—of this secular faith was contained for Herder in one word: *Humanität*.

V

FROM NATIONALISM TO
INTERNATIONALISM: *HUMANITÄT*

HERDER was not the first to indulge in visions of building God's Kingdom on this planet; but few of his predecessors went to such lengths as he did in bringing down the divine to the human level, or, more precisely, in denying the existence of any dualism or antithesis between the religious and the secular realm. To bring secular values to religious fields and religious values to secular fields appears to have been his main resolve: 'What a wonderful idea it is to apply religion for the benefit of man and society!'[1] Religion, if it was to constitute an active element in social life, had to be directed to human and social aims. The better it strove to achieve these, the more conducive it became to the furtherance of the highest of social ideals, of *Humanität*.[2]

This supreme social ideal was more than a 'concept' for Herder. It expressed for him the *summum bonum* of this world; it enshrined all that was pure, lovely, and of good report, as Kühnemann remarked, not without irony.[3] *Humanität* was the alpha and omega of Herder's social philosophy. Herder went so far as to declare that the surest test of the moral worth of any religion was its promotion of *Humanität*: 'The purer a religion was, the more sincerely it strove to promote the common good of humanity. This indeed is the very touchstone . . . of the diverse religions.'[4]

At this point it would seem appropriate to enquire a little further into Herder's philosophy of religion. For Herder's ideas on religion are not only of relevance to the issue under discussion; they bear also on his approach to history and social development.

I. RELIGION AND *HUMANITÄT*

In his philosophy of religion, no less than in his philosophy of history,

[1] VI, 63.

[2] XVII, 121–2. The word has no precise equivalent in the English language. I propose, therefore, to use the German term throughout.

[3] E. Kühnemann, *Herder*, München, 1927, p. 536.   [4] XVII, 121.

Herder was anxious to reconcile the providential determinism inherent in his view of the universal order with the idea of human freedom.

In many respects Herder's religious views are barely distinguishable from deistic ideas, in particular from those of John Toland and Matthew Tindal. Like Toland and Tindal Herder deplored uncritical devotion and 'supernatural' beliefs: 'May God protect me from miracles! . . . Do not strive towards the supernatural. . . . Belief in magic is a senseless chimera, an unnatural impulse.'[5] The Bible was a human and historical document, to be read and judged in terms of human values, and not made an object of blind and uncritical worship.[6] Man should have a questioning attitude, even an intransigent spirit.[7]

The most characteristic feature of religion, Herder insisted, was its being truly and entirely human.[8] Man was an active and conscious part of creation and was not intended, therefore, to forgo the freedom of choice. It was not the purpose of the Bible to induce or even allow him to place his life passively in the hands of Providence; it did not teach him predestination, or blind Providence. On the contrary, man should, in a sense, be his own god upon earth, conscious of the rôle he played in his own destiny. No hypothetical future life should deprive him of, or even mar, his present life. It was upon this earth that man had his origin, his native land, his kingdom; it was here that he had his purpose and his destination.[9]

Herder's interpretation of revelation was, like Lessing's, in terms of illumination, the attainment of a clearer understanding, enlightenment: 'The purest form of revelation . . . is to see things as they really are: without images; without delusions, face to face.'[10] Revelation was not a unique event of the distant past; it was a process; it went on. '*Each* period is a period of unveiling, of revelation.'[11] In Christ Herder saw primarily a great *Aufklärer*, a determined fighter for the freedom of the spirit: 'A noble enthusiast for universal enlightenment and for the freedom of the spirit against all prejudices.'[12]

Institutional Christianity, with its ecclesiastical hierarchy, its set

---

[5] XIX, 53 and XX, 75. It must be stressed that these views were not occasional outbursts, but the considered statements of the highest church official in Weimar, to which he accorded detailed treatment in a collection of essays, entitled *Christliche Schriften* (1794–1798), in no less than five volumes. It should be noted, however, that during the period in Bückeburg (as Chief Pastor to the Count of Schaumburg-Lippe, 1771–6) Herder inclined at times towards a more mystical interpretation of religion.

[6] VIII, 543, 544; see also XI, 178.   [7] VII, 264.

[8] VIII, 235; see also XX, 178, 232, 239, 265.

[9] VI, 64; see also XIV, 322–4, and XVII, 120–1. See further Herder's letter to Lavater, dated 30 October 1772. (Düntzer, *Aus Herders Nachlaß*, op. cit., vol. II, pp. 15–16.)

[10] XX, 128.   [11] XX, 131.   [12] XX, 47.

dogmas, found little favour in Herder's eyes. Church and religion were not one.[13] Herder also questioned the argument that Christianity had helped to establish more peaceful and friendly relations between States and denied the validity of the thesis which claimed ecclesiastical authority to have its *raison d'être* in acting as a check upon political power. The Church, Herder maintained, had done nothing to restrain the despotic powers of the princes. Indeed, far from curbing political absolutism, the hierarchical organization of the Church had in fact served as a model for its emergence and development.[14]

Religion and dogmas, Herder insists, must be sharply distinguished.[15] Religion unites men, dogmas divide them. For dogmas breed fanaticism and intolerance.[16] In his plea for tolerance, for 'free untrammelled enquiry into truth', Herder warmly applauds the efforts of the *Aufklärer*, of men such as Lessing and Mendelssohn. He also pays tribute to the German translators who had introduced the great English protagonists of the principles of toleration—Hutcheson, Shaftesbury, Butler, and Locke—to the German reading public.[17]

Herder's approach to religion, as to any other facet of human endeavour, is strictly relativist. Religion, he argues, is the innermost concern of each individual; it is inalienable.[18] It cannot, therefore, be exactly the same for any two persons, still less for different nations.[19]

What, then, is Herder's definition of religion? Although his general theological position is somewhat ambivalent, he is remarkably specific on this point. This is how he formulates it in the *Christliche Schriften*: 'Religion is the conviction, that is, the innermost awareness, of ourselves as parts of the universe, of what we ought to become, of what we ought to do as human beings. . . . Religion means conscientiousness in all our human duties.'[20] Religion, as Herder views it, is essentially man's consciousness of his social obligations. Christianity, in its purest form, is the expression of this consciousness in social conduct and in man's

---

[13] XIV, 541–2; see also XV, 130–1.   [14] XIV, 411.   [15] XX, 135.
[16] XV, 130–1; see also XVII, 273; XX, 145; and XXII, 10.
[17] XI, 204; see also XV, 33; XVII, 233; and XXIII, 133–4. Herder's own broad-mindedness goes quite far. Shaftesbury had attacked Locke for having encouraged free-thinking. Herder comes to the defence, not only of Locke, but also of free-thinking (XXIII, 134–5). Even atheists are not considered beyond the pale. 'Far too many cruel and inhuman games have been played with the expression "a man without religion" ' (XXIV, 97). It is Herder's conviction that more harm has been done to the true purpose of Christianity by its pious, uncritical, and frequently hypocritical supporters than by its opponents in the course of history. (See Herder's essay on the 'pious lie' ('Die fromme Lüge'), in the *Christlichen Schriften*, 'Vom Geist des Christentums', XX, 5.)
[18] XX, 141, 225; see also XVII, 273 and XXIV, 49. (See further Düntzer, *Von und an Herder*, op. cit., vol. I, p. 281.)
[19] XXIV, 49.   [20] XX, 159–60, 264.

ROUTE ITEM

Title: Herder's social and
political thought; from
enlightenment to
nationalism, by F.M.
Barnard.

Author:

Call Number: PT2354 .B3 1965

Enumeration:

Chronology:

Copy: 1

Item Barcode: 00000000302554

Route To: Rockville

potentiality, but an actual creative energy or *Kraft*.[50] What is less easy to account for, however, is Herder's apparent distinction between his concept of mind and his concept of *Besonnenheit*. For although all that he has to say about the latter concept would be equally applicable to the former, Herder nowhere suggests that these concepts are in fact interchangeable.

Somewhat less perplexing, if not altogether free from ambiguity, is the closely associated concept of *Besinnung*, which could be best rendered perhaps as conscious discernment or awareness. Herder is presumably making use here of the Leibnizian distinction between 'apperception' and the *petites perceptions*. For the reason for introducing this additional term appears to be the desire to draw attention to activities of the mind, such as dreaming for example, which do not entail *Besinnung*, but which still presuppose *Besonnenheit*, since we are still thinking even though not so coherently or distinctly as when we are awake.[51]

But Herder suggests a further, and quite different distinction between *Besinnung* and *Besonnenheit* when he says: 'Man is from the very first moment of his existence a human being and not an animal because he is right from the start a creature of *Besonnenheit* (i.e. a thinking being) even though he is not yet a creature endowed with *Besinnung* (i.e. conscious awareness).'[52] Now, although this further distinction introduces an element of ambiguity into the meaning of *Besinnung*, it lends at the same time an added interest to the concept. For it implies that the self is not only logically but also temporally prior to its consciousness and hence reinforces Herder's contention that knowledge can never be *a priori* nor wholly subjective. Consciousness, that is to say, is not innate, but rather a function of *development*. It is the result of the peculiar manner in which the growing self receives, and reacts to, the *stimuli* of its environment. The significance of this implication is a matter which will receive attention in the subsequent section in which we propose to turn to Herder's second main reason for postulating his concept of *Kraft*. Before doing so, however, let us briefly sum up the main arguments by means of which Herder sought to refute the traditional doctrine of faculties or mental powers.

Applying his principle of active inter-relation to the activities of the mind, Herder comes to the conclusion that the diverse organs of the mind and the activities which they perform are not separate entities existing in isolation from one another. Reason, for example, which hitherto has been treated as a distinct and dominant faculty of the

[50] V, 32-3.   [51] V, 99.   [52] V, 93.

mind, is presented as a process of thinking which cannot be divorced from other processes such as feeling or willing. The mind, therefore, is not to be thought of as an assembly of separate faculties but rather as an integrated whole. And since the mode of operation of the interlinked processes is not to be envisaged in terms of the working of a mechanism, but as a creative activity, Herder postulates the existence of a vital power which constitutes the *internal* energizing source of this activity. As such it represents the principle of unity within the diversity of the inter-related processes through which it manifests itself. Herder's theory of the organic unity of the mind, then, which is advanced in place of the doctrine of faculties, no less than his notion of the unity of the universe conceived as an organic whole, is directly derivative from his metaphysical concept of *Kraft*.

2. THE PROBLEM OF CONTINUITY

Change as 'growth'

To deny the tenability of Locke's theory of power was, we suggested, Herder's second aim in postulating his basic concept of *Kraft*. When Locke used the term 'power', he understood by it a capacity for producing change *and* a capacity for receiving change. 'Thus we say', Locke explained, 'fire has a power to melt gold . . . ; and gold has a power to be melted . . . ; the one may be called "active" and the other "passive" power.'[53] In order to bring out the contrast between Locke's concept of power and Herder's concept of *Kraft* it may be convenient to make use of the concepts of *vis* and *potestas*. These, as we noted earlier, were frequently used interchangeably by the 'faculty' school. We propose to draw a distinction between them by identifying *vis* with an internal energy corresponding roughly to the Aristotelian concept of 'entelechy', and *potestas* with 'power' in the sense in which Locke employed the term, implying by it both an active and a passive connotation.

Now it is not difficult to realize from what has been said so far about Herder's concept of *Kraft* that he could hardly entertain a belief in the possibility of a passive power. If 'being' entails 'activity' then it also implies the existence of an energizing source. And to speak of such an energizing source as a passive power would, in Herder's view, constitute a contradiction in terms. What is more, the acceptance of the possibility of an active *and* a passive power would militate against the

[53] Locke, *Essay*, op. cit., Book II, ch. XXI, sect. 1 and 2.

monistic philosophy of organic unity which Herder wishes to advance in opposition to dualistic interpretations of reality. It is this consideration as much as the first which underlies Herder's determination to postulate a single creative power as his metaphysical support in place of the traditional Substance.

But, it may be objected at this point, in disposing of the dualism which the Lockean conception of power apparently implies, Herder is far from establishing his own case. For it remains to be explained how we can conceive of the universe or of reality as a whole or unity, if the 'stuff' of this reality is not an unchanging Substance but a creative power manifesting itself through continuous activity. How can we, that is to say, reconcile the universe's fundamental unity with the notion of continuous activity and *change*? For are we not by postulating the latter denying the former, since the universe as it is and the universe as it may become are not one but two? By raising these questions we are of course questioning the very legitimacy of Herder's undertaking in postulating an active *Kraft* in place of Substance. The latter, as Spinoza clearly saw, had to be conceived as unchanging, for if it were not so conceived, one state of Substance would be different from another and hence could no longer constitute a single all-embracing unity. Moreover, if Substance is the same as God, as Spinoza maintained, change is equally inconceivable. For there cannot be change other than movement from one state towards another. If, therefore, we mean by God that which is wholly perfect, we would, by postulating a changing Substance, either have to admit that God is other than Substance or that He is not wholly perfect. To admit the former would mean denying the postulate of unity on which Spinoza's theory of monism rests; whilst to admit the latter would render the concept of God meaningless.

Now Herder regarded himself as a Spinozist.[54] He even went so far as to identify *Kraft* with God, as we remarked earlier, in the belief that by substituting *Kraft* for Substance he succeeded in making the Spinozist system so much more coherent and intelligible.[55] Apart from the light this throws upon Herder's somewhat ambivalent theological thinking, it also suggests that Herder hardly seemed to realize how very different his metaphysical presuppositions were from those of Spinoza, and how profoundly, therefore, in spite of superficial similarities, his brand of monism differed from that of his 'precursor'.

[54] See Herder's letter to Gleim, dated 17 February 1786. (H. Düntzer and F. G. v. Herder, *Von und an Herder*, Leipzig, 1861-2, vol. I, p. 116.)
[55] XVI, 458, 549.

Indeed it would not be wrong to say that Herder's notion of 'unity' was as fundamentally at variance with that of Spinoza as his concept of *Kraft* was with the Lockean conception of power.

Let us explore now briefly how Herder came to replace the notion of static unity by that of a dynamic whole; how, that is to say, he attempted to reconcile the principle of one-ness with the principle of activity and change.

We may recall that Herder conceives of the universe in terms of an organism or, more precisely, in terms of a plurality of inter-related organisms, each of which is necessary to the existence of the other so that we must think of the totality of these connected organisms as constituting an integrated whole. We have noted, too, that the inter-relationship is held to be one of interaction rather than one of a passive 'being-in-relation'. Indeed, we have seen, it is the process of this inter-action which is presented as the core or 'stuff' of reality. The *nature* of interaction is that of organic activity and hence by implication fundamentally homogeneous. In order to maintain this claim, Herder denies the distinction between mind and matter or between material and immaterial 'substances', and stipulates instead a single psycho-physical force or energy (*Kraft*) as the common source of activity. This force, however, is not to be thought of as an external agency acting *upon* the universe but as an *internal* force acting *through* the universe. The universe, in other words, is the manifestation of *Kraft*. This being so, it cannot be a changeless universe. For *Kraft* entails activity and activity entails change. We arrive, therefore, at the conclusion that the universe as the embodiment of an immanent vital energy (*Kraft*) is a stream of continuous change.[56]

A corollary of this conclusion—and one which is of considerable relevance to Herder's philosophy of history—is the notion that 'time', far from being something imposed upon reality by the human understanding, is in fact a necessary function of reality. For if reality is a flux of change, time is of its very essence.[57] Phenomena, therefore, are not timeless in reality, but are instead 'agents of time'.[58] It follows also that time or duration (Herder uses both terms) must be conceived as an active and vital force and, as such, as the very principle of existence.[59] It is not surprising, therefore, that time or duration is treated by Herder as a notion which is implicit in his concept of *Kraft*.[60]

[56] IX, 371 and V, 512.   [57] IX, 371–2.   [58] XXII, 314.
[59] XVI, 566 and IX, 371.
[60] XXI, 64. Herder is not altogether consistent, however, in his treatment of time. (See, for example, XVII, 80, where time is defined as a 'thought-image'.)

Kraft, Herder's metaphysical support for his principle of interaction, is conceived, then, as a *process in time*. By identifying this process with 'becoming' or development, Herder hopes to succeed in presenting his concept of 'unity' as the relational unity of a process. At this point we may introduce the distinction between *potestas* and *vis* to which we made reference at the beginning of this section. Herder's treatment of *Kraft* does not make it difficult to decide to which conception of power his own concept more closely approximates. His theory of development finally settles the matter. If by *vis* we mean, as we have stipulated, an internal energy corresponding roughly to the Aristotelian 'entelechy' then the *direction* which the process of change assumes is inherent in the nature of the changing 'thing'. Development, accordingly, is a process in which that which is already latent becomes actual. This is precisely what Herder understands by development which he, there-fore, identifies with 'growth': 'Within every grain of seed there lies the plant with all its parts; within every animal seed the creature with all its limbs.'[61] Even if environmental factors are recognized as having a modifying influence, it is primarily the innate, or, as Herder prefers to call it, the 'genetic' propensity towards the attainment of a thing's end which is said to constitute the determinate driving power of its growth.[62] For it is the genetic propensity that determines what manner interaction will assume and to what extent external influences will succeed in affecting the process of growth by means of which a thing will realize its full nature.[63]

Growth and human development

But if the end towards which things develop is implicit in the unfold-ing of the genetic propensity, then, surely, the result of the process is virtually pre-determined by the initial nature of that which undergoes the process of change. This Herder does not deny. At the same time he realizes that the application of this sort of blind teleological determinism or functionalism to human development would offer little scope for the exercise of choice. He carefully distinguishes, therefore, human and social development from other forms of growth. Whereas the latter develop in an unconscious or instinctive manner,[64] human beings, as creatures of *Besonnenheit*, are capable of realizing consciously the nature and direction of their development.[65] The extent to which they

---

[61] II, 62. In using the Aristotelian notion of 'entelechy' I do not wish to imply that the Aristotelian psychology as a whole admits of being reduced to biology.

[62] XIII, 273, 276, 277.   [63] ibid.   [64] V, 98; see also XIII, 102.

[65] V, 29.

do will differ, however, from individual to individual according to the degree to which *Besonnenheit* results in *Besinnung* or actual consciousness.[66] The process of human development is envisaged, therefore, as the unfolding of *Besonnenheit* into *Besinnung*, by virtue of which it ceases to be a 'blind force' and becomes instead the expression of a conscious self-determining mind. Environmental factors are again not overlooked but their significance is secondary in that their effective influence is dependent on the active apprehension by the individual mind. Thus while everything in the total environment (to which Herder applies the term *Klima*[67]) is of some relevance to the development of the self towards its fullest realization (to which Herder applies the term 'individuation'[68]), different things will be relevant in different degrees. Man's recognition of what is most relevant to his own development in the light of individually conceived purposes constitutes presumably what Herder means by conscious becoming.

The life of the individual, then, is seen as a process of activity in which internal and external factors are inter-related and blended according to their relevance to the individual's conscious aims or purposes and not merely in accordance with the functional requirements of his physical needs. The realization that life is not a mere succession of separate and random psycho-physical states, but rather the flow of connected purposive activities is one of the most distinguishing features of human existence.[69] Without this realization there could be no sense of *continuity* and hence no conception of human *history*. By the same token, there would be no point in speaking of man's capacity for self-determination and self-perfection unless he was in a position to grasp the inter-connexions and the directional determinants of his own development.[70]

Herder's theory of development and self-determination contains, however, in spite of its attractiveness, a very fundamental difficulty. I think Herder is right in distinguishing the self from an aggregate and in stipulating the relational unity of a process in place of a mere succession of psycho-physical states. We do not, as a matter of empirical fact, think of the self as 'nothing but a bundle or collection of different perceptions'.[71] We do, that is, envisage some sort of identity of the self within its changing states. And I suggest that we do so on grounds not unlike those advanced by Herder's theory. For what we generally

---

[66] XXI, 152.   [67] XIII, 272.
[68] XVI, 574. See also XXI, 106 regarding this passage.   [69] V, 98.
[70] XVII, 115 and XVI, 574.
[71] Hume, *A Treatise of Human Nature*, Book I, Part IV, sect. VI ('Of Personal Identity'); Everyman ed., p. 239.

regard as the identity or unity of the self is a measure of consistency in the purposive direction of its changing states. Nevertheless, it is somewhat of a mystery how we can account for that 'something' which 'recognizes' the purposive relationship of the changing states. For this presupposes that the 'something' is distinct from the self's states. In postulating the concepts of *Besonnenheit* and *Besinnung* as two *distinct* ideas, identifying the former with the power of thinking as such, and the latter with a capacity for conscious self-awareness, Herder seems to make an attempt to meet this difficulty. For 'conscious awareness' could conceivably apply to that state of the self in which it is aware of the purposive relationship of its other states, in view of which it recognizes the relational unity of the 'mind', i.e. (in Herder's terminology) the totality of the self as an individual personality. But the matter is not entirely clear.[72]

3. UNITY AND CONTINUITY

Continuity as the relational unity of a process

If the plurality of diverse parts is said to be a prerequisite for the existence of the whole, and if it is also maintained that the existence of the whole is inconceivable unless 'existence' is envisaged in the form of continuous activity or change, then it is the nature of the relation between the 'parts' and the 'whole' and between the 'now' and the 'later' which constitutes the decisive issue. The problem of unity and the problem of continuity, therefore, which we have singled out as the core problems in Herder's philosophy of organism, are, it would appear, in fact reducible to a single problem, the problem of relation. Herder's answer to this problem is, as we have seen, the principle of interaction. According to this principle all that exists does so in a state of continuous becoming, in which the 'now' and the 'later' are inseparably fused, the 'now' containing the 'later' in the manner in which an acorn 'contains' the oak. The relation characteristic of this process therefore, is one of growth, i.e. of continuous activity directed by an internal end or purpose.[73] At the same time the activity of any

[72] It may, of course, be argued that this 'difficulty' arises from asking an illegitimate question, i.e. a question to which one simply cannot expect to get an answer on any theory.

[73] I am using the words 'end' and 'purpose' as alternatives and not as synonyms, to distinguish teleological processes such as the growth of a plant or an animal, where the 'end' does not imply a conscious aim, from those where it does. In the former case *telos* implies simply a tendency towards biological completion; in the latter case *telos* implies conscious striving towards the attainment of envisaged goals. (For an extremely lucid treatment of this distinction, see Dorothy Emmet, *Function, Purpose and Powers*, London, 1958, pp. 46–51.)

individual unit is inseparably linked with that of every other in such a manner that the existence of one is indispensable to the existence of the other, even though no single unit is exactly like any other. The nature of the relationship, therefore, is also one of mutual inter-dependence. Growth and functional inter-dependence, accordingly, constitute the joint characteristics of Herder's principle of active inter-relation or 'interaction'. They are characteristics which are associated with organisms rather than with mechanical bodies, for they presuppose the existence of an *internal* source of activity. It follows, therefore, that growth and inter-dependence are but a function of an active energizing force or power which underlies the organic activities of which they are the relational characteristics. To this single force or power Herder applies his concept of *Kraft*. This concept, then, which Herder intended as a synthesis between Spinoza's monism and Leibniz's pluralism, represents the basic presupposition of what unquestionably constitutes the central idea of Herder's philosophy of organism: the principle of interaction. This principle implies, we have found, a state of continuous change or flux between inter-penetrating events. Accordingly, every event must itself be conceived as a continuous process within this flux. What we are confronted with, therefore, is not a series of separate events but a network of relations. Moreover, and this is highly important, the relations themselves are not distinct from the things they relate, but are held to be inherent in their very nature. This is implicit in the postulate of *organic* inter-relation from which Herder draws the consequence that no single thing can be studied or understood when treated in isolation, that is, in abstraction from the context in which it occurs.

In order to realize the methodological import of this consequence it must be remembered too, that the nature of the relationship is held to be teleological. For from this it follows that the 'meaning' or 'significance' of any one thing, said to be deducible only if it is studied within its context, is its end or purpose. Now both the postulate of continuous process and the concept of functional or purposive relation[74] raise the question of how far Herder's principle of interaction by-passes, if it does not supersede, the law of causation as it is ordinarily

[74] Again I wish to stress that the 'or' expresses a distinction, and not an identity, between functional and purposive relations. Both functional and purposive relations are inter-connecting links in a system or structural 'whole'. But the 'meaning' of the former will be interpreted in terms of their functional effects within a system, whilst the 'meaning' of the latter will be interpreted in terms of purposive intentions. This formulation is not wholly satisfactory, but I hope it is sufficiently clear to bring out the point I wish to make here, namely that the *nature* of the explanation in each case will be different.

understood. For if things are not really separate from one another, to speak of *a* cause and *an* effect would mean the arbitrary singling out of two events from what is in fact a continuous series. What is more, if an event is not an isolated occurrence in space or time, then, really, there would appear to be no need to invoke a causal law in the form in which it is commonly known.

Teleological causation
Herder's ideas on historical causation, to which we propose to return in a later chapter,[75] are undoubtedly the most difficult as also the most controversial aspect of his social philosophy. In the present context we merely wish to draw attention to the connexion between Herder's 'organic' conception of the universal order and his approach to the problem of causation.

The ordinary view of causation presupposes that an event, a cause, which is separate from another event, the effect, and earlier than the effect in point of time, brings about or determines the latter. When, therefore, we say that 'A causes B' we not only mean that B follows A, but also that B results from A, in that A is the sufficient condition for the occurrence of B. We mean, that is, that there is a determinate connexion between the two events. But what precisely is the nature of that which is said to link two separate events in this determinate manner? Surely, to have causal effect it must possess causal *power*. Now the action of this power constitutes, as it were, if it is something external to A and B, an additional event, the separate existence of which is causally inexplicable unless we resort to an infinite regression. But if it is not something separate, then A and B cannot be separate either for we have no way of distinguishing their separate existence. The alternative is to stipulate the existence of causal characteristics as something inherent in the events themselves. In the former case, where A and B cease to represent separate events, the law of causation in the customary sense is rendered inapplicable, whilst in the latter case the postulate of an internal power is necessitated. Hume, rejecting the second alternative, could not, therefore, but conclude that the law of causation was either unnecessary or unfounded. By postulating it we are not talking about something which is inherent in, or derivable from, reality. All we do and can do is to link in our imagination events which past observation has shown to occur regularly together as if they were necessarily related. Accordingly, all we *should* mean when we say that A is the cause of B is that A is regularly followed by B.[76]

[75] Ch. VI.   [76] Hume, op. cit., Book I, Part III, sect. VI; Everyman ed., p. 163.

At first sight Herder's own view on causation appears to coincide with that of Hume. We merely assume, he says, the existence of a causal relation with the aid of mental constructions based on analogy and observation.[77] Yet on further examination it becomes evident that what Herder questions is not the reality of causation as such but the acceptance of causation as something simple and readily intelligible. When he agrees, therefore, with Hume that finite minds may only be able to construct causal hypotheses based on the observation of 'outside' relationships, that is, of sequences which appear to reveal regularity, he does so for different reasons. For Herder, it will be remembered, *does* presuppose the existence of an internal causal power and hence the causal relation which he stipulates is that of an *internal* relation. Furthermore, since he only denies the separateness but not the individuality of phenomena, the mode of causation which he puts forward in place of 'simple causation' is that of pluralistic causation of an exceedingly complex and varied pattern. It is this complexity which occasions Herder's doubt of the possibility of gaining a true or complete knowledge of causal relations. For to gain such complete knowledge we would have to be able to penetrate into the inner being of things. To succeed in this, however, is clearly beyond our ken. In the natural sciences all we can do is to stand outside and observe from the outside.[78]

It is not difficult to see why, if 'internal causality' is something essentially unknowable, Hume found himself unable to accept such a postulate. But the same cannot be said of Herder. Two related reasons account for this. The first is that Herder invokes his metaphysical concept of *Kraft* to support his 'empiricism' and the second is the teleological element in his theory of causation.

In spite of his desire to think as an empiricist and his declared distrust of metaphysics, Herder could not dispense with his metaphysical 'support' of *Kraft*. It was not only the unifying principle of his philosophy of organism; it was also the basic concept in his theological cosmology. In *Kraft* he saw both the First Cause and the continuous energizing power of 'becoming', which he identified with existence. *Kraft*, therefore, embodied for Herder the continuous manifestation of God.[79] The principle of internal relation, similarly, entailed for Herder the existence of an inherent harmony in the universe;[80] but he advanced no argument in support of this belief. Presumably he regarded the internal harmony of the universe as the necessary corollary of the postulate of *Kraft*—the divine source of all existence.

[77] XVI, 522.   [78] XVI, 551.   [79] XXXII, 228.   [80] XVI, 547-51.

Herder, in short, unlike Hume, was not a thoroughgoing empiricist at all. At heart, whether he knew it or not, he was not only a metaphysician, but a religious metaphysician at that. This fact needs stressing, for it is exceedingly relevant to Herder's approach to politics and history.

Closely allied with the metaphysical element in Herder's theory of causation was the teleological element. Herder's model of causation was that of an organism, the operation of which he held to be activated by a directional power. 'Cause', according to this view was, therefore, not wholly, or not even necessarily, explicable in terms of the origins of an event, but rather in terms of its end or purpose. That Herder wished to emphasize the causal efficacy of the end was not surprising in view of his theory of becoming, in which the end or purpose of a process was held to be implicit in the process of its development. To explain a process we must, in other words, not only look backwards to that which occasioned its existence, but also forwards to the end towards which it is tending. For 'becoming' not only reflects its past, but also foreshadows its future.

Natural scientists in particular and empiricists in general may (and on the whole do) share Hume's doubts about the methodological value of teleological approaches. Yet in the field of human study it may well be asked whether it is not the Humean, that is, the so-called 'scientific' pattern of causation which gives equal cause for doubt. And I would venture to submit that in this sphere Herder revealed a truer insight into the nature of historical and sociological explanations than the great Scotsman whom he so deeply admired. But this is not the place to enlarge on the relevance of Herder's teleological approach to the study of man and society and, in particular, to the interpretation of history. Our main concern in this chapter was to elicit the epistemological and metaphysical strands in Herder's philosophy of organism and, more specifically, to show how, by combining the Aristotelian notion of teleological development with his own conception of *Kraft*, Herder arrived at a position which enabled him to identify the idea of unity with that of the unity of a process, and thus to demonstrate the essential one-ness of the principle of unity and the principle of continuity.

III

ORGANIC POLITICS

THAT in spite of the plurality and diversity of its constituent parts the world forms a single integrated whole, is, we have found, central to Herder's 'organic' interpretation of the universal order. Applied to the human realm, this doctrine attempts to reconcile the uniqueness of man as an individual with his dependence upon other individuals within the larger whole of his social setting: he is a microcosm in himself and yet he cannot exist by himself alone. Diversity *and* relatedness, these are the basic features, therefore, that confront the social philosopher no less than the student of nature.[1] The problem is to discover a manner in which men can associate and co-operate without sacrificing their distinct individualities.

Herder is not the first to perceive the challenge of this problem. Of this he is perfectly aware. Rousseau is uppermost in his mind: 'His great theme is most closely akin to mine', he remarks in one of his early notebooks.[2] But although he shares with him the basic premise asserting man to be a social animal, born in and for society,[3] he differs from him in significant details.

When Herder asserts man to be born into society, he means by 'society'—and here he echoes Justus Möser—an already integrated social unit such as the family, the clan, the *Volk*—a kind of 'family writ large', as he terms it[4]—or one which is in the process of social integration.[5] In either case it is a social setting arising out of human interdependence, i.e. out of a natural need. There is no cause, therefore, Herder feels, to postulate a 'social contract', conceived historically or, as with Rousseau, hypothetically.[6] We cannot but regard social life as something that is given: the state of society *is* man's state of nature. To think of the individual as something outside society is to think in terms of an abstraction. It deludes one into treating him as a repository of

---

[1] On the passage as a whole see: IV, 37; VIII, 210, 226, 314; XIV, 227.

[2] XXXII, 41.

[3] IX, 313. These are not, of course, original ideas; they recall those of the thinkers of antiquity; nearer home, they are not so very different from those of Shaftesbury, the continental idol of the eighteenth century.

[4] XIII, 384.   [5] IV, 369.   [6] VII, 294.

natural inalienable rights to be maintained against the encroachments of
'society'. It is this misconception which, Herder believes, underlies the
doctrine of natural rights. But there is no ground for positing a fundamental antithesis between the individual and society. The two are
inseparable; they are complementaries, not opposites. This view does
not, in Herder's opinion (as we shall see later), rule out the possibility
of social conflict. What it does preclude is the supposition of an *a priori*
antagonism between an isolated unit—the individual—on the one hand,
and a collective body—society—on the other.[7]

But Herder goes further. Man is not only a social animal but also of
necessity a political creature.[8] For his life in society necessitates some
form of organization, some regulative device for the ordering of his
relations. Government, conceived in this sense, is therefore an integral
part of man's social existence: 'Man has never existed without political
organization; it is as natural to him as his origin.'[9] Hence it is nonsense,
Herder declares, to speak of a non-political state of nature.[10]

The ordering of social relations and the accommodation of wants and
interests by rules and regulations, essential though they are, represent
for Herder, however, only the outer forms of political activity. He
searches for the inward springs of socio-political life, for its inner
Kraft. For, like Shaftesbury, Herder sees in the inwardness of a thing
the source of its strength and staying power. And—rather paradoxically
perhaps—he comes to identify this inner sustaining force of socio-
political association with what most strikingly reflects the individuality
of a human being: his native language.

I. LANGUAGE AND POLITICAL ASSOCIATION: '*VOLK*'

Herder's prize essay *Ueber den Ursprung der Sprache* (1770, published
in 1772) has rightly been acclaimed as an outstanding contribution to
the study of language.[11] But it was more than that. The issues which it
raised transcend the confines of philology.

The subject of the *Essay* (the origin of language) had long fascinated

---

[7] IX, 538; see also V, 509 and XIV, 227.   [8] XVI, 48, 119; see also IX, 311–19.
[9] IX, 313.   [10] V, 44.
[11] It has been variously described as 'the first psychological and philosophical beginning
of a theory of language' (Ernst Cassirer, *Freiheit und Form*, op. cit., p. 199); as the 'foundation of a true philosophy of language' (R. Haym, op. cit., vol. I, p. 408); as the 'basis of the
science of philology and the comparative study of languages' (R. R. Ergang, *Herder and the
Foundations of German Nationalism*, New York, 1931, p. 106); and as Herder's 'most
ingenious creative work' (H. A. Korff, op. cit., vol. I, p. 115).

Herder. The heated polemics which the subject aroused in the 'fifties and 'sixties of the century could not, therefore, escape his attention. He decided to join battle, for he felt that neither of the two contending theories was tenable.

Herder dismissed the hypothesis of the divine origin of language as 'humanly inconceivable' and as 'historically and philosophically insupportable'.[12] At the same time, he denied that language could be attributed to human invention. Reason no more than God had 'devised' language. For the emergence of language was not consequent upon, but simultaneous with, the power of reason; reason and language were co-terminous: 'Each nation speaks in the manner it thinks and thinks in the manner it speaks. . . . We cannot think without words.'[13] Herder had already made these points quite clear in the *Fragmente* (1767), which in several important respects foreshadowed the major themes of the *Essay*.

Man, then, was *naturally* endowed with the capacity to speak and the ability to reason. The one implied the other. Whilst Herder did not dispute that man expressed his strongest emotions in sounds and inarticulate cries in a manner indistinguishable from that of an animal, he failed to see what relevance this had to the origin of human language.[14] Were not language and sounds two totally different phenomena?[15] To agree about the animalistic elements in language was one thing; to trace its origin, however, to these elements was quite another. For how was the transition from primitive animalistic 'speech' towards the emergence of intelligible human language to be explained?[16]

That neither Condillac nor Rousseau could convincingly account for the 'jump' from primitive sounds to intelligible language did not surprise Herder since he saw no justification for postulating such a jump.[17] There was no transition from an animalistic to a human stage of language. Man *fundamentally* differed from animals. In place of the animals' instincts, he was endowed with *Besonnenheit*. In view of this, man was not simply an animal with reason superimposed, but a being *sui generis*, whose energies were developed in a wholly different direction.[18] Human language did not evolve from animal sounds. It was not the mere result of a peculiar formation of the mouth and throat, not simply the imitation of the cries of birds and beasts, but rather the corollary of a reflective mind. With the very first sign of consciousness man was a creature of language.[19] The idea, therefore, of an in-between

[12] II, 67.   [13] II,18 and I, 420.   [14] V, 5.   [15] V, 20.
[16] V, 9.   [17] V, 20.   [18] V, 29.   [19] V, 35.

or semi-human state of language, a kind of 'gibberish', as Blackwell had suggested,[20] preceding man's entry into political society, was wholly unfounded, apart from invoking again the 'phantom' of 'natural man'.[21]

Herder approaches the problem of language in terms of three of the dominant conceptual categories which have engaged us in the previous chapter: the principle of interaction, the concept of self-consciousness, and the doctrine of diversity. What is significant, too, is that by viewing language in its widest context Herder succeeds in fusing the epistemological and socio-political implications of *Kraft*, the basic concept of his philosophy of organism.

Herder not only stresses the closest inter-relationship between a community's language and its habits of thought and modes of life; he even draws attention to the interacting influences of such factors as climate and food: 'Climate, water and air, food and drink, they all affect language. . . . Viewed in this way, language is indeed a magnificent treasure store, a collection of thoughts and activities of the mind of the most diverse nature.'[22]

Language is the medium through which man becomes conscious of his inner self, and at the same time it is the key to the understanding of his outer relationships. It unites him with, but it also differentiates him from, others. Imperceptibly it also links him with the past by revealing to him the thoughts, feelings and prejudices of past generations, which thus become deeply ingrained in his own consciousness. He, in turn, again by means of language, perpetuates and enriches these for the benefit of posterity. In this way language embodies the living manifestation of historical growth and the psychological matrix in which man's awareness of his distinctive social heritage is aroused and deepened.[23] Those sharing a particular historical tradition grounded in language Herder identifies with a *Volk* or nationality, and it is in this essentially spiritual quality that he sees the most natural and organic basis for political association.

A language, then, is the criterion by means of which a group's identity as a homogeneous unit can be established. Without its own language, a *Volk* is an absurdity (*Unding*), a contradiction in terms.[24] For neither blood and soil, nor conquest and political fiat can engender that unique

---

[20] Thomas Blackwell, *Enquiry into the Life and Writings of Homer*, 1735. (Page references are to the second edition, London, 1736.) In the third chapter of the *Enquiry*, Blackwell describes the beginnings of language as 'broken, unequal and boisterous', a kind of 'gibberish' (p. 42). Only in the course of political development, during the 'infancy of states' is there a beginning of language properly so called (p. 43). Herder's references to Blackwell: I, 78, 289; V, 330, 341, 398.

[21] V, 44.   [22] V, 125, 136.   [23] V, 135.   [24] I, 147.

consciousness which alone sustains the existence and continuity of a social entity. Even if a *Volk*'s State perishes, the nation remains intact provided it maintains its distinctive linguistic traditions.[25]

Herder's faith in the sustaining and integrating power of language even led him to expect a higher measure of social cohesion to result from the conscious fostering of a common linguistic medium. Thus when he was asked in 1787 to draw up a plan for an 'Institute of German National Enlightenment', he thought of it not merely as an association for the promotion of the German language, but also as a kind of cultural parliament which, by developing and propagating German, would tend to reduce the gulf separating the diverse social classes and thus help to promote the expression of a 'general will'.

Germany has only one interest: the life and wellbeing of the whole; not the sectional interests of the princes or the Estates, not the interest of this or that class. All these divisions only give rise to oppressive restrictions. We Germans still do not understand the importance of a national language. The bulk of our people still think of it as something that only concerns the grammarian. To consider it as the *organ of social activity and co-operation*, as the bond of social classes and a means for their integration: this is something of which most of us have only the remotest notion.[26]

But if language is capable of arousing a sense of identity within a community, it will, in doing so, simultaneously give rise to the community's consciousness of difference from those speaking another language. This, Herder feels, is as it should be. For diversity is the fundamental characteristic of the universal order. The world must be a world of many nationalities.[27] Diversity, not uniformity, is the design of the Almighty. Emperor Joseph II is taken to task for ignoring what patently is a law of Nature and a decree of God: 'Truly, just as God tolerates all languages of this world, so too should a ruler tolerate, nay, treasure, the diverse languages of his subject nations.'[28]

A *Volk*, on this theory, then, is a natural division of the human race, endowed with its own language, which it must preserve as its most distinctive and sacred possession. Language is as much the embodiment of a *Volk*'s 'soul' or character, as it is the expression of an individual's unique personality. By forsaking it, a *Volk* destroys its 'self' for language and the national consciousness to which it gives rise are inseparably joined. Intermixture with other nationalities, therefore, is to be avoided. The situation most congenial to the preservation of the natural order of things is that analogous to the growth of a plant rooted in the soil.[29]

[25] XIV, 87.
[26] XVI, 607 and XVIII, 384; see also R. Haym, op. cit., vol. II, p. 486.
[27] XIV, 67, 84.   [28] XVII, 59.   [29] IV, 212.

association of autonomous nations, co-operating in matters of common interest on a basis of equal partnership, irrespective of size, economic development and other individual differences, without a common political authority or formal agreements to bind them. The essential presupposition for peaceful international *Zusammenwirken* Herder saw in the growth of common interests and common purposes, which would, he felt, have a moderating effect on purely nationalist tendencies. *Humanität*, once it became an integral part of patriotism, would guard against chauvinistic excesses.

Nations, Herder thought, were in a sense, comparable to individuals. Just as the self-realization of the individual was an interactive process, inconceivable in isolation, so also, Herder believed, did national self-realization necessitate international co-operation. The recognition of inter-dependence in each case would, Herder hoped, act as a brake on egoism and chauvinism respectively.[95] In each case Herder looked upon the principle of *Billigkeit* as the light that will guide man to find new and better ways of social and political existence: 'Hence, love of our own nation should not prevent us from recognizing the good (in man) everywhere. . . . The tendency of human nature is to embrace within itself a universe. An infinite diversity, striving for a unity that lies in all things and which urges all things forward.'[96] Unity amidst diversity, not uniformity or 'mechanical' unification, was Herder's operative principle of international *Zusammenwirken*. He conceived this 'unity' essentially as the unity of a common desire, the will to behave in matters of international concern according to the unwritten law of *Billigkeit*.

But whereas the political transformation from the 'mechanical' to the 'organic' State is held to be 'naturally' pre-conditioned by the existence of a common language, this is not so in the sphere of international relations. In the former case, language, being an already existing 'spontaneous' force, will provide a natural basis for socio-political association. It is *there*; it need not be created. The natural basis for the political transformation in the international sphere, on the other hand, is *not* 'there'; it has to be *developed* from the very outset. *This* is the supreme task of 'humanization' and, in Herder's view, the surest criterion of a State's political worth and maturity: 'The better a State

---

individual identity and autonomy as also the notion that men can govern themselves without becoming slaves to the machinery of government. The correspondence between the Herders and the great Swiss historian Johannes v. Müller is instructive on this point. (*Briefwechsel mit J. G. Herder und Caroline v. Herder*, op. cit.)

[95] XIII, 346; see also XIV, 227; XVI, 119, 551; XVII, 116; XVIII, 302, 408; XXIV, 375; XXIX, 133, 139.

[96] XVIII, 137, 300; see also XVIII, 271.

is, the more favourable will be the climate for the cultivation of *Humanität.*'[97]

There is a curious, even paradoxical, but for Herder not uncharacteristic, mixture of doubt and faith, of realism and idealism in his political application of the concept of *Humanität*. There is also in his political judgment an equally paradoxical combination of insight and almost prophetic vision on the one hand, and a somewhat defective grasp of political realities on the other. In his yearning for a transformation of politics he was led astray at times into a manner of political reasoning which cannot be described as other than exceedingly naïve. 'Cabinets may deceive each other; political machines may be positioned against one another, until one destroys the other. Yet fatherlands never oppose one other in this manner.'[98] Remarks such as the one just quoted may also suggest that beneath Herder's political speculation, presented as reasoned principles, there was a strong emotional undercurrent of personal discontent, due in some measure to unsatisfied political ambitions and attributable in part to the prevailing social and political conditions. This, indeed, cannot be ruled out. At the same time, Herder's hostility to political 'machinery' was the reflection of a positive and firmly held conviction about man's social and political 'destiny', and about his capacity to order his political life in a more 'natural' manner.

Herder saw his chief task in endowing *Humanität*, the leading notion of his age, with a new vitality: *Humanität* was to be both what man *had* achieved and what he *could* achieve. Therein lies its logical weakness as a concept, but its strength as a social ideal. For the inspirational power which it was to exercise stemmed precisely from this fusion of past, present and future, of reality and potentiality.

[97] XVII, 121.   [98] XVII, 319.

VI

HISTORY AND SOCIAL DEVELOPMENT

IN SPITE of ambiguities, due largely to the absence of a precise definition of its principal term, Herder's doctrine of *Humanität* nevertheless succeeded, we found, in endowing the word with a significance that was new. *Humanität* now came to mean *continuity* as well as unity. From being a fixed norm it became a dynamic principle, a kind of protean manifestation of human striving throughout the ages. At any given time and place *Humanität* would reflect the particular mode in which man aspired to achieve that attitude to social life which befitted his nature as a human being. To trace the manifold ways in which such aspirations were pursued, if not necessarily attained, was, in Herder's view, the proper concern of the social philosopher and historian.[1]

I. CONTINUITY AND PURPOSE

Such an undertaking presupposes, however, two distinct considerations. One is that human striving is of necessity purposive, and hence a directional process; the other, that this process has a moral orientation. The former may conceivably claim recognition as an empirical hypothesis. But the same cannot be said concerning man's moral inclinations. It is one of the chief weaknesses of Herder's philosophy of history that these two considerations are not clearly kept apart.

Herder's failure to distinguish clearly the empirical from the moral and metaphysical realm stems partly from his essentially religious conception of the universal order, in which he viewed history as the unfolding of a divine plan.[2] To a large measure, however, it springs also from a widely shared conviction about the pragmatic and didactic use which history is supposed to serve. Herder's remark that history which merely narrates the deeds of kings and generals provides no useful example to youth is characteristic of this attitude to the study of history.[3] To be a fruitful subject of study, history must render proof of the moral orientation of human conduct; it must be morally satisfy-

[1] XIII, 161 and XVII, 259.   [2] V, 513.   [3] XVI, 587.

ing by driving home the lesson that right always ultimately earns its due reward and wrong its just punishment.[4]

But although Herder shared the didactic, morally oriented attitude to history, he none the less rejected the apocalyptic manner in which many of his contemporaries approached the study of the past. His polemical essay *Auch eine Philosophie der Geschichte zur Bildung der Menschheit* (1774) was a direct attack upon those who saw in the past nothing but a prelude to the present and who evaluated its errors and achievements wholly in terms of current standards or in the light of super-historical absolutes.[5] Each individual event, Herder insisted by contrast, was not merely a means to an end but of intrinsic value in itself, carrying within itself its own immanent validity and justification.[6] To be able to discern this 'inner' significance, the historian had to re-live the past, to reconstruct and re-think for himself its thoughts and feelings, and thus to recapture the spirit of the age which he was studying.[7] In order to succeed in this, psychological insight into human motivation was an essential prerequisite. Herder therefore closely linked the development of historical methodology with the advances in scientific psychology. The extent to which psychology became capable of attending to each empirical detail under investigation would, he believed, materially determine the scope of historical understanding and the historian's ability to 'feel himself into everything'.[8]

Yet, emphatic though he was in his demand for minute attention to empirical facts before any generalizations were drawn from which men could derive practical benefit, he also realized that historical understanding required more than the mere accumulation of facts. He saw, that is, that the notion of history as an objective compilation of facts was just as untenable as the belief that facts can be arbitrarily marshalled into an *a priori* framework of the historian's choosing. What he

---

[4] To meet this requirement, Herder advanced the concept of *Nemesis* (XVIII, 283 and XXIV, 326). See also XVIII, 321 and XIII, 256. On the other hand, in one of his early works (*Fragmente*) Herder criticized Winckelmann severely for presenting history as a didactic system (II, 123).

[5] V, 524–5; Herder seems to have reached a position similar to that of Vico quite independently. Vico is not mentioned by Herder before 1797, and even then Herder's reference to him, though eloquent in praise, suggests that he is only superficially acquainted with his thought, hardly realizing its similarity to his own (XVIII, 246). Vico was little known in Germany at the time. The contention that some of his ideas had percolated, mainly through the writings of Montesquieu (see Paul Hazard, *European Thought in the Eighteenth Century*, trans. by J. Lewis May, London, 1954, p. 246), does not seem well-founded. (I am indebted to Sir Isaiah Berlin for his observations on this point.)

[6] V, 527.   [7] III, 470; see also IV, 202–3. (Similarly, I, 137.)

[8] II, 257; IV, 364 and V, 503; see also his fragmentary sketch written in 1766: 'Politics, history . . . , the kernel is psychology' (XXXII, 58).

therefore advocated was a most subtle and careful synthesis between the 'objective' material and the 'subjective' ordering of it into a coherent and intelligible account. In this fusion of 'fact' and 'interpretation' the historian, Herder readily conceded, could not dispense with his own judgment. The historian could only see what *he* could see. Of himself Herder wrote to this effect: 'I only write history as it appears to me, as I come to know it.'[9]

In admitting the subjective element in historical interpretation, Herder did not doubt, however, the possibility of attaining objectively warranted explanations of historical events. On the contrary, he held that the historian's awareness of the personal factors liable to affect his judgment may actually enhance this possibility, in so far as it would assist him to mitigate if not entirely eliminate their influence.[10] None the less, the recognition of subjectivity does mean—and herein lies Herder's chief contribution to historiography—that the only objectivity attainable in historical interpretation is *relative* objectivity. However successful he may be in divesting himself of personal bias, the historian must ultimately rely on his own sense of interpretative perspective.

But even more fundamental than the problem of objectivity is the question of historical understanding as such. In what sense, it may be asked, can the past be understood or made intelligible? It may or may not be granted that the explanation of historical sequences, once undertaken, should, as Herder suggested, yield useful lessons. This does not, however, meet the question as to the possibility of arriving at such explanations in the first place.

Any answer to this question invariably rests on a number of assumptions about the nature of the universal order in general and about human nature in particular. These assumptions, therefore, be they factual, in the loose sense of being empirically verifiable, or conceptual, in that they are derivative from a more comprehensive 'metaphysical' scheme of things, will vitally bear on the interpretative perspective of the historian. It is they which fundamentally determine his approach to the problem of intelligibility in history.

[9] VIII, 466.
[10] See V, 435 and XVIII, 137. Although it is undoubtedly true that Herder in many important respects transcended Voltaire's conception of history, he nonetheless shared with his contemporaries an enormous intellectual debt to this conception which in its most developed form found expression in Voltaire's epoch-making *Essai sur les moeurs*. Voltaire's influence is particularly in evidence in Herder's emphasis on psychology as the key to history, in the importance which he attaches to social history, conventions, customs, and to the history of ideas, and in his disdain for military glory and 'heroes'.

Confronted with this problem, Herder invokes at one and the same time the conceptual framework which underlies his providential theory of history and the empirical hypothesis which he posits about the nature of human actions. In the light of the former, history is held to be analogous to nature. The God of nature is also the God of history.[11] If unity and continuity are observable in the realm of nature, why should they fail to be discoverable in the realm of human events? Even if we have to suspend judgment about the ultimate design of the providential order, why should we refrain from seeking meaning and purpose in what is so manifestly purposive?[12] Moreover, is it not a fact that man thinks and acts in terms of purposes? We may or may not espy the purposes and operations of divine creation by a study of history, but at least we may come to understand the operation of human motives and desires under the most diverse conditions of time and place.[13]

This parallelism between an essentially man-centred view of history, seeking the operative forces of historical change in a spirit similar to that in which natural science attempts an understanding of the factors governing the events of nature, and a providential conception of history which looks upon historical events as the inexorable working out of transcendental purposes gives rise to one of the most perplexing problems in Herder's philosophy of history. For whereas his 'naturalist' approach to history can still be classified as merely 'deterministic' in that it is based on the acceptance of causal relationships, his 'providential' theory presupposes a doctrine of historical fatalism.[14]

Accepting for the present Herder's assurance that in embarking on his *Ideen zur Philosophie der Geschichte der Menschheit* (1784–91) he

[11] XIII, 7–9; see also II, 127; IV, 200 and XXIV, 334. It was, of course, Herder's declared aim to vindicate man's place in the world of nature. What was less clear was the meaning which the concept of 'nature' was intended to have. Herder was aware of the proliferation of meaning which this word had undergone: 'No word in human language is more ambiguous than "nature" ' (IV, 181). Yet his own use of the concept exemplified as ambivalent an attitude as that of his contemporaries. Nature was what one could observe, but more often it was what one wished to observe: it was good (XVI, 570), reasonable (XXIV, 333), orderly (XXX, 283), rich yet simple (XVI, 463), and never arbitrary (XVI, 546). Nature was God in His works (XIII, 10). When used in this manner, 'nature' simply served as a sanction of value judgments or as a dialectical device for their concealment.

[12] XIII, 7–8.   [13] V, 589.

[14] On this point I feel indebted to G. A. Wells's article on 'Herder's Determinism' in the *Journal of the History of Ideas*, vol. XIX, January 1958. I am inclined to think, however, that the conflict is not merely one between determinism and fatalism. I have put 'deterministic' in inverted commas to indicate that a further distinction may have to be borne in mind since Herder did wish to distinguish between the mode of causality in the world of natural phenomena and that applicable to human affairs.

did so not as a theologian following in Bossuet's footsteps but from the point of view of the social scientist,[15] we must next ask how Herder set about arriving at historical explanations in strictly human terms, with the aid of which he hoped to be able to trace an intelligible and continuous pattern in the sequence of human events.

2. CAUSE AND PURPOSE

The *Ideen* make it quite evident that Herder was not merely, nor even chiefly, concerned with the discovery of factors occasioning the occurrence of an event. It is its value or 'significance' that he wished to establish. His search for intelligibility and continuity in history, therefore, was a composite and, in a sense, a two-dimensional undertaking. It aimed at the *explanation* of an event in terms of the antecedents operative at a given time and place, and at the *evaluation* of it in terms of its direction or orientation.

Each of these inter-related processes of historical interpretation is concerned with the tracing of connexions, but they may be broadly distinguished by reference to the main perspective that comes into play in each. Thus whilst the explanatory search is essentially backward-looking, the evaluative search is forward-looking. The former concentrates on an event's *origins*, the latter centres on its *development*. What complicates matters, however, is that for Herder 'evaluation' also implies the assessment of an event's *moral* orientation. Apart from the difficulty this raises concerning the application of moral criteria which are not at the same time super-historical norms, it also involves the identification of the idea of development with the idea of moral progress. On the other hand, this 'complication' renders Herder's advocacy of evaluating each individual event as an end in itself less inconceivable. If the human motive that has given rise to its occurrence is singled out, as it frequently is by Herder, as the most relevant evaluative factor, it does make sense to speak of an event's intrinsic value in terms of the moral criteria that are applied to it. None the less it remains obscure how the notion of the intrinsic significance of an historical event can be reconciled with the notion of continuous development.

At this stage it may be helpful to recall, and enlarge upon, some of the points made in an earlier chapter (ch. II) about Herder's theory of

[15] XIV, 569.

causation and his attempt to equate development with organic growth.

Herder's model of causation, we found, is that of an organism activated by an internal driving power. 'Cause', accordingly, is not discoverable, chiefly, by tracing the occurrence of an event back to its antecedents, but rather by recognizing its end, i.e. the *direction* in which it is moving. That Herder should focus attention on the causal efficacy of ends or purposes follows logically from his theory of development which, as we indicated earlier, maintains that the purpose of a thing is implicit in its unfolding, i.e. in the process of actualization of that which is already latent.[16]

If we apply Herder's principle of internal teleological causation to the sphere of human events, then, bearing in mind his axiom asserting human behaviour to be purposive, the internal driving or motivating power sustaining them are the ends which are aimed at. Assuming that when dealing with human events in history we are principally concerned with deliberate actions, rather than purely accidental ones, the ends or purposes which are involved will constitute the *reason* for their occurrence. No doubt, the psychological and circumstantial grounds that have given rise to the reason for a particular decision may be of relevance to its total causal explanation. But the degree of relevance of these antecedent causes will be determined by the nature of the reason itself. Even if the possibility is granted of a reason being determined by antecedent circumstances, it can never thus be wholly determined. For it would then be an act devoid of purpose. Reason, or purpose, therefore, cannot simply be a function of antecedent causes. But the converse does not necessarily hold good. When a course of action has been decided upon, the means chosen will be those that are deemed most suitable to the purpose in hand. The series of events preceding an act will therefore be determined by their relevance to the end aimed at. None of these events may have the slightest bearing on the reason that has prompted the occurrence of the act, in the absence of which they might never have come into being at all. It is the end which occasioned the means to occur. The less adequately a reason helps to explain an event (in the sense of making it intelligible in terms of customary—or 'normal'—habits of thought and feeling), the more importantly significant will be the circumstantial antecedents, including the state

---

[16] In adopting the Aristotelian conception of causality Herder obviously assumes a pre-Cartesian or, more probably, an anti-Cartesian position; a position, that is, which had little appeal to scientific minds of his own and the subsequent period. But, as applied to human affairs, it cannot, we attempt to argue here, fail to be of interest to the *social* scientist.

of mind of the agent. Conversely, in closely integrated means to end sequences (e.g. wanting to get up early to catch an early train to attend an important meeting) we shall expect a given set of actions (e.g. going to bed earlier the preceding night, setting the alarm clock, etc.) to occur that are likely to facilitate the desired end. We would be surprised to hear that someone made all these careful arrangements without knowing what end or purpose they were intended to serve. We would be equally surprised to find that, although X wanted to attend an important meeting in town at 10.30 a.m., he made no attempt to ensure his prompt attendance. But whilst the making or not-making of proper arrangements to facilitate the desired end may have a vital bearing upon its attainment, it will in no way provide a clue to the reason which occasioned the end in question to be desired, nor will it provide a basis for its evaluation. What we therefore earlier distinguished as the explanatory search, not only contains within itself, but is in fact logically preceded by the evaluative search, since the latter determines the causal perspective (as to range and order of significance) that is applicable to the former.

It may rightly be objected that the evaluative procedure may involve an infinite regression in tracing the determinate reason or reasons in any sequence of events, as well as pose serious problems regarding the selection of relevant antecedents. None the less, the distinction between 'cause' as a temporal antecedent and 'cause' as a purposive direction is, I believe, an important one in the treatment of human affairs. For by drawing this distinction it seems perfectly admissible to uphold a form of causal determinism without subscribing to a theory of fatalism. We can, that is to say, admit the relevance of causal antecedents to explanations of human behaviour without committing ourselves to the view that any particular action is necessarily inevitable. One can go even further and argue that the knowledge of causal antecedents may preclude rather than favour the inevitability of occurrences. This is what Herder presumably had in mind when he said that we can learn from the mistakes of the past and that by gaining historical insight, we may arrive at results which are both descriptive and prescriptive. But to argue thus implies of course that what happened in the past was in a sense avoidable. It presupposes man's ability to recognize purposes and his freedom to pursue or to shun them.

Now, Herder's teleological treatment of causation looks at first as if it implied determinism in both the sense of causal explicability and in the sense of inexorable inevitability. For by attributing to the inherent or, in Herder's terminology, 'genetic' force in a thing the determining power of its development, on which environment has but a modifying influence, the end of its development is, as it were, predetermined from the outset. Such a theory of development leaves no room for the exercise of human choice. Only by clearly setting apart human development from other forms of organic growth and by investing man with the capacity consciously to realize ends and to choose between them, does it make sense to speak of purposes as being something that is not merely given but aimed at.

Herder, we have seen, advances the concepts of 'reflection' (*Besonnenheit*) and 'consciousness' (*Besinnung*) to meet this requirement. By means of reflection and consciousness man is held to be capable of acknowledging purposes and of being actuated by self-chosen ends. He is thus enabled to reflect upon the past and to draw inferences and 'lessons' from what happened before under what circumstances and for what reasons. Since such knowledge can, and possibly will, affect future situations, there will always be an incalculable element in the causal relation of human events which militates against the inevitable repetition of causal sequences.[17] It would appear, then, that Herder's principle of teleological causation, applied to human affairs, weakens rather than supports the case of that form of determinism which conceives of events as being inevitable or predictable.[18]

The preceding account may also help to throw some light on the problem inherent in Herder's demand for treating an event not merely as a means within historical sequences but as an end in itself. For it suggests that in interpreting the past a distinction can be drawn between the sheer temporal sequence of events and their continuity in terms of intended purposes, in so far as their temporal consequences differ from these. Since, clearly, not all consequences of human actions are intended consequences, there is a sense in speaking of a 'gap' in the continuity of purposive actions. There is, by the same token, a sense in speaking of an event's intrinsic meaning or significance in abstraction

[17] Thus the Marxist interpretation of the events following the French Revolution for example—in particular the rise of Napoleon—palpably affected Trotsky's position in post-revolutionary Russia. Or, to take another example, the Munich Agreement of 1938 undoubtedly made post-war thinking so much more sensitive to the dangers of 'appeasement'.

[18] When talking about teleological causation in this context one must guard against confusing the argument for teleology *in* history with the argument for teleology *of* history. The latter is, no doubt, no more than a 'form of faith capable of neither confirmation or refutation by any kind of experience (since) the notions of evidence, proof, probability and so on, are wholly inapplicable to it' (Isaiah Berlin, *Historical Inevitability*, London, 1954, p. 16). But the former, I feel, cannot be denied the status of a heuristic or regulative principle capable of empirical scrutiny.

of its temporal inter-connexion with subsequent events. If *ex hypothesi* we can isolate what lies within an event (i.e. the intended purpose) from what lies beyond it, and regard this internal self-directive element as a basis on which we can rest an interpretative judgment of its significance, Herder's demand for treating an event as an end in itself seems adequately warranted even without recourse to the motive's moral evaluation.

3. CONTINUITY AND SOCIAL DEVELOPMENT

In his philosophy of history Herder applies his concept of development (as a continuous process of 'becoming' or growth) to the group rather than to a single individual. The group he has in mind is the *Volk* which, as we noted earlier, he regards as the most 'natural' socio-political unit, identifying it with a community sharing the consciousness of its own distinctive socio-cultural traditions, the determinate feature of which he sees in the possession of a common language. His main interest, therefore, centres on the formation and growth of such a language community.[19] Notwithstanding the extensive use made of biological terms,[20] there can be no doubt that he is less concerned with physical than with socio-cultural characteristics, for what he primarily wishes to trace are the social customs, folk-lore and literary traditions of a people. Hidden and elusive though these may be, they constitute, in his view, that element of consistency in a *Volk*'s changing states, by means of which it can preserve and perpetuate its identity as a distinct social entity: 'This is the invisible, hidden, medium that links minds through ideas, hearts through inclinations and impulses, the senses through impressions and forms, civil society through laws and institutions, generations through examples, modes of living and education. It is through this medium that we actively establish a continuum between ourselves and those that follow upon us.'[21] The task of the philosopher of history is to discover this 'invisible medium', this

[19] Herder's interest in the development of a *Volk*'s distinct collective consciousness, to which he also refers in terms of 'national character' and 'national spirit', forms the central theme of the *Ideen*. But this interest can be traced to his earliest works, e.g.: I, 23, 147, 261, 276; II, 8, 13, 19, 28, 32, 79, 160; III, 30, 62, 398, 414, 425; IV, 168, 213, 253, 371; and V, 134, 506, 539.

[20] A *Volk*'s arts and sciences, for example, are said to grow, produce buds, bloom, and wither (I, 151). In the *Ideen* the history of mankind is pictured as a series of national organisms (XIV, 67, 84). See also IV, 212 and XX, 136.

[21] XVI, 35. Herder defines 'philosophy of history' as the study of the chain of tradition (XIII, 352).

continuum between past, present and future. He must study, therefore, the mode and manner in which national traditions are transmitted and assimilated.[22]

The function of transmitting national traditions Herder assigns to education. But since a given generation may not wholly assimilate, but partly also challenge, the traditions transmitted to it, education necessarily involves a certain dialectic in its operation. It entails not only the passing on, but also the re-appraisal and revaluation of a *Volk*'s socio-cultural heritage.[23] In view of this, Herder speaks of education as a continuous spiritual 'genesis', investing it with both 'genetic' and 'organic' attributes: 'The education of our species is thus in a twofold sense genetic and organic: genetic in view of the manner of the transmission, organic in view of the nature of the assimilation and application of what is being transmitted.'[24] As the vital link in the chain of social development, relating the living with the dead and with those who are to come, education is at once the guardian of tradition and the herald of progress.[25]

The chief medium of transmission in this educational process of social interaction is language which, as we remarked earlier, Herder regarded as the most distinctive element in a *Volk*'s cultural heritage. It is through language that a community's sense of its separate existence is both awakened and sustained. Language and education, therefore, constitute for Herder the most determinate factors in the fashioning of a community's social consciousness by which it becomes aware not only of its own existence but also of that which differentiates it from the rest of humanity.

The manner and form which at any given stage the development of a *Volk*'s collective consciousness assumes, Herder termed its national 'culture'. This was a new conception of the word, wholly at odds with the prevailing outlook of the Enlightenment which tended to identify culture with civilization and intellectual sophistication, opposing it to the original simplicity of nature. Herder, by contrast, held it to be applicable to a wide and varied range of human activities, provided its purely relative significance was recognized in each individual case: 'Nothing is more indeterminate than this word and nothing more deceptive than its application to all nations and to all periods.'[26] One must always specify the sort of culture one has in mind in relation to what period and to which section of society.[27] Thus one could speak, for

[22] XIII, 352.   [23] XIV, 234.
[24] XIII, 348; see also XIII, 346 and XIV, 84.   [25] XIV, 89.
[26] XIII, 4; see also XIII, 348.   [27] XIV, 35.

example, of a political culture, or of the culture of intellectuals as distinct from the culture of *Bürger*.[28] Or again, one could distinguish different forms of culture existing side by side and developing at different rates, some attaining their optimum level or 'maximum' before others.[29] The most decisive factor, however, from the political point of view, Herder interestingly remarks, is not the number of cultural maxima, nor the degree of perfection achieved in any single cultural sphere, but rather the *balanced relationship* of a *Volk*'s diverse social cultures.[30]

We noted earlier that Herder's theory of social development visualizes a 'dialectic' in the mode of transmission of social cultures. We must now ask what it is that, given that social cultures are not passively assimilated by one generation from another but creatively applied and progressively re-oriented, confers on the process as a whole a relational unity, in the light of which one can discern a directional continuity which is more than the sheer temporal succession of events.

Herder, it is true, does not provide a systematically formulated answer to this question. He does indicate, however, throughout the *Ideen* (as also in the *Briefe*) that he is thinking in terms of certain basic determinants, with the aid of which he conceives it possible to trace significant connexions in a *Volk*'s historical development. How precisely he envisages the manner of inter-connexion and interaction between these determinants emerges rather well in a work of a much earlier period. In the *Fragmente* (1767) Herder suggests that continuity between historical determinants manifests itself in a two-dimensional manner: 'horizontally', in so far as *at any given time* a number of factors exercise upon each a reciprocal influence; 'vertically', in so far as by succeeding each other they influence the course of events in a particular *direction*: 'A series of causes act together, reciprocally and in succession to one another; one wheel interlocks with the other; one motive spring acts against the other.'[31] The inter-relation and inter-

---

[28] XIV, 34–5.

[29] Herder mentions the Greeks and Hebrews as contrasting examples. (See XIV, 67 and XIV, 227.)

[30] XIV, 149. Herder must certainly be ranged among the early pioneers who attempted a sociology of culture.

[31] II, 65. In the *Ideen* the idea of two-dimensional interaction in history receives its most developed elaboration in Herder's interpretation of Greek history. It takes the form of four basic hypotheses (in the sense of provisional generalizations) which are intended to serve as the theoretical framework for the study of historical continuity. They are:

(i) 'That which can come about in the realm of mankind within the compass of given national, temporal, and local conditions, does in fact come about.'

(ii) 'What is true of one nation is also true of the inter-relation of several nations; they

action between what Herder regards as the persistent forces in history —he applies to them the term 'genetic'—and the environmental factors —to which he refers as '*Klima*' (climate)—can be said to correspond to the horizontal dimension. The forward propelling power of the historical motive forces (*Triebfedern*), on the other hand, can be said to correspond to the vertical dimension. The distinction between horizontal and vertical inter-connexion is in a sense arbitrary, but it helps, I think, to clarify Herder's distinction between causal antecedents (*Ursachen*) and causal motive forces (*Triebfedern*). It also suggests a line of procedure to be followed in singling out what Herder considers to be the dominant determinants in historical development.

Let us then examine briefly, in turn, the chief determinants in Herder's two-dimensional conception of historical continuity, starting with the 'genetic' forces.

(i) *Genetic Forces*

Most of the social and political thinkers of the century, accepting as self-evident Locke's epistemological assumption of *tabula rasa*, turned a blind eye to innate and hereditary factors. Instead they tended to place unbounded faith in the power of environmental forces to effect the regeneration of man and society. Herder by no means disregarded the potency of environmental influences. But he insisted on treating them as secondary factors. The primary factor was the 'genetic' force or energy (*Kraft*), by which he understood an inherent characteristic distinguishing one individual and, in its extended application, one *Volk* from another, independently from, or even in spite of, external circumstances: 'The genetic force is the mother of all creations on earth, to which the climate can only contribute, favourably or unfavourably, as the case might be. . . . But whatever the climatic influence, every human being, every animal, every plant has a climate of its own; for each absorbs and adapts the external influences in its own organic manner.'[32] That he could not account for the origin of this genetic force,

---

stand together just as time and place have brought them together; they influence one another, just as the conjunction of vital forces has determined.'

(iii) 'The civilization of a nation is the flower of its existence, its most pleasing yet transient manifestation.'

(iv) 'The health and permanence of a State are founded not upon its highest point of culture, but upon a wise or happy balance of its vitally operative forces. The deeper its centre of gravity is within the striving of these forces, the more stable and durable it is.' (XIV, 144–9.)

These generalizations also exemplify most revealingly Herder's tendency to think almost simultaneously in terms of both a more extreme and a more restrained form of determinism.

[32] XIII, 273, 276–7.

or even describe its inner nature, Herder freely admitted. At the same time he was quite convinced about its existence. He identified with it that creative power by means of which an individual was able to assimilate and apply what had been transmitted to him in his own peculiar manner. It is not clear which, if any, physical characteristics Herder associated with this inborn force.[33] But to judge from Herder's own application of the concept to the origin and development of *Volk*-communities, it would appear that he was thinking primarily in terms of psycho-social characteristics. For what he singled out as the differentiating factor between nations was a particular habit or mode of thinking (*Denkart*).[34] The mode of thinking among different individuals of any one nation had more in common, or differed less, than the mode of thinking of any two individuals of two different nations.

At this point Herder's theory of genetic forces threatens to become circular. For it is impossible to tell which is the really determining factor, the fact that an individual is born with a given national mentality, or the circumstance that he is born into a given national *milieu*. It is also difficult to see, incidentally, how the idea of an inborn mentality is reconcilable with Herder's epistemological anti-*a priorism*. What, finally, complicates matters even more is Herder's suggestion that, as a result of the interaction of inborn traits and environmental factors, the inborn traits may undergo change so that inborn and acquired characteristics would become intermingled.[35] Herder realized this difficulty, but none the less insisted that in spite of such inter-mingling there would remain a 'hard core', as it were, which was immune to the influence of environmental factors.[36]

Herder was clearly faced here with a dilemma. To insist on the unchanging nature of genetic forces would have involved the denial of the dynamics of historical change. To allow, on the other hand, for the complete changeability of genetic forces would have seriously threatened, if it would not have invalidated, the notion of a persistent 'national character'.

(ii) *Environmental Factors*

The chief weakness of Herder's environmental theory lies in the excessively comprehensive sense in which he employs the term 'climate' (*Klima*). For Herder does not confine its applicability to

---

[33] XIII, 274. When on one occasion (XIV, 39) Herder does make reference to physical characteristics he does not seem to think of them as inborn or hereditary.

[34] XIV, 84.   [35] XIII, 280–4.   [36] XIII, 273.

meteorological phenomena. Nor does he restrict it, as Montesquieu had done, to such physical influences as are attributable to geographical, geological, or biological causes. He simply identifies it with the total *milieu* into which an individual is born. He includes in it elements of the most diverse nature: educational institutions, natural products, the standard of living, political systems, dress, posture, amusements, the arts; he even calls for a 'climatology' of human thought and feeling.[37] Indeed, one cannot help wondering at times whether Herder is still thinking of environmental factors at all, when, for example, he speaks of '*Klima*' as the 'global sphere of interaction', reflecting, as it were, the effect of the interplay of human 'genetic' forces and their physical environment.[38] For, clearly, viewed in this way, man is at one and the same time moulding, and moulded by, the forces of his environment. *Klima* changes man, but man also changes *Klima*.

None the less, Herder's concept of '*Klima*' is of interest to the student of social and political development in that it emphasizes the plurality and inter-relatedness of the most diverse aspects that bear upon the shaping of socio-political life and, in doing so, calls attention to the need for the utmost care in the treatment of historical causation. In the second place, by the manner in which it insists on *organically* relating the physical and the human aspects of social development, it goes beyond Montesquieu's doctrine of environmental causation. Herder sought to bring out the contrast between physical environment as such, and environment which had been 'energized' by the human factor, in order to demonstrate what he considered to be an essential element in the historical development of human societies: the *process* of fusion between the 'merely objective' and the 'merely subjective', the continuous emergence of a continuum between man and his environment.

(iii) *Historical Motive Forces*
Although Herder recognized the importance of political, economic and technological factors as directional determinants in human history,[39]

---

[37] XIII, 269.   [38] XIII, 272.

[39] As regards the political factor there is little that can be added here without the risk of repetition. The quotation below, however, seems worth inserting for it sums up rather neatly Herder's assessment of the rôle of politics in social development.

Klima may be regarded as the soil in which the seed of human knowledge develops; . . . national character as the factor which helps to determine more closely the type of the seed; whilst the political constitution of a nation—understood in its widest sense—represents without question the further

he attributed the chief historical driving power to what he called the 'force of ideas' (*Drang der Ideen*).[40] By 'ideas' Herder mainly seems to understand what Kant meant by categories of thought (*Denkformen*), although in a less formal and perhaps more dynamic sense. Ideas were those conceptual categories which the human mind was evolving in its endeavour to understand, explore and enlarge the range of human possibilities and the world in which it can realize these. They are both the basic means in terms of which the external world is perceived and the conceptual tools with the aid of which man can give expression to his own relationship to this world. Whilst in one sense they bring to his notice the limits of what he can hope to achieve, they urge him in another constantly to transcend these limits. In the interplay of these opposing tendencies Herder saw a vital driving source of human development.[41] And it was essentially by virtue of these immanent 'ideological' forces that Herder viewed the stream of history as a directional or purposive movement.

This belief in the primacy of thought in human affairs and its efficacy in transforming social and political institutions no doubt led Herder to reject revolution as an instrument of political change in favour of gradual and peaceful reforms. Coupled with this belief, if not underlying it, was his notion that 'time' itself was pressing for change in the desired direction.

Herder's treatment of time is perhaps the most interesting, if also the most perplexing aspect of his theory of directional determinants. 'Time', far from being empty space in which events 'occur', is in fact presented as an historical motive force in its own right. It has its own causative existence *sui generis* which Herder identifies with a forward-propelling, 'progressive' tendency embodying by its very nature the progress of humanity.[42] But Herder hesitated to commit himself, as we shall see in the next chapter, on the question whether the mere progress

---

cultivation of the soil, the sowing of the seed and at the same time the influence of all those natural factors without which nothing can prosper and grow (IX, 311).

Herder seems fully aware of the intimate relationship between economic conditions and socio-political change. (See, for example, XIII, 295; XIV, 69; or XVIII, 289.) As to technical inventions and scientific discoveries, Herder was particularly impressed by the 'as yet unrealized possibilities of electricity', which he regards as a *Triebfeder* of 'truly tremendous historical importance' (V, 533).

[40] XIII, 186.

[41] XX, 90. Indeed, Herder goes so far as to regard all human organizations as 'systems of ideological forces' (XIII, 181).

[42] XIV, 236.

of time *ipso facto* implied social amelioration and human perfection. None the less, in postulating an immanent progressive force within historical sequences he comes perilously close to the brink of fatalism. The quotation below certainly suggests that he was not far from thinking in terms of 'objective necessity': 'Whatever is to happen at any given time, does in fact happen. ... Thus, let each one strive in his own place to be what he can be in the course of things; for this is what he has to be and anything else is impossible for him.'[43] Herder struck a similar fatalistic note when he spoke of *Zeitgeist* (a concept which he is alleged to have been the first to use in its German form)[44] in almost mystical language. He identified it with the 'genius of *Humanität*', with a 'mighty genius', or even, more ominously, 'with a powerful demon'.[45] But he shrank from accepting the inference that would have to be drawn from such a conception of historical change. His rhetorical question 'should the spirit of the times rule or serve',[46] reveals his uneasiness in the matter. By replying that the *Zeitgeist* should do both: that it should rule and serve at the same time,[47] Herder cannot be said to face at all squarely the issue raised in his question. His alternative interpretation of *Zeitgeist* as the 'sum of the thoughts, attitudes, strivings, drives, and living forces, expressing themselves with given causes and effects in a definite course of events',[48] whilst it suggests that Herder was anxious to reduce the concept to more manageable proportions, only helps to confuse the issue further. It simply remains unresolved whether Herder's notion of *Zeitgeist* was merely a metaphysical way of expressing the essentially empirical idea of the 'temper' of a society at a given time, or whether it was indeed a wholly metaphysical or transcendental concept.

The matter is not made any clearer by Herder's treatment of the rôle of the individual in history. At times Herder seems to believe that individuals can never hope to achieve success if their ideas cut across the prevailing bias of a community.[49] Thus Luther's Reformation, for example, was successful, not because of what Luther said or did, but because the time was ripe for it.[50] Joseph II (of Austria), on the other hand, failed because the *Zeitgeist* was against him.[51] At other times, however, Herder puts his trust in 'the few' to guide the spirit of the times.[52] Once again, so it seems, Herder is faced with a dilemma. Whilst he is anxious to recognize individual merit and accord praise to

[43] XIV, 149, 248.   [44] Suphan makes this claim (see XVIII, 609).
[45] XVII, 77–9.   [46] XVII, 78.   [47] XVII, 78.
[48] XVII, 80; see also XVII, 95.   [49] XIV, 408.   [50] V, 532.
[51] XVII, 56.   [52] XVII, 79.

individual achievements, he is at the same time reluctant to concede that history is made by individuals.[53] In view of these discrepancies, it is difficult to resist the conclusion that on the basic issue in this matter, the efficacy of 'time' (and hence of history with a capital 'h') as a creative force *sui generis*, Herder was both confused and undecided.

Herder's ambiguous treatment of the concepts of 'chance' and 'fate' gives rise to difficulties similar to those which result from his vacillating attitude towards the concept of *Zeitgeist*. At times 'chance' is presented as a real motive power of historical sequences,[54] whilst on other occasions the mere possibility of chance is categorically denied.[55] It could, of course, be argued that by 'chance' in the former case Herder simply means that which is not deliberately willed by man, without denying that it is causally determined. But such an argument is hardly convincing in view of Herder's attempt at identifying chance with fate.[56]

In spite of these difficulties, which constitute the main source of controversy regarding Herder's theories of historical causation and historical continuity, it would not be wrong to say that by and large chance and the purely accidental factors in history were only of marginal interest to Herder. The historical determinants to which he chiefly had recourse were those which he held to be more generally applicable at different times and places. Whilst he stressed the uniqueness of each historical event, he also believed that there were certain basic factors common to diverse historical situations, which helped to provide clues to historically significant connexions.

[53] There are, no doubt, temperamental reasons for Herder's inability to view history as the work of individuals. Like Voltaire, Herder had a distaste for 'heroes' and for 'glory'. But to a sizable extent Herder's dislike of 'dramatic' history in which individuals—great men—are the prime movers of historical change must be attributed to his determination to advance a historical method of causal determinism comparable to the empirical method of the natural sciences. More often than not, however, his 'scientific' aspirations clashed with his 'humanistic' impulses. The latter revolted against regarding historical individuals as mere products of their times. Hence he could not resist describing Luther, for example, as the greatest teacher of the German nation (XVII, 87), or Joseph II as a ruler who had a profounder vision of the needs of his country than any other ruler at any other time (XVII, 57).

[54] See, for example, II, 64–5; V, 531; and XIV, 69.

[55] See, for example, XVI, 488.

[56] Thus, for example, in *Auch eine Philosophie*, chance, fate, and providence appear to be used interchangeably (V, 531). Herder's treatment of 'fate', however, is again far from consistent. There are times when Herder draws a clear distinction between fate and providence: 'Providence . . . (which) has placed human fate in human hands' (XIV, 213); on this view, man determines his own fate. What appears to him as fate is in reality the natural result of his own actions (XVIII, 405, 410). At other times, however, fate is treated as a hostile power—history is then viewed as the story of man's struggle with fate (XXIV, 326)—or as objective necessity (XIV, 85–6).

By the same token, whilst Herder insisted upon the essential unity of the realm of physical nature and the realm of human endeavour, he also recognized the special position of history as a study in which man was at once the observer and the object of observation. Thus, whereas in the natural sciences causal hypotheses could be based on the observation of external relationships only, in history there was the possibility of gaining an understanding of what Herder regarded as real and causal *power*, the *internal* relations between events. The measure of consistency that was discoverable in the mode of their purposive direction indicated, in his view, the relational unity, and hence the *continuity*, of historical processes.

Acting on his own principle of inter-relation, according to which nothing could be understood unless it was studied within the context of its relations, Herder became involved at times in perplexities which, as the preceding pages reveal, he found himself unable to resolve. In his determination to advance a causal system in which a multiplicity of the most diverse factors was held to be mutually inter-related, he did not always observe the lines that separate politics from biology, metaphysics from empirical fact, ethics from psychology, and history from science. Putting it crudely, Herder's desire for fusion led at times to confusion. Similarly, the shifting emphasis on what he considered to be the key determinants of historical change, make it difficult to decide whether Herder's approach to history was merely deterministic or outright fatalistic. Did Herder, in other words, merely believe historical events to be causally connected or did he also hold them to be inevitable, and thus beyond the control of human volition? It must be admitted that the second possibility cannot be lightly dismissed. When the area of free choice is as circumscribed as it appears to be at times in Herder's system of historical causation, it is indeed hard to see how it can function at all. If man can only be what he *must* be according to the circumstances of time and place, then surely it seems that his freedom to act merely consists in conforming to what objective necessity demands.

At the same time, Herder's distinction between causal antecedents and causal motive forces, and the causal efficacy which he attributed to the latter, as also his emphasis on man's capacity for acknowledging purposes and for being actuated by self-chosen ends by virtue of the possession of a reflective consciousness, hardly suggest that he was anxious to 'suppress the free play of man's intelligent will', as one writer has remarked.[57] It would, I feel, be nearer to the truth to say

[57] J. B. Bury, *The Idea of Progress*, London, 1920, p. 241.

that like others possessed of a reforming zeal, Herder believed that by investing what he deemed desirable with the attribute of 'objective necessity', he would succeed in making it psychologically more compelling. If men could be convinced that their goals and ideals were not utopian dreams, but the product of a subjective realization of what was objectively necessary, there was no limit to what they could achieve.[58]

Had Herder not thought that men at least acted *as if* they were free, that when they cherished purposes they did so out of a consciousness of having chosen them, he would scarcely have viewed history as the expression of man's continual striving for the attainment of that *Humanität* of which he was capable.

[58] Presumably this is what Meinecke's concept of 'inner necessity' could be taken to mean in this context. (Friedrich Meinecke, *Die Entstehung des Historismus*, Munich and Berlin, 1936, vol. II, p. 403.)

VII

PROGRESS AND PERFECTION

HERDER'S belief that one could elicit certain basic determinants in the history of mankind, comparable to those governing events in nature, was symptomatic of an age which, in spite of its moralistic and metaphysical tendencies, displayed a profound faith in the empirical method of the natural sciences. Allied with this belief, if not inherent in it, was the conviction that a proper understanding of past human behaviour would render possible a wider measure of control over social phenomena in a manner similar to the physical scientist's ability to control nature. If Newton, by discovering the operative laws of nature, could extend man's power over physical nature, why, men like Herder asked, should others not do the same for morals and politics?[1] This was the question and the challenge of the century.

One attempt to answer this question, Herder thought, was to subject the known facts of human history to careful examination. Such a study, he felt, would provide the empirical data from which psychology could draw valid inferences not only about human events in the past but also about human nature generally. Psychology would reveal to man the laws operative in human nature. Once these became known, morals and politics should become much less intractable than they were for so long.[2] Psychology, therefore, Herder remarked as early as 1766, must be treated as the pivotal science among the social sciences.[3] Indeed, in the *Journal* Herder went so far as to declare the true purpose of history to lie in the study of the human mind.[4]

The view that factual discoveries about human nature would be of vital assistance to the solution of social and political problems was widely shared.[5] It rested, however, on a number of suppressed premises which cannot be taken for granted.

[1] VII, 270; see also II, 257; IV, 445; V, 503; and XXXII, 37–8, 52, 61.
[2] II, 257; IV, 445; and XXXII, 37–8.   [3] XXXII, 58; see also IV, 445.
[4] IV, 364.
[5] The most representative contemporary writers who advanced this view in England were Hartley and Priestley. (See the former's *Observations on Man, His Frame, His Duty and His Expectations*, 2 vols., London, 1749; fourth edition, 1801, vol. I, p. 512—and the latter's *An Essay on the First Principles of Government*, London, 1771, second edition, p. 4.)

Even if it were plausible to assume that what had occurred (especially since the seventeenth century) in the physical sciences could be emulated in the social sciences, it does, nevertheless, not follow that the knowledge gained would inform man how to shape his own moral and political life or how to control that of his fellow-man. The assumption that it would, rested on two further premises. One was that there was an intimate connexion between knowing about human propensities and purposes and knowing about what one ought to do. The fallacy involved was that of making the connexion one of logical deducibility: moral knowledge was to be *deduced* from a factual understanding of human nature. The other premise implied that the acquisition of knowledge about human nature would in itself give power over human nature too. This presupposed, in turn, a belief in the constancy of human nature and in its infinite malleability.

Although Herder questioned the belief in the constancy of human nature, he fully shared the reformers' faith in the malleability of human behaviour. He also accepted the Baconian notion that 'knowledge' meant 'power', and that, therefore, the direction and moulding of human progress lay in the extension of man's knowledge about human nature.

1. THE IDEA OF PROGRESS

To take the idea of progress first. The chief impetus behind Herder's preoccupation with this idea stemmed from two distinct sources. One was his theory of development, which begged the question whether change was in any sense tantamount to a forward movement and, if so, in what sense. The second reason was essentially negative, but, in point of fact, the more compelling: Herder was determined to dispel the complacency of the age. *Auch eine Philosophie* was first and foremost an indictment of that idea of progress which viewed all the centuries preceding the present age as a period of darkness. What infuriated Herder most was that *raisonnement* which regarded this 'darkness' as the necessary prelude to the present 'Age of Light'. Had there been no contrast, so the argument ran, man might never have realized the meaning of progress; he might thus have failed to recognize the wonderful portents of his own times. Fortunately it all just happened as it should; and now the whole earth was radiant with light—Voltaire's light, of course—Herder exclaimed with irony and added: 'The savages everywhere will adopt our civilization and, God willing, will become just like ourselves: good, strong, happy men!'[6]

Above all Herder questioned the belief in an inevitable linear progress in human affairs.[7] History, he felt, did not provide evidence for so optimistic a view. At best, human progress could be compared to human walk, since it appeared to consist in a continuous falling from the left to the right.[8] One simply could not rush things. Joseph II, in his attempts at political reform, tried to do too much all at once and hence was doomed to fail.[9] For progress, if it was to have enduring effects, had to be a concomitant of social *growth*; it had to emerge, that is, out of a given social tradition. Without tradition, progress was like a plant without roots.[10]

But whilst Herder insisted that enduring progress was necessarily an 'evolutionary' process rooted in a people's historical traditions, he also stressed that a living tradition was inconceivable without the progressive emergence of new goals. If progress without tradition was like a plant without roots, tradition without progress was like a plant without water.[11] Indeed, Herder went so far as to postulate a kind of dialectic in the relationship between tradition and progress, identifying each progressive movement in history with the attainment of a reconciliation between 'the old' and 'the new' at increasingly higher levels.

. . . It is the same with cultural progress among social groupings and whole nations. . . . The generations renew themselves in a continuous flux and in spite of the linear and prescriptive tendencies of tradition each son continues to write in his own particular way. Thus Aristotle differed most assiduously from Plato and Epicurus from Zeno, until finally the calmer succeeding generations came to see and use both extremes more dispassionately.[12]

This synthesis, though it superseded the two original opposites, also in a sense absorbed and enriched them: 'The opposites assist and promote one another; only by their reconciliation there emerges a (new) world.'[13]

In this dialectical process of combining opposites and of reconciling 'the old' with 'the new', education, we have found, is held to play a vital rôle. For it is through education—in the widest sense—that the individual is said to become aware of his relation to the past no less

----

[6] V, 546.   [7] IX, 540.   [8] XIV, 234.   [9] XVII, 51.
[10] XIII, 347.

[11] Tradition without progress, Herder pointed out, can be a 'real opium' of the spirit and spell the doom of States no less than of individuals (XIV, 89).

[12] XIV, 234.   [13] XVI, 571 and XXIII, 9.

than of his relation to the present and future. He learns what he may receive from, or add to, his social heritage, and it is thus that he acquires the capacity for conscious and creative development (*Bildung*).[14] It is thus, too, that education, by combining the function of assimilation with that of revaluation and renovation, acts at once as the guardian of, and the conspirator against, tradition.

By virtue of the conscious element which attends this creative dialectical process, Herder distinguishes the causal determinism governing human progress from that governing events in the rest of nature, *Bildung* from mere development. Without this capacity for *conscious* development man would be a mere tool in the hands of a fathomless Providence.[15] At the same time, Herder warns, man must not delude himself into thinking that social progress is solely determined by the conscious actions of individuals, there being so many interacting 'outer' and 'inner' circumstances—including chance—which help to fashion it.[16] Nor must he (man) blithely assume that progress is tantamount to improvement, that with every passing stage the world is progressing towards increasingly higher levels of material or moral perfection. Each period bears within itself its own standard of perfection and amelioration, and the philosopher of history must therefore resist the temptation to treat earlier periods as subservient or inferior to later periods.[17] Instead he must accept that there are a thousand different purposes for man to aim at under different circumstances of time and place, and content himself to evaluate these in terms of the historical and psychological forces at work rather than in the light of super-historical criteria. To assess human progress, then, Herder concludes, is to trace the effect of changing influences and conditions upon the formation and development of human propensities and to establish whether these reveal a degree of continuity in their purposive direction.[18]

The assumption underlying this conclusion is that social and political values are derivable from human propensities. Since psychology is the proper discipline for the study of human propensities, educators and politicians (Herder's political leaders—the 'aristo-democrats' are intended to be both) should, by invoking the aid of psychology,

---

[14] V, 539; see also XXIII, 517.   [15] V, 580, 586.   [16] V, 589–93.
[17] V, 509, 559.
[18] V, 589 and XIV, 202. It cannot be gainsaid that Herder himself frequently failed to adhere to his maxims of historical relativism. But it is of interest to note that in his treatment of the impact of European 'progress' on the development of 'backward' peoples Herder consistently maintained his relativist approach to progress. (See, for example, VIII, 210, 303; XIII, 333, 455; XVII, 237; XVIII, 290; and XXIII, 505.)

acquire greater knowledge about human propensities and thus find themselves in a position to influence and guide a nation's social and political progress.

2. HUMAN VARIABILITY AND PERFECTIBILITY

In linking ethics and politics with empirical psychology, Herder was one of many in his century. But he was one of the first amongst eighteenth-century thinkers to question the belief in the immutability of human nature. Even 'relativist' writers such as Helvetius and Montesquieu never doubted that 'man in general has always been what he is', as Voltaire had remarked.[19] When Hume wrote that 'mankind are so much the same, in all times and places', and that, therefore, the chief task of the historian was 'only to discover the constant and universal principles of human nature', he merely expressed what practically everyone else took for granted.[20]

Herder challenged the validity of this view. Time and again throughout his writings he insisted on the variety and changeability of human nature. As early as 1769 he formulated what remained the basic principle of his relativist psychology: 'Human nature under the diverse climates is never wholly the same.'[21] Later, in the Essay *Auch eine Philosophie*, he elaborated further on this principle: 'Human nature . . . is not the vessel of an absolute, unchanging and independent "happiness", as defined by the metaphysician; everywhere it attracts that measure of happiness of which it is capable; it is a pliant clay which assumes a different shape under different needs and circumstances.'[22]

The belief in the *malleability* of human nature, as distinct from the *variability* of human nature, was not, however, an original idea. That this belief was so widely held was in part a testimony to the influence of Locke's writings.[23] But it was also an expression of the widespread desire for social and political change and the outcome of a boundless faith in education as *the* instrument of socio-political amelioration. In spite of his scepticism and misgivings regarding the prevalent belief in

---

[19] Voltaire, *Oeuvres*, ed. Lequieu, Paris, 1820, vol. XI, p. 19.

[20] Quoted by Carl L. Becker, *The Heavenly City of the Eighteenth Century Philosophers*, Yale, 1932, p. 95; cf. also Priestley, quoting Bolingbroke, in his *Lectures on History*, London, 1826, pp. 31–2.

[21] IV, 38.   [22] V, 509.

[23] Helvetius remarked: 'You can count on your fingers the people who have not read, thumbed, and admired him.' (Quoted by Hazard, *European Thought in the Eighteenth Century*, op. cit., p. 41.)

linear progress, Herder wholly shared his contemporaries' faith in the perfectibility of human nature through education, when he wrote: 'In all his activities man is a flexible quantity. This fact is basic to the very idea of education.'[24]

At the same time Herder was aware that the plasticity of human nature also provided scope for abuse. Men could be influenced for evil purposes, they could be induced to act against their own interests, even against their own feelings. Education can be for good or for ill, for happiness or for unhappiness, for the individual or for mankind.[25] The notion of 'perfection', too, acquired in Herder's use a more restrained meaning. Man could perfect only propensities that were inherent in his nature and even this he could do only as the conditions of time and place permitted.[26]

Herder's theory of perfectibility receives its most coherent treatment in the *Briefe* (nos. 24–6) of the Second Collection of the *Briefe zu Beförderung der Humanität* (1793). The subject is treated in the form of a discussion between imaginary correspondents. One of the feigned correspondents is made to ask whether the whole idea of a continuously progressing perfection of mankind is not a mere dream. What, he asks, is its path and purpose? 'And the aim of perfection? Is the line leading to it an asymptote, an ellipse, a cycloid, or some other curve?'[27] To which Herder replies that 'perfection' must be conceived in a relative sense only. It does not aim at the development of 'superman' or at producing 'extra-human' beings (*Ueber- oder Außermensch*).[28] If that were the case, Herder remarks, there would be no point in writing even a single line on the subject. Perfection simply means the process by which a thing becomes what it can and should.[29] To aim at perfection, individually and in co-operation with others, means utilizing one's natural potentialities. The extent to which one succeeds in this process of self-realization will determine the identity and continuity of one's 'self' as a single personality. One *can* achieve self-development because one is by nature capable of it (*bildbar*).[30] The initial stimulus, however, Herder curiously insists, must come from 'outside'.[31] Although man is born with purposive and self-directive energies, he must learn from others how to apply them. Perfection, therefore, is both an individual and a social process, and any social and political framework which neglects the development of its members or directs it into the wrong channels is deemed by Herder to have lost its *raison d'être*.[32]

---

[24] XVI, 44.   [25] XVI, 44.   [26] XVII, 115; see also V, 505.   [27] XVII, 113.
[28] XVII, 115.   [29] XVII, 115.   [30] XIII, 147.   [31] XXI, 152.
[32] XIV, 209; see also VI, 104; XVII, 116; XXIV, 109 and ch. IV, pp. 78–80 above.

To the question whether technological advances also entail human perfection and social progress, Herder gives a conditional reply. By itself, technology merely consists in augmenting man's tools and instruments; the nature of their use depends wholly on the goals and purposes that pervade a society at any given time.[33]

Perfection, then, like progress, is conceived by Herder as purposive development towards goals which at any given time appear as socially desirable objectives capable of realization. Whereas absolute perfection is regarded as an article of religious faith only, as a 'Christian hypothesis' to which man can only hope to approximate, relative perfection is put forward as a necessary constituent to social and political progress.[34] If man, within his particular circumstances of time and place, ceases to aim at, and to work for, tangible objectives to his further development, he cannot but degenerate. The alternative to striving for perfection is drifting into corruption.[35] 'Not to get worse, we must continuously strive to get better.'[36] At the same time, Herder insists, man is not expected to strive for super-human ends or to sacrifice himself or his generation for the benefit of posterity.[37] On this point Herder is most anxious to refute Kant, who in his brief treatise *Idee zu einer allgemeinen Geschichte in weltbürgerlicher Absicht* argued that the individual existed for the good of the species. Herder, by contrast, urges that striving for perfection must be envisaged as a process where the *telos* is not beyond a generation's social development but rather *within* it. Each generation is to interpret its operative goals in the light of what he calls the 'inner and outer circumstances' prevailing at any given time.[38] This means that each generation has to face anew the challenge of its self-development and amelioration, that perfection cannot be achieved once and for all but has to be struggled for time and again within its own historical context.[39]

3. CONFLICT AND HUMAN STRIVING

The idea that human and social development must not be thought of as a smooth advance towards absolute and unchanging goals, but rather as a *struggle* towards ever-emerging ends, is an integral element in Herder's theory of progress and human perfectibility.

Herder traced the seeds of this 'struggle' to the contrariness and

[33] XVII, 113.　　　　[34] XVII, 122 and XVIII, 328; see also XIII, 345 and XV, 326.
[35] XVIII, 61.　　　[36] XVIII, 370.　　　　[37] XVIII, 283; see also XVII, 120-1.
[38] XVII, 138 and XXVI, 365.　　　[39] XIII, 196.

duplicity of human nature. He used the term 'double creature' (*Doppel-geschöpf*) to describe what he held to be an inherent polarity within the human mind. Man embodied, as it were, two opposite 'worlds'.[40] This contrariness within his own nature gave rise to an inner struggle on the one hand, yet on the other it also urged him to discern more clearly the nature of the conflicting forces in order to reduce, if not to eliminate, their incompatibilities. Owing to the intimate proximity of these opposing elements, however, man had considerable difficulty in disentangling them.[41] This difficulty in turn led to an acute feeling of tension and restlessness and it was to this state of restlessness that Herder attributed the most active driving force, the 'inner necessity' of man's striving for progress and perfection.[42]

Herder, however, also suggests that, by the very nature of things, there is inherent in all struggles and conflicts a tendency pressing for their reconciliation: 'These (conflicting forces) oppose one another temporarily; eventually they contain each other according to the infallible laws of nature and bring about a kind of equilibrium and harmony of movement.'[43] Man's task, it would appear, is to assist nature by devising means whereby the destructive propensities in society can be effectively controlled and modified so as to serve the constructive propensities.[44] Simply to crush the former is categorically ruled out by Herder as both futile and dangerous; futile, because it cannot hope to succeed in the long run, and dangerous, because it provokes and encourages the recourse to blind force and unreason which is only likely to enlarge the area of conflict in the short run and thus retard rather than assist an ultimate solution.[45] Tensions, antagonisms and conflicts must be accepted, therefore, Herder argues, as vital and necessary forces in human and social development. It is their presence, and the full recognition of their presence rather than their denial which, to him, affords the possibility for man's conscious shaping of his life in society. Just as there is no evil in nature, so also is there in the social realm no failing that cannot be turned into a blessing.

Not only is there an antidote for every poison, but there is also a persistent tendency inherent in all vital forces with the effect of transforming the most harmful poison into the most wholesome remedy. . . . No evil that befalls

---

[40] XIII, 195–6; see also V, 558 and IX, 536.   [41] XVII, 27.
[42] V, 98; see also VIII, 230; XIV, 205; XV, 263; XVI, 567; XVII, 27 and XVIII, 298.
[43] XIV, 227.   [44] XVII, 119.
[45] XVII, 119. There are distinctly Freudian overtones in these statements that will not escape the modern reader.

man, can and shall be any other than salutary; for even vices, faults, and weaknesses of man are, as natural occurrences, subject to nature's ordinances and are or can be calculable.[46]

Herder's optimistic approach to the problem of conflict is in the purest Leibnizian tradition. The view that the destructive forces must ultimately serve the constructive and preserving forces breathes the cosmic optimism of his age. Conflict is not only inevitable; it is also necessary. Indeed, it is the essential presupposition of social progress and human perfection. Like other apparent ills and calamities it is a force making for good. Antagonism performs a decidedly beneficial function in human and social development in that it helps towards the release of constructive energies. Yet this optimistic approach is in marked contrast to Herder's earlier writings where he voiced strong disapproval of the Leibnizian notion of pre-established harmony.[47] Even as late as 1778, in his treatise *Vom Erkennen und Empfinden*, Herder confined himself to merely posing the problem: 'Contradictions in man's heart and mind: what nourishes and strengthens these divergences? Is it the work of nature or the work of artifice and corruption?'[48] By the time he came to write the *Ideen*, however, his reforming zeal had got the better of him. He could no longer view things with philosophic detachment. He wished to point the way. If there was conflict and strife in man and society, there must also be a method of so modifying human propensities as to bring them into harmony with desirable ends. By stipulating that there could be no evil in nature, by insisting that what appeared pernicious did so only on first sight, Herder sought to deepen man's faith in his own regeneration and in that of the society in which he lived.

The *tour de force* in Herder's outlook, if such it can be called, was not, however, necessarily a case of optimism taking the place of relativism as has been suggested.[49] For Herder, in spite of the 'optimism' of his later years, still insisted in both the *Ideen* and the *Briefe* on a strictly relativist interpretation of progress and human perfectibility. It would, I think, be more correct to say, therefore, that in his treatment of conflict Herder was not so much a relativist turned optimist, but rather a campaigning reformer anxious to transform the somewhat complacent optimism of his age into the nostrum of a fighting creed. And the first article of faith in this nostrum was to establish that man can actively help to shape the course of human

---

[46] XVII, 27, 122.
[47] XXXII, 225; see also Herder's letter to Hahn, cited in Haym, op. cit., vol. I, p. 665.
[48] VIII, 268.   [49] Rudolf Stadelmann, op. cit., p. 65.

events by gaining an insight into the working of human propensities. The second article—though implied by the first—was to regard such knowledge as *practical* knowledge, i.e. as something directly applicable to the direction and control of human and social development. The will and determination to gain such knowledge, coupled with the belief in its practical use, seemed to Herder—as to many reformers since— firmly grounded in the results achieved by the natural sciences. Herder, like many of his younger contemporaries, increasingly felt that the methods of empirical observation when applied to the study of society would progressively yield comparable results, in the light of which tangible and realizable social goals would emerge. Assuming, as he did, that a knowledge of human and social goals and values was directly deducible from the factual discovery of human propensities, Herder hoped that these specific ends would become ever more clearly discernible with the aid of a systematic application of psychology to the study of human development.

Indeed, so great was his confidence in the progressive scope of psychology and in the possibility of plotting future action as a result of empirical investigations of past human behaviour that he tended to lose sight of the fallacy inherent in such a belief and of its incompatibility with his own theory of teleological causation. It was this failure to realize that neither psychology nor any other science could tell man what he ought to do which makes the assumptions underlying Herder's ostensibly empirical reasoning so indistinguishable from acts of faith.

But to question thus the empirical and, indeed, logical foundations of Herder's theory of progress and human perfectibility is not to deny its historical significance or its importance as a political doctrine. In identifying the idea of progress and perfectibility with an *operative* ideal related to a specific social and historical setting, as distinct from an ideal aiming at a distant goal, Herder's philosophy of social development parts ways with the utopian progressivism of his age and ushers in a period of a more restrained, yet—paradoxically perhaps—more militant form of political optimism. Likewise, the curious but ingenious marriage of the idea of moral striving with the idea of natural development could not but add to its persuasive political appeal.

That nature and its laws were identifiable with what was orderly, moral, and rational, was an undisputed principle of long standing. It took some time before biology and psychology began to question this comforting principle. None the less, the natural 'growth' element in Herder's theory of progress lent point to the view that advance in the desired direction could be effected without sudden and violent breaks in a society's historical development, and, in so doing, urged reformers to devote their efforts to thoroughly preparing the soil out of which a regenerated society was to grow. It was in the light of such an 'evolutionary' theory of progress that Herder envisaged his proposed transformation from a 'mechanical' to an 'organic' form of social organization. In view of his conviction that there was a social wisdom which could be learned and of the 'organic' properties which he attributed to this process of learning, education was, as we have seen, accorded a crucial importance in his evolutionary theory. But whilst education in the Platonic sense was confined to a select few, it was held to be the birthright of all members of a State in Herder's theory, without which neither the individual citizen nor the community as a whole was thought to be capable of the fullest development. Herein lies Herder's contribution to that conception of social progress in which political change is viewed in essentially democratic and evolutionary terms.

At the same time, however, Herder can be said to have contributed to another and quite different line of political thinking. Admittedly, it could be argued that when Herder spoke of struggle as an integral constituent of social progress he did so as a moralist and not as a writer on politics. But even if this is granted, Herder's ideas on conflict and strife, coinciding as they did with the French Revolution, could not but drastically affect the temper of political theorizing. For they not only provided an ideological justification for revolutionary changes, but also intimated that such changes were an essential ingredient of political development.

Herder's doctrine of progress gave rise, then, to two conflicting interpretations of political change and development. Henceforth each interpretation played its part in the expression and propagation of Herder's social philosophy and of his nationalist creed.

VIII

SIGNIFICANCE: SUMMARY AND ASSESSMENT

HERDER did not formulate a systematic political theory. What we have attempted in the preceding pages was a systematization and analysis of ideas which were rarely worked out in detail. These ideas taken as a whole may not constitute a theory of government comparable to any of the 'classical' juristic or philosophical interpretations of the State. They are, nevertheless, we believe, of interest mainly for two reasons. They represent an attempt to explore the basis of, and justification for, statehood outside the traditional field of approach; and, secondly, they reveal a method of political and historical thinking that was novel in the eighteenth-century world of ideas.

The chief impetus behind Herder's pioneering work in these two directions was a feeling of discontent. Herder was consumed by an intense sense of dissatisfaction with the social and political conditions of his time. Personal frustration in not finding a political outlet for his creative aspirations may well have been a contributory factor. Outside the church and the universities there was virtually no field of public activity in which men of humble origins like Herder could hope to make any headway. There were no political parties, no effective parliamentary life, no political clubs or societies in eighteenth-century Germany. 'Germany' itself was a geographical area, not a political unit. With some notable exceptions, Germany was an agglomerate of absolutist or semi-feudal States. To describe it, as Herder had done, as a *terra obedientiae* was no undue exaggeration; for submissiveness was undoubtedly its most pervading socio-political characteristic.

Herder found himself unable to accept the *status quo* in silence. He assailed it with a virulence and moral fervour, the intensity of which was not always matched by political insight and sheer political sense. Irresponsible and excessively emotional though his tirades at times were, they do evidence a degree of radical sentiment which was not common in the political literature of contemporary Germany.

The chief targets of his wrath were the hereditary system of political rule, the nobility, the institution of serfdom, despotism and political censorship, and all forms of arbitrariness in the ordering of political life. In international affairs attempts at political and economic domination by one nation over another seemed to him the prime source of war. His anger was particularly aroused by those who, in claiming cultural superiority for European civilization, felt themselves justified in subjugating and exploiting non-European peoples. Herder saw in slavery and colonialism the greatest blots in the history of mankind.

But Herder did not denounce war and contemporary methods of political rule on merely humanitarian grounds or simply because he found them intrinsically bad and at variance with the dictates of 'reason' and 'nature'. What he abhorred most was the consequences which he attributed to their existence. Thus he inveighed against war because he saw in it the circumstance that had given rise to serfdom and to the emergence of hereditary government. Similarly, he condemned political censorship because he believed it to lead to dullness, hypocrisy, fear and resentment which could not but harm the political health of a nation. He detested despotism because he held it to breed uniformity, arbitrariness and lawless force, and was thus certain to undermine the morale of the citizens.

Herder's opposition to colonial oppression and to the slave trade, likewise, was not grounded entirely in the prevailing idolization of the Noble Savage. When he denounced slavery and colonialism, he did so chiefly because in them he saw a threat to the existence and survival of national entities. He was convinced that their subjugation could not go on indefinitely. One day the awakening of their national consciousness was sure to occur. Herder was fearful that when this happened it would entail a savage desire for vengeance on the part of the oppressed against their rulers.

But Herder's discontent with things as they were did not find expression only in emotional indignation and destructive criticism. It also prompted him to advance positive principles. Consumed as he was by hatred for the *status quo*, he was also imbued with a political creed aiming at its amelioration and eventual transformation.

Herder's political creed drew for its main sustenance upon the Judeo-Christian tradition and on the secular humanism and humanitarianism of the Renaissance and the Enlightenment.

The Biblical account of early Hebrew society in particular, we have found, played an important rôle in Herder's political thinking. In the Hebrew people Herder saw the oldest example of a *Volk* with a developed national consciousness and of an 'organic' community in which socio-political organization grew naturally out of the socio-economic functions of its members. Here was, he held, a substantially undifferentiated society that was at once a community of interests and a community based on a common language and on common beliefs and traditions; a kind of extended family, held together not by the power of coercion but by the co-operation (*Zusammenwirken*) of its members; a homogeneous entity without a single focus of power; a many-centred as distinct from a monolithic organization, where there was no division into rulers and subjects, and where the 'law', essentially in the sense of customary rules, reigned supreme.

In one sense, it is true, Herder repudiated the political traditions on which he had fed. Like Hume he could not accept the postulate of a 'social contract' as a satisfactory basis of, or justification for, political obligation; he held it to be historically unsound and logically untenable. He rejected on similar grounds the concept of Natural Law as he knew it, which was the then widely current interpretation of Pufendorf; and, like Justus Möser and Edmund Burke, he had little use for the belief in absolute individual rights and for 'general principles'.

Yet although Herder formally rejected these traditional notions, he nevertheless upheld their moral implications. For consent rather than force, law and reason rather than arbitrariness and personal whim, and the Aristotelian premise that the State existed for the good of its individual members and not *vice versa*, were principles which Herder never doubted. Without these he could not envisage the maintenance of a healthy political life.

These principles, however, Herder held, were only the desirable *result* of socio-political processes; they did not in themselves constitute or account for what, he felt, was of the essence in social and political organization, if it was to be conceived in terms of organic growth: national character. For Herder a State without national character was a political machine without life, a phantom without organic existence. The natural and organic basis of statehood, in his view, was *Volk*, a people with its own peculiar national character which embodied for him the one and only effective cohesive force (*Kraft*) in socio-political association. What mattered, therefore, Herder argued, was to elicit and analyse those elements and processes in social and political life which furthered the development of this cohesive *Kraft*.

Language was singled out by Herder as the most determinative characteristic of a *Volk*. Statehood, to be 'natural', had to coincide with nationhood, that is, with an ethnic community. This was a new conception of the basis and nature of nationhood and statehood. A nation was no longer simply a group of people owing political allegiance to a common sovereign; a State was not merely a legal and welfare institution, but a community bound by spiritual ties and cultural traditions, a *Kulturstaat* as well as a *Rechtsstaat*.

A *Volk*, on this theory, was a natural division of the human race, a community *sui generis*, endowed with its own language by means of which it became aware not only of its own existence but also of that which differentiated it from the rest of humanity. A *Volk*'s language, for Herder, was not something detachable, for he saw in it the embodiment of a *Volk*'s inner being, its inner *Kraft*, without which it ceased to exist. This inner and essentially spiritual quality constituted, in his view, the most vital, and hence 'organic' basis of nationhood and statehood. States which comprised a mixture of ethnic communities lacked this inner spiritual bond and were, therefore, held to be devoid of life. As mere 'mechanical contrivances' they were politically doomed from the outset.

The themes in terms of which Herder approached the question of language also formed the framework of his social and political philosophy, the central idea of which was his theory of 'organic' nationalism. These themes, we found, were the concept of self-consciousness, the doctrine of diversity, and the principle of interaction. Herder considered language to be at once the expression of the individuality of each human being and the psychological matrix in which man's consciousness of his distinctive social heritage was aroused and deepened. In a world in which diversity was said to constitute the fundamental characteristic of the universal order, language was held to be the criterion by means of which a group's identity as a separate social unit could be established and, at the same time, the source from which its claim to political recognition derived its legitimate sanction. Even when Herder recognized that factors other than language partook in fashioning the national character and the political consciousness of a *Volk*, he nevertheless regarded the linguistic element as the most decisive determinant.

This stress on language as the 'natural' basis of socio-political association had immense political consequences. It not only provided the ideological foundation of subsequent nationalist agitation, but it also led to the prodigious philological research which accompanied it. Henceforth professors of language and literature were to play an important part in shaping the political fortunes of emerging 'national' entities. What is more, the intimate link between language and politics helped to give rise to the belief that many of the social and political ills that afflicted empires comprising diverse language communities could be successfully cured once each of these communities acquired their own political independence.

It took some time before it was realized that the identification of a territorial State with an ethnic community or *Volk* was capable of posing as many problems as it was aiming to solve. A spontaneous feeling and consciousness of being an integral part of a social 'whole' such as the State may well be inconceivable without the existence of some kind of 'spiritual' bond. But this recognition does not in itself establish language as the sole and indispensable condition for its existence. Likewise, the world may 'naturally' be one of diversity—a world of many nationalities—and yet it does not follow that the pre-eminent mark of distinction is or ought to be the possession of a separate language.

Herder, in advancing his theory of 'linguistic' nationalism, strove to draw attention to the *inward* forces of socio-political cohesion. In so doing he hoped to point the way to the creation of a political order that could dispense with the use of force and with the institution of governmental 'machinery'. For he held that the only mode of 'government' that was compatible with the dignity of the human spirit was self-government or 'self-determination'. Man was only free when obeying the laws which he found in himself in the absence of any physical coercion from outside. By the same token, nations were only free when they were obeying laws that were inherent in their historical traditions. Herder believed that once the State coincided with an ethnic community or *Volk*, legislation would have no need of coercive sanctions, because the laws would be an expression of a people's social consciousness. Underlying this belief was the view that politics was but an integral part of social education and social culture.

By 'education' Herder principally understood the transmission of those value patterns and habits of thought that sustain the historical continuity of an ethnic community. He conceived this transmission as a 'dialectical' process, involving opposition to, as well as acceptance of, what was handed down from one generation to another. Education, therefore, Herder argued, was at once the guardian of tradition and the herald of progress.

'Culture', like education, was not confined in Herder's use, to literary and artistic pursuits, but applied to a wide range of social activities. It represented the diverse forms and stages of a *Volk*'s historical development or 'becoming'. Culture was held to be capable of attaining different levels of development (or 'maxima') in diverse directions. It was, however, the balance attained between diverse fields of culture rather than the excellence achieved in any one direction, which Herder considered to be the decisive factor in the growth of political stability.

Although Herder applied biological terms like 'genetic' and 'organic' to the process of transmitting social cultures, he did not think of this process in a specifically biological sense. For he was not really concerned with physical characteristics attending heredity but rather with the origin and development of communal attitudes and habits of thought. His chief interest as a philosopher of history lay in tracing the historical 'continuity' of national traditions, by which he understood the measure of consistency that was discoverable in their purposive direction. Similarly, when making use of biological metaphors, Herder did not thereby imply that no distinction was to be drawn between the nature that characterized membership of a social 'whole' or 'organism' and that which characterized the relation of parts of a single human organism. Instead he insisted on co-ordination between units which, although they were inter-dependent, were none the less *individual* and *active* wholes in themsleves. In view of these internal energizing forces Herder looked upon the State as an organism rather than as a combination of aggregate units comparable to a mechanical assembly.

'Government', in the sense of a political authority *sui generis*, Herder confined to the period of transition between the 'mechanical' *status quo*, consisting of dynastic States, and the emergence of 'organic' nation-States. The *form* of government during this transitional period was not clearly specified by him. Herder had, however, unlike many of his contemporaries, little faith in the enlightened rule of princes. Social and political improvement, he felt, would have to come 'from below'. He visualized the emergence of 'popular leaders', so-called 'aristo-democrats', who were to undertake the task of helping the *Volk* to attain a more developed sense of social and national consciousness and political responsibility.

By *Volk* Herder most often meant the whole of an ethnic community. When, however, he spoke of the transition from the 'mechanical' to the 'organic' State, *Volk* was identified with a certain section of the population only. This section Herder regarded as the most valuable part of the nation, partly because it was the most numerous and the most productive, but chiefly because he held it to represent most truly those characteristics which he associated with a *Volk*'s national character. Herder used the term *Bürger* to differentiate this part of the population from the rest, i.e. from the aristocracy, the learned class and the 'rabble' (*Pöbel*). He included in this part those occupations which figure prominently in folksong, such as those of the farmer, the artisan, and the shopkeeper. In these 'working folk' he saw the 'national salt' of the earth. Whilst it is not clear whether Herder envisaged the *Bürger* as a homogeneous group without marked socio-economic distinctions, he does seem to think of them as sharing a common mentality (*Denkart*). The 'rabble' presumably, therefore, refers to a minority of people of a somewhat lower mental outlook rather than to members of a lower economic 'class'. The aristocracy, on the other hand, though it was identified with another minority, was nevertheless held to be the most powerful social element by virtue of its hereditary prestige and its accumulated wealth. The intellectuals, by contrast, were thought to be the most disinterested section of the population since they were held to be free from property interests. As in the case of Plato's guardians, they were expected to be the most clear-sighted and public-minded men and hence eminently suitable for political leadership. Their immediate and principal function was to promote such conditions as were likely to foster a sense of homogeneity among all members of the nation: *Volk* and nation were to become one. Their ultimate function, however—and here Herder parted with Plato—was to make themselves dispensable. To bring this about, the *Volk* itself was to participate actively in the political transformation from 'mechanism' to 'organism'.

'Humanization' was the term Herder applied to this period of transition. He understood by it a gradual process of conscious development (*Bildung*). Though Herder had hailed the French Revolution as the most momentous event since the Reformation, he saw in it a poor substitute for *Bildung*. The purpose of 'humanization' was to replace force by co-operation. Political organization was to be dissociated from an 'apparatus of power'. This presupposed above all that a *Volk*'s national aspirations entailed respect for the national aspirations of another *Volk*. Herder therefore insisted that the *Bildung* of *Volk*-consciousness and of *Humanität* must be regarded as essentially *one* process. *Volk* and *Humanität* were inter-dependent and not incompatible notions. 'Humanization', therefore, meant the promotion of conditions that were conducive to *both* national self-determination *and* international co-operation.

By *Humanität* Herder primarily had in mind the recognition of social inter-dependence within, as also between, States. But he distinguished *Humanität* from 'cosmopolitanism', in which he saw a threat to, and denial of, national character, and hence the negation of his organic conception of politics. *Humanität* did not oppose patriotism, conceived as love for one's own *Volk*; it aimed at enriching patriotism, at enlightening it. *Humanität*, in short, Herder argued, had to become an integral part of patriotism.

Herder had no faith in diplomacy, in alliances, in international treaties and inter-governmental institutions. Even the creation of a world government had little appeal to him. He saw in all these devices 'mechanical contrivances' which, though they might temporarily succeed in effecting a measure of international unity, were nevertheless doomed in the long run. Instead Herder visualized a loose association of autonomous nations, co-operating in fields of mutual interests on a basis of partnership without a common political authority or formal agreements to bind them. His aim was the unity of co-operative processes and interests, not the formal unification of political entities; unity amidst diversity, not uniformity. And the only 'unity' that he found meaningful was that which found expression in an attitude of mind, in a *Gesinnung*. In this he saw the essence of *Humanität*.

The growth of national consciousness and of *Humanität* Herder regarded as the unfolding of a spontaneous *Kraft*, of 'becoming' in the Aristotelian sense. He conceived 'becoming' as both an individual and a social process, for, although he agreed that it was only meaningful to speak of 'becoming' in terms of the development of individual human beings, he also insisted that man can develop his potentialities only as a member of society. And the social *milieu* that seemed to him the most conducive to man's 'becoming' was that of an ethnic community or *Volk*. Herder's emphasis, therefore, on the rights of nations rather than on the rights of individuals was not a denial of the importance of the individual. He was too much a child of his century to have thought of the moral and political *summum bonum* other than in terms of individual happiness. Nevertheless, in making the right to individual happiness and the development of individual potentialities contingent on man's membership of a national community, Herder marked the watershed which divides the 'liberal' thought of the Enlightenment from nineteenth-century liberalism in Europe.

In his attitude to social and political change Herder wavered between scepticism and optimism, and between outright fatalism and a more restricted form of causal determinism. But the prevailing tenor in his views was optimistic and non-fatalistic. Man *was* capable of determining his own destiny within given fields of activity, the limits of which could only be defined with reference to 'genetic', environmental, and historical forces. Human nature was not a constant, and hence social and political behaviour was susceptible to conscious human control and amenable to progressive improvement. Man's purposes were made, not found. Man's cosmos was not a finished article, but a complex of interacting and developing *processes*.

Herder's treatment of 'interaction' was not, however, free from ambiguities. It suffered particularly from a tendency towards circular argument. His indecision on historical causation constituted another weakness. The doctrine of *Zeitgeist* bears this out especially. Nevertheless, Herder succeeded in drawing attention to the psycho-physical nature of the relationship between man and his environment and in pointing out the limits to which environmental factors could be regarded as effective instruments of socio-political change.

Whilst Herder's optimism was not unqualified, he hoped that by combining the idea of natural development with the idea of moral striving he could make what seemed to him 'objectively' desirable subjectively more compelling. But it was this combination between natural 'growth' and social and moral 'struggle' which helped to give rise to two conflicting interpretations of Herder's theory of socio-political progress, namely, one which viewed political change in essentially non-militant and evolutionary terms, and another which regarded 'struggle' as its indispensable pre-requisite.

A belief in absolute perfection was of necessity, Herder agreed, an article of faith only, but the idea of human perfectibility in terms of limited human purposes was, in his view, a useful and even essential element in a philosophy which saw scope for human volition in the shaping of human history. For it was such a philosophy which Herder, in spite of his fatalistic moods, wished to see adopted; a philosophy which was not satisfied with interpreting the world but which also aimed at changing it.

Although we would agree that fatalism is incompatible with a belief in man's ability to effect an amelioration of his social and political life by his own volition and effort, we do not share the view that the same must be said in respect of causal determinism. For there is surely no reason why human volition could not be regarded as a constituent factor among historical determinants. We believe that Herder's theory of historical causation with its emphasis on the distinction between purposive and functional development strongly suggests that Herder was a determinist in this sense. Those who have equated Herder's determinism with the negation of human freedom have either confused his determinism with his occasional lapses into fatalism or they have insufficiently recognized his distinction between function and purpose.

That the vistas of human progress seemed brighter to Herder than would appear justified in the light of a sober analysis of human history could be attributed mainly to three reasons. Herder was one of the first to question the belief in the constancy of human nature. Given greater knowledge of the variety and plasticity of human nature, there was no saying, he felt, what conscious control of human propensities could not attain. For Herder fully shared the current conviction—and that was the second reason for his optimism—that morals and politics would become less intractable once man gained a deeper insight into their psychological origins. That morals and politics were ultimately reducible to psychology was the confident maxim of the century. It was also one of the basic presuppositions of Herder's theory of progress.

The third reason for Herder's optimism was his reformist zeal. Not to aim at human progress and social improvement was tantamount to sliding back. To cease to work for *Humanität* was to fall victim to *Brutalität*. To forsake the belief in human perfectibility meant opening the door to human corruptibility. The idea of social progress and human perfectibility, therefore, Herder argued, was not to be identified with an utopian ideal, but was to be conceived rather as an 'operative ideal', related to a specific social setting at a given time.

It was in this relativist interpretation of progress and human perfectibility that Herder's philosophy of social development parts company with the optimistic progressivism of his age.

Relativism and the notion of inter-relationism are the cardinal features of Herder's methodology which we have elicited as the second significant aspect of Herder's contribution to political thought. It is difficult to assess it justly. For a great deal of what Herder wrote on the limits of human knowledge, on historiography, on interaction and inter-relatedness has become part of an intellectual background which we simply take for granted. Not that all that Herder had to say in this respect was entirely new even in the eighteenth century. What was original in conception and novel in its application to the study of social and political affairs was the synthesis which he succeeded in fusing out of the most diverse currents of thought.

Furthermore, Herder's 'conceptual tools' were so much part of his ideas on nature and society that it is almost misleading to speak of his method as something apart from his doctrines. They both originated from a common source: discontent. What primarily provoked Herder into evolving a new method of viewing history and social development was the intellectual complacency and arrogance of his age; its tendency to measure past human endeavour in the light of its own value criteria, arrogating to itself a right which it denied previous periods. It found these wanting simply because their values and purposes were not in accord with its own. The relativity of time and place did not seem to matter greatly; it was ignored or inadequately recognized.

Historical and geographical relativity, however, does matter. Each age, each civilization, each nation, even each plant is unique and incomparable. The past must not be approached with preconceived ideas; the historian must feel himself into the events of the past. Above all, causation in history is a most complex phenomenon. Events are closely inter-related and hence must be studied within the context of their relations.

These were the central themes of Herder's polemical Essay of 1774, which was a frontal assault on eighteenth-century methodology and historiography.

Herder was aware that absolute objectivity was unattainable and that the degree of empathy of which the historian and social philosopher were capable was limited. He realized that subjective elements could not be entirely eliminated. One's value judgments were necessarily coloured by one's geographical, historical and personal circumstances. Yet the degree of objectivity realized, Herder insisted, would be enhanced if its limiting and distorting factors were clearly recognized.

Herder's relativism and inter-relationism were not confined, however, to historiography. They found application also in his epistemology and in his approach to social and political questions.

In his epistemology Herder was anxious to refute what he considered to be the more facile forms of rationalism: its *a priorism*, its abstractionism, its love of system-building, its dogmatism and, above all, its 'faculty' psychology. Things were far too inter-related to lend themselves to arbitrary separation. Herder hoped that by expanding the Aristotelian theory of purposive development and linking it with his own organic conception of *vis*, he would be able to replace the faculty approach and the philosophical dualisms current in his day by the notion of psycho-physical and relational unity. With the help of this notion he sought for a synthesis between 'mind' and 'matter' and between the 'merely subjective' and the 'merely objective' in the problem of the relationship between man and his environment.

Applying his relativism to politics and social development, Herder rejected such 'general' political principles as the theory of natural rights, the concept of a state of nature, the idea of a 'best form' of government, and the notion of a model civilization. Even the universal concept of *Humanität*, the leading idea of the age, underwent a change of meaning in his use. By relating it to contemporary political problems he not only gave it concrete significance but also exemplified its historical relativity. Whilst his theory of social development was frankly teleological, the nature of its teleological elements was conceived in a strictly relativist sense. The *telos* was not held to lie beyond human 'striving' but within it. It was that which, at any given time, prompted man towards realizing what was latent in him to become. It was both the essence *and* the function of human 'development', and it was both determining and determined. For it determined man's endeavours within a given historical and geographical setting and, at the same time, in view of Herder's principle of continuous interaction, it also assumed the form it did *because* of the prevailing conditions of time and place. Social processes were, accordingly, the expression or embodiment of historical and environmental forces 'energized' by human purposes. It would not be wrong, therefore, to say that Herder's teleology was but a corollary of his theory of internal relations which, applied to history and social development, was again, as in his epistemology, an attempt at integrating the 'inside' and the 'outside' of the human condition. This 'condition' was for Herder a continuous 'becoming', activated by its internal springs (*Triebfedern*) and its external circumstances (*Umstände*).

Finally, Herder's theory of historical causation, in distinguishing between 'cause' as a temporal antecedent and 'cause' as a purposive direction, is of considerable methodological significance in its bearing on the treatment of human affairs. For by means of this distinction it is possible to maintain a system of causal determinism without subscribing to a doctrine of fatalism.

We have attempted to summarize those of Herder's ideas which we believe to represent his main contribution to socio-political thought. When all is said, it must be admitted that Herder's emotional discontent and its corollary, the intense desire for a political transformation, impaired, at times, his vision and warped his critical judgment. He underestimated the efficacy of political expertness, *per se*, and the resilience of established political institutions as much as he exaggerated the rôle of language and 'national consciousness'. He also seriously underrated the strength of dynastic loyalties and the psychological significance of purely *political* traditions, even if the latter happened to be no more than myths hallowed by usage or sheer symbolistic projections.

In his longing for the removal of 'government', and in his distaste for, and distrust of, contemporary politics and politicians, Herder was led

astray occasionally into a manner of political reasoning which cannot
be described as other than surprisingly naïve. Thus he could argue, for
example, that international friction was purely the work of governmental 'machines', that national diversity naturally led to international
harmony, or that the establishment of folk-law meant the reign of
supreme justice. Yet, as we have shown in the last two instances, the
belief in diversity as the *sine qua non* of harmonious social and
international co-operation as also the credal affirmation of folk-law can
be questioned on both empirical and logical grounds. Diversity may be
the natural order of things, but it may have disintegrating as well as
unifying characteristics. Laws that are in harmony with a people's
historical traditions and indicative of its collective consciousness, may
be good laws, but they may equally be very bad laws. Neither diversity,
therefore, as such, nor folk-law can be relied upon as infallible safe-
guards against social and political ills.

What may also help to account for this lack of political realism was
Herder's inability to differentiate sufficiently between the wider
community of the State and the natural unit of the family from which it
conceivably originated. Having adopted—and adapted—Aristotle's
account of the growth of States, Herder believed it would further his
argument against political 'mechanism' if he invoked the image of a
'political family'. In this he was clearly mistaken. For the family is a
model of an hierarchical pattern of authority which, with its vertical
structure of responsibility, not only fundamentally conflicted with his
notion of horizontal co-operation, but also left unanswered the crucial
problem of defining and delimiting the spheres of authority of the
diverse centres of activity in his pluralist scheme.

Since Herder's theory of community, unlike Möser's, aimed at the
removal of élitist politics, it had to project into the future the kind of
'natural development' which the past so far had refused to reveal.
Hence, Herder's 'traditionalism' could not dispense with the idea of
progress. If social and political life had failed to emerge so far in a form
that befitted the nature of man, it was because the process was as yet
incomplete, because somehow, somewhere, the chain of continuity had
been broken. It was the very task of the philosopher of history to discover, with the aid of social psychology, the gaps in the purposive
direction of social development and to trace by means of sociological
hypotheses the causes that have brought about the divergence between
the actual and the 'natural' course of the historical process. The
knowledge thus gained should help to steer the course of progress in the
desired direction, in the direction, that is, in which the true end of

social association (which for Herder as for Aristotle meant its true *nature*) would become more fully realized. That men could learn from the study of history, from social psychology, and from sociology, how to solve social and political problems, is still a common enough notion. For Herder and many of his contemporaries it was a firm conviction, a matter not of faith, but of empirical and 'scientific' truth.

In making these criticisms we must not lose sight, however, of the conditions of Herder's Germany, its political censorship, the personal rule of dynastic princes, and the dearth of channels into which political ideas and political activity could be directed. It must also be remembered that in both his theory of community and his relativist methodology Herder was exploring regions that were largely uncharted.

If his ideas were not always free from vague speculation, we must not on this account dismiss Herder as a mere dreamer, unaware of political realities. In questions of such crucial significance as the growing political rôle of the middle classes, the importance of language, historical consciousness, folk-lore and customs as cohesive factors in political life, and, not least, in his appraisal of the French Revolution, Herder revealed not only a sound grasp of contemporary realities, but also remarkable political imagination and foresight. He was quick to realize that the French Revolution was the most important historical event since the Reformation and, unlike many of his German contemporaries, he never went back on his verdict. Likewise, the depth of detail with which Herder anticipated the failure of colonialism—fully apparent only in our own day—evidences an almost prophetic degree of perspicacity. It is remarkable, too, how many key concepts of modern political sociology can be traced, directly or indirectly, to Herder's concern with 'patterns of culture', and how close recent thinking on administrative processes and decision-making comes to his notion of co-ordination free from norms of centrality and hierarchy.

Herder's political thought represents the link between the Enlightenment and the era of modern Nationalism. It was both the culmination of an age and the beginning of a new epoch. In his negative attitude towards the contemporary 'mechanical' State Herder was one of many. In preaching the gospel of the nation-State, however, and in advancing an 'organic', community basis of statehood, Herder was one of the first of modern political thinkers, whose ideas have not lost relevance to current discussions in politics and sociology.

IX

IMPACT

THE nature and extent of Herder's influence on subsequent political thought and activity is clearly a subject of too broad a scope to be treated at all adequately within the limits of this study. We shall confine ourselves, therefore, in the first part of this chapter to the political ideas of those who frequently are regarded as Herder's immediate successors in Germany, whilst in the second part we shall attempt to indicate briefly Herder's political influence outside Germany.

I. HERDERISM AND GERMAN POLITICAL ROMANTICISM

When Haym, nearly a century ago, surveyed the writings of the Romanticists, he felt that his generation could not but lack in understanding of most of their political utterances.[1] He may well have been justified in this belief. Politics, we are told on good authority, is always charged with emotion, unless it be entirely corrupt.[2] But the degree of political emotionalism varies from age to age and so does our capacity to understand the diverse forms and modes of expression which it assumes. A world that has witnessed the ravages which excessive emotionalism and political mythologies have brought upon mankind is unlikely to reveal more sympathy than Haym's generation for ideas that have contributed their fair share towards their espousal. Yet at the same time it may find itself less startled by their occurrence and more discerning in an appraisal of their nature and origins.

For the purpose of our enquiry we shall be chiefly concerned with the views of such leading representatives of German political Romanticism as Novalis, Wilhelm and Friedrich Schlegel, Adam Müller, Schleiermacher, Savigny and, with some reservations, Fichte.[3] Whilst Schelling

---

[1] R. Haym, *Die romantische Schule*, Berlin, 1870, p. 340.

[2] Sir Ivor Jennings, *Party Politics*, Cambridge, 1962, vol. iii, p. 230.

[3] Hegel, like the Romanticists, borrowed heavily from Herder, yet he was neither a nationalist nor a Romanticist. His notion of the organic state, nonetheless, comes closer to that of the Romanticists than to that of Herder.

may rightly be regarded as one of the most profound exponents of the organic conception of nature after Herder and Goethe, his contribution to political thought was too slight to deserve special attention. Gentz, Arndt and Görres, on the other hand, although they took an active part in practical politics, espoused views which corresponded closely to those of Novalis, Savigny and Adam Müller, so that their separate treatment would only involve tiresome repetition.

On first sight it may seem a curious paradox that, considerable though the influence of Herder's organic conception of politics and his relativist methodology was on German political Romanticism, it nevertheless failed to transmit the very ideas which essentially constituted Herder's political creed. Indeed, it would not be wrong to say that Herder's 'ideological' approach to politics which so strongly appealed to his immediate 'successors' unwittingly helped to nurture a political tradition that was the very opposite to what he politically stood for.

The discrepancy between Herder's political outlook and that of his 'followers' is not, however, so surprising if the changed circumstances with which the latter tried to come to terms are taken into account. The men who principally appropriated Herder's organic philosophy of nationalism were not ignorant of his 'liberal' and 'democratic' sentiments even if they were hardly aware of his more 'anarchistic' leanings, since these only became known with the publication of his uncensored drafts in the subsequent century.[4] Indeed, there is no dearth of evidence that a number of them would have preferred to pursue a liberal and democratic path towards the achievement of their nationalist aspirations. Thus Fichte in his earlier writings proclaimed the rights of the individual, Wilhelm and Friedrich Schlegel espoused republicanism, and Gentz and Görres demanded democracy during the Wars of Liberation. If these writers eventually felt that they had to change course and even abandon their erstwhile path, they did so, not because of ignorance of, or ingratitude towards, Herder's political heritage, but out of a real conviction that Herder's advocacy of middle-class leadership, reform from below, co-operation rather than sub-ordination and popular participation in government had little relevance to the condition with which their country was faced.

But even though the political content of their ideologies was fundamentally out of tune with Herder's political creed, it was not without native roots. The emphasis on 'subordination', for example,

---

[4] Suphan's was the first complete and authentic edition of Herder's works. It appeared in print over the years 1877–1913.

which was a dominant characteristic of political Romanticism, was well in keeping with a political tradition which had remained unbroken in spite of the Lutheran Reformation. For Luther, although he challenged the ecclesiastical authority of the Pope, never questioned the principle of obedience to political *Obrigkeit*.[5] Similarly, the religious mysticism and the stress on 'feeling' rather than on reason, which are features common to a number of Romanticists, could be traced back to the Pietist movement, or, even further, to medieval Catholicism.[6] The 'imperial' conception of nationalism, too, had its links with the past and with a political tradition that was still kept alive in the eighteenth century by jurists and historians such as J. J. and F. K. Moser, Pütter, and A. L. Schlözer. When the Romanticists glorified the German State, they were still frequently thinking in terms of the Empire centred on Vienna. Even Hegel held that view when he wrote *Die Verfassung Deutschlands* in 1802. Finally, when a number of Romanticists favoured the revival of a feudal order of society, they used ideas that had been developed by Justus Möser nearly half a century earlier, although in doing so they misinterpreted, if they did not also misunderstand, Möser's traditionalism as frequently as they failed to grasp Burke's empiricism.[7]

At the same time it cannot be denied that in spite of their political re-orientation the Romanticists owed much to Herderian ideas, however disguised these became by exaggeration or outright distortion. The veneration of the past—in particular the medieval past; the viewing of 'history' as a 'force' no less powerful or real than that of 'nature'; the notion that 'creative activity' is of the very essence of human existence: they can all be traced to Herderian origins. Likewise, on the political plane, Herder's denial of Natural Law and of a pre-political state of nature, as his affirmation of language as the most vital source of a people's collective consciousness, found expression in the basic premises of Romanticist thought.

It may strike the reader as odd that in their desire to come to grips

[5] It is not suggested that Luther was blind to the personal faults of some of the princes; that did not prevent him, however, from insisting on complete and unconditional submission to the political authority in a State. (See his *Schriften*, Weimar, 1853, vol. II, p. 267.)

[6] See H. S. Reiss, *The Political Thought of the German Romantics*, op. cit., p. 2 and Reinhold Aris, *History of Political Thought in Germany*, (1789–1815), London, 1936, p. 286.

[7] Adam Müller, for example, regarded himself as a true follower of Burke. He simply venerated him. He called him 'the last prophet who had come to this disenchanted earth'. (*Ueber König Friedrich II*, Berlin, 1810, pp. 52–3; see also his *Elemente der Staatskunst* 3 vols., Berlin, 1809, vol. I, pp. 31–2.) But did he really understand him? I wonder.

with the problems of their time the Romanticists should have found it compelling to turn their gaze to a bygone age. Yet it was precisely this odd combination of an intense desire for realism and an almost poetical nostalgia which characterized Romanticist ideology.[8] To men such as Novalis, Josef Görres and Adam Müller the Middle Ages were the golden age of the past, medieval society the ideal socio-political order. With these ages they associated the national glory of a unified German Empire grounded in a common religion and fortified by a common faith in its political destiny. By reviving the social and economic forces on which it had rested they hoped to restore the national unity which their country so sorely lacked.

In order to fuse the medieval conception of a social unit with the philosophy of political organism, the latter had to undergo a distinct change from its Herderian meaning. The 'organism' that emerged in Romanticist writings displayed a decidedly hierarchical anatomy. The State, said Novalis, was a *macro-anthropos*, the anatomy of which was composed of the different social orders that formed a community: 'The State has always been a macro-anthropos: the guilds were its limbs and (physical) energies, the estates its (spiritual) faculties. The nobility represented the moral faculty, the priests the religious faculty, the scholars the intellectual faculty whilst the king embodied the power of the will.'[9] Only the monarch was more than the summation of a community's functional parts since he symbolized the living idea of the State. As a being born into high office he was by nature accustomed to rule, yet at the same time he was, by virtue of his noble birth, impervious to the corrupting influence of power.

Neither giddiness nor over-excitement will afflict him who is thus born. . . . The king is the very life-force of the State; he is to the State what the sun is to the planets. . . . Every citizen is a civil servant and only thus earns his income. Yet one is quite wrong to describe the king as the first servant of the State. The king is not a citizen and hence he is not a civil servant either. The characteristic which distinguishes monarchies is the belief in, and the acceptance of, the higher-born individual as the embodiment of ideal man.[10]

According to such a conception of the body politic, the inequality of man was a necessary presupposition, obedience and sub-ordination a

---

[8] Benno von Wiese, in a penetrating analysis of German political poetry, has drawn attention to this paradoxical combination which, in his view, is but an instance of a feature common to all ideologies. (See his *Politische Dichtung Deutschlands*, Berlin, 1931, pp. 15–64.)

[9] Novalis, *Gesammelte Werke*, ed. Carl Seelig, 5 vols., Zürich, 1945, vol. IV, p. 158. (See also vol. II, p. 193: 'The State is a person like an individual.' Similarly, vol. III, p. 298.)

[10] Novalis op. cit. vol. II pp. 53–5. (See also ibid., p. 62: 'The king and queen protect the monarchy more effectively than 200,000 men.')

natural corollary. Some individuals were born to rule as others were destined to serve; each had to perform the rôle that Providence had assigned to him. Novalis wrote in his *Die Christenheit oder Europa* (1799) of the 'joy of obedience', and Friedrich Schlegel, in a letter to him, was full of praise and admiration for these sentiments and the royalism underlying them.[11] Likewise, Adam Müller spoke of obedience as the most vital element in effective government and as the essence of political liberty: 'The secret of government lies in obedience; the soul's craving for elevation in voluntary surrender; freedom in complete devotion to the fatherland.'[12] Müller and Gentz advocated a return to feudalism because they saw in it a beautiful equilibrium between government and obedience and a safeguard against the rule of the rabble and the intelligentsia.[13] The land-owning nobility was generally identified with a natural ruling class and most favourably contrasted with commerce and trade.[14]

Allied with this glorification of the medieval structure of society was a somewhat incongruous notion, namely the idea of the supremacy and all-pervasiveness of the State. For the Romanticists the State represented an all-embracing organic whole, outside which human existence was held to be wholly inconceivable.[15] Adam Müller spoke of the State as the interest of all interests, as the supreme end, and as the totality of all human affairs.[16] It was a thing beyond dispute, for only those who looked upon the State as a means only could dare to question its use and purpose: 'Should anyone ask: "what is the purpose of the State?", I would ask in return: "you look upon the State as a means? ... do you still maintain that anything exists outside the State which it should serve, like the structure supporting the building or like the shell enclosing the kernel?" '[17] Man entirely belonged to the State, in mind and in body and with all his earthly possessions: 'If only the whole

[11] Novalis, *Werke*, op. cit., vol. V, pp. 32–3. As to Schlegel's letter to Novalis, see *Novalis Briefwechsel*, ed. by J. M. Raich, Mainz, 1880, p. 129 f.

[12] Müller, *Elemente*, op. cit., vol. III, p. 327.

[13] Müller, *Elemente*, op. cit., vol. II, p. 99; F. Gentz, *Briefwechsel zwischen F. Gentz und A. Müller*, Stuttgart, 1857, p. 244.

[14] It may be of interest to note here that among English Romanticists S. T. Coleridge was probably the most outstanding writer who championed the agrarian nobility. See particularly *The Constitution of Church and State*, London, 1829, pp. 20–32, and his *Lay Sermon*, London, 1817, p. 414.

[15] Müller, *Elemente*, op. cit., vol. I, p. 62: 'There is no human endeavour that is conceivable outside the State.'

[16] See Müller, *Ueber König Friedrich II*, op. cit., p. 270, and *Elemente*, op. cit., vol. I, pp. 66–8.

[17] Müller, *Elemente*, op. cit., vol. I, p. 67.

human being would dedicate himself to the State and not merely offer his worldly goods.'[18]

There is a strong temptation to apply the word 'totalitarian' to such a conception of the State. For we commonly associate this word nowadays with a political doctrine which denies the value of the individual as a being other than that of a member of a State and which treats of the latter as the supreme end and as the sole arbiter of all human values, whose right to pronounce on all spheres of human activity is beyond question. But it is only fair to bear in mind that the word 'totalitarian' is one which belongs to the vocabulary of the twentieth century, and is not one to be found in the writings of the Romanticists. Hence to apply it readily to Müller's, to Wilhelm Schlegel's or, for that matter, to Hegel's philosophy of the State may not only rightly be considered inappropriate, but also ambiguous. None the less it is difficult to think of a more suitable term, especially in view of the fact that the Romanticists also subscribed to what is generally regarded as another corollary of totalitarian doctrine: the affirmation, if not the glorification, of war.[19]

The theory of the political origin of society further strengthened the argument in favour of the omnipotence of the State. According to this theory the State was not the result of human association but its very accompaniment. In the words of Adam Müller, the State was as old as the human race.[20] It reflected, therefore, a union not only of those who at any given time constituted its members but also of those who had gone before and those yet to come. The State, in short, was the living embodiment of historical continuity: 'The State is not an association of merely those families who live side by side of one another but also of those who follow on.'[21]

In the light of such a theory of the State it is hardly surprising that the conception of Natural Law as the supreme arbiter over human

---

[18] Müller, *Elemente*, op. cit., vol. II, p. 85; see also Novalis, *Werke*, op. cit., vol. IV, pp. 225, 274.

[19] See Oskar Walzel, *German Romanticism*, trans. by Alma Elise Lussky, New York/London, 1932, pp. 136-8, and B. von Wiese, *Politische Dichtung*, op. cit., pp. 62-4. Müller spoke of war as a political teacher: '(Observe) how war serves as a teacher of political ideas, how it enlivens politics and economics' (*Elemente*, vol. I, p. 94). It must be conceded, however, that to say that war has some merits is not the same as to advocate it. This could perhaps be said in defence of Hegel's attitude to war in particular, for Hegel nowhere in his writings argued in favour of continuous warfare. He did not, it is true, favour perpetual peace either; but he never presented war as man's noblest pursuit. For an interesting discussion of Hegel's thoughts on war, see Shlomo Avineri, 'The Problem of War in Hegel's Thought', *Journal of the History of Ideas*, October 1961, pp. 463-74.

[20] Müller, *Elemente*, op. cit., vol. I, p. 75.

[21] Müller, *Elemente*, op. cit., vol. I, p. 84; see also vol. II, p. 63.

rights had little appeal to the political Romanticists. Müller, Görres, Arndt, as Savigny and the Historical Law School after him, insisted that positive law, that is the law peculiar to, or promulgated by, a given State, was the only 'natural law'. There never was, they maintained, a law prior to, or apart from, positive law, and hence there was no sense in speaking of such a law as being superior to political legislation. Müller wrote: 'We may therefore confidently deny Natural Law as something outside, over or beyond positive law; we may indeed recognize all positive law as natural.'[22] Positive law, Savigny maintained, was the only genuine basis of a State, since it was firmly rooted in the collective consciousness of a nation (*Volk*).[23] Indeed, he argued, in promulgating it, the law-giver was merely giving expression to the popular will. His legislative action, therefore, was not an arbitrary act but rather the inevitable result of forces that grew organically out of a given social environment and national tradition. In short, positive law was nothing but an organic growth which determined, rather than was determined by, the action of the legislator.[24] The crucial, and twofold question, however, concerning (a) the conditions under which a given positive law could be expected to correspond to the collective will (whatever that may mean) of a community, and (b) the coincidence between good and effective laws on the one hand, and communal customs and beliefs, on the other, was left unanswered. But it is evident that Savigny, like Herder, thought of Law in essentially medieval terms, as an expression of the communal ethos to be discovered and declared rather than made.

A further characteristic of political Romanticism was the determination to view the State as something that was far more than a purely utilitarian institution serving particular human and social needs. The Romanticists wished to envisage it in metaphysical terms, as an 'idea', which in a sense was outside and beyond the sphere of empirical experience. Thus Müller wrote of the State as the 'eternally moving realm of ideas',[25] and Hegel identified it with 'the mind on earth' unfolding itself to be the actual shape and organization of a world.[26] For Schleiermacher the monarch was the embodiment of the

[22] Müller, *Elemente*, op. cit., vol. I, p. 75.
[23] Friedrich Carl von Savigny, *Vom Beruf unsrer Zeit für Gesetzgebung und Rechtswissenschaft*, Heidelberg, 1814, p. 11.
[24] ibid., pp. 11-12, 17. Ernst Moritz Arndt (1769-1860)—a close friend of von Stein—put forward very similar views as early as 1803 in his *Germanien und Europa*.
[25] Müller, *Elemente*, op. cit., vol. I, p. 63.
[26] Hegel, *Naturrecht und Staatswissenschaft* (1821), trans. by T. M. Knox (*Hegel's Philosophy of Right*), Oxford, 1953, pp. 165-6.

divine idea of the State.[27] Like Müller he also denied the validity of a utilitarian or empirical justification of the State, presenting it as something that wholly eluded definition because it was entirely beyond the grasp of finite minds. Indeed, Müller went so far as to regard this inherent indefinability as the most profound and distinctive hall-mark of the State.[28]

I would not wish to dispute Friedrich Gundolf's statement that by and large the Romanticists' approach to the State was of a poetical rather than of a strictly philosophical nature.[29] But care must be taken lest one overlooks what was politically significant beneath the mist of poetical theorizing. Both the assertion of positive law and the 'idealistic' interpretation of the State aimed at establishing principles, the political importance of which cannot be gainsaid. In intimately linking Law with the historical traditions of a nation Savigny was anxious to emphasize that Law was not simply the expression of the arbitrary whim of a ruler, or something external like the Roman Law to be imposed on a people without due regard being had to its own peculiar customs and national characteristics. By endowing the State with a mystique and transcendence of its own, the Romanticists wished to distinguish it from all other forms of human organization, and present it as something quite unique and incomparable.[30] In contrast to the political thinkers of the Enlightenment, the political Romanticists 'rejected analysis and speculation as the best means of acquiring ultimate knowledge'.[31] Analysis may be applicable to 'concepts', Müller maintained, but not to 'ideas'. For a 'concept' refers to a particular static condition at a given point in time. An 'idea', on the other hand, refers to a dynamic, living object, to something that 'moves and grows'.[32] Since the State is held to be an 'idea', and not a 'concept', true knowledge of the State can only be gained by direct intuitive insight and not as a result of analytical speculation or theoretical definitions.

In both directions—the assertion of positive law and the 'idealization' of the State—the Herderian concept of 'Volksgeist' played a significant rôle. It embodied for the Romanticists that essentially

[27] Schleiermacher, *Vorlesungen über den Staat* (1829), trans. by H. S. Reiss, op. cit., p. 198.

[28] Müller, *Elemente*, op. cit., vol. I, p. 27.

[29] Friedrich Gundolf, *Romantiker*, Berlin, 1930, p. 177.

[30] In their determination to present the State as something unique and incomparable, the Romanticists succeeded, however, unlike Herder, in drawing a clear and fundamental distinction between the 'organism' of the family and the 'organism' of the State.

[31] Robert W. Longee, 'German Romanticism and Political Thought', *The Review of Politics*, October 1959, p. 634.

[32] Müller, *Elemente*, I, p. 20.

indefinable, yet decisive spiritual characteristic, by virtue of which a collection of men acquired a distinct personality of its own. They saw in the State no less than the inexorable historical manifestation of the emergence of such a collective personality. Once a people had become conscious of its distinct personality, it had not only the right, but also the duty to claim recognition for its separate and independent existence as a political entity.

For the Romanticists, as for Fichte and Hegel, the source and the expression of a people's collective spirit, its *Volksgeist*, lay in the possession of a common language. Fichte, in his *Reden an die deutsche Nation* (1808), assured his compatriots that once the Germans became conscious of the power and unique quality of their language, they would rally together and form a unified State.[33] Likewise, Hegel, in his *Vorlesungen*, insisted that the concept of 'Volksgeist'—which for him was basic to any theory of the State—was inconceivable without the identification of language and nation.[34] Savigny saw in language the matrix of a people's collective consciousness out of which the idea of law came to emerge,[35] whilst Schleiermacher and Friedrich Schlegel viewed language as the means by which true political reality could be grasped.[36]

Finally, Herder's impact on Romanticist historiography was unmistakable. In particular, Herder not only anticipated the historicism of Friedrich Schlegel who raised history to the queen of the sciences, regarding it as the supreme source of knowledge, but he also significantly foreshadowed in his theory of opposites Hegel's dialectic. The Historical Law School of Savigny, too, was substantially influenced by Herderian ideas. The quotation below most strikingly recalls in its formulation Herder's arguments in support of historical relativism: 'But this organic inter-relation between Law on the one hand and the

---

[33] Fichte, *Werke*, ed. by I. H. Fichte, 8 vols., Leipzig, 1845-6, vol. VII, pp. 458-80. The philological researches of the brothers Grimm, but even more so their collection of German fairy-tales did much to deepen the kind of 'consciousness' which Fichte had at heart.

[34] Hegel, *Vorlesungen über die Philosophie der Weltgeschichte, Werke*, ed. by G. Lasson, Leipzig, 1920-1, vol. I, p. 219; see also Theodor L. Haering, *Hegel, sein Wollen und sein Werk*, Leipzig and Berlin, 1929, p. 96. For a different interpretation of Hegel's conception of *Volksgeist*, see Shlomo Avineri, 'Hegel and Nationalism', *Review of Politics*, October 1962, pp. 461-84.

[35] Savigny, *System des heutigen Römischen Rechts*, Berlin, 1840-51, 9 vols., vol. I, p. 17; and *Vom Beruf unsrer Zeit*, op. cit., pp. 11, 14.

[36] G. Halstein, *Die Staatsphilosophie Schleiermachers*, Bonn and Leipzig, 1923, pp. 92-4. Regarding the importance which language assumed in Friedrich Schlegel's 'conceptology' —to coin a term which seems to me exceedingly appropriate in this case—see F. Gundolf, op. cit., pp. 59-100.

nature and character of a people on the other, proves true also in the
progress of time. . . . Just as there is no absolute standstill for language
or any other facet of a people, so also do we find Law to be constantly
subject to change and development.'[37] By the time Savigny wrote these
lines, however, the diverse Herderian notions—organism, national
character, continuous development and activity—had become common
stock, and frequently those who used these notions were no longer
aware of their Herderian origins.

Carl Schmitt has described the political Romanticists as the spokesmen of the middle class.[38] This view needs to be qualified if it is not to
mislead. Most of the representatives of political Romanticism were, it
is true, middle-class intellectuals, but they took no pride in this fact.
Men such as Friedrich Schlegel or Adam Müller suffered even from
an acute sense of social inferiority and were obsessed by a craving to be
raised to the rank of nobility.[39] The Romanticists felt that they could
not count upon the support of the middle classes. They were
'reactionaries', not because they favoured absolutism as such, but
because they were convinced that political initiative could only be
expected from 'above' and that it could only be effective if it was
glorified and mystified. Hence they revived the belief that monarchs
were by virtue of their noble birth divinely ordained to rule. It was this
aspect of their conviction which was reactionary in the literal sense of
that much-abused word. The conviction itself, however, was not
unfounded in a country which, unlike contemporary England and
France, had no self-respecting and politically conscious middle class
even at the close of the Napoleonic Wars.[40] The reign of terror following in the wake of the French Revolution, moreover, had engendered so
widespread a fear of anarchy as well as an intense feeling of doubt about
the possibility or desirability of reform from below, that arguments of
functional subordination did not fall on deaf ears. Coupled with the
disillusionment over the viability of 'rational' social ideals was an acute
sense of national humiliation. The middle class intellectuals who had
formed the vanguard in the struggle for social and national emancipation during the Wars of Liberation felt betrayed. And, rightly or
wrongly, many of them regarded this betrayal as something they had

---

[37] Savigny, *Vom Beruf unsrer Zeit*, op. cit., p. 11.
[38] Carl Schmitt, *Politische Romantik*, second edition, München and Leipzig, 1925, p. 16.
[39] R. Aris, op. cit., p. 306.
[40] Franz Schnabel, op. cit., vol. I, p. 283 and vol. II, p. 8,. See also Ralph Flenley,
op. cit., pp. 139–42.

inflicted on themselves by arrogating to their class what time-honoured usage had confined to the nobility. Thus an imagined sense of self-betrayal bred a real sense of self-abasement. Under these circumstances it was small wonder if men preferred the idols of the past to the gods that failed.

I would be inclined to submit that in the last analysis the class origin of the political Romanticists is largely a matter of indifference. For I believe that the really significant thing about the Romanticists was their uprootedness. They were men without social roots in quest of ideas and ideals that, primarily, were to meet their own social and psychological needs. That these needs were intimately connected with the social and political ills of their time is not being denied. Indeed, it is the close identification between the personal and the public spheres which made the Romanticists in question *political* Romanticists. But they were not so much spokesmen of a particular class as spokesmen of a particular mood; a mood which was at once highly personal and yet widely shared too. It was a complex mood: a mood of disenchantment *and* defiance, of degradation *and* elevation, of despair *and* yearning. It was a mood, above all, which brooked no delay. The political Romanticists were visionaries, but they were also imbued with a sense of practical urgency. The ideals for which they searched were ideals that seemed realizable in the here and now, within the existing structure of society. In this sense they were 'reactionaries' and 'revolutionaries' at one and the same time.

This is not as paradoxical as it may seem. The essential nature of revolutionary activity does not lie in the novelty of the ideas that animate it, but in the sense of urgency and determination in converting ideas into reality. The men of the anti-Reformation were no less revolutionary than the leaders of the Reformation. By the same token, the Romanticists, in their determination to resuscitate the scale of values which the French Revolution had well nigh succeeded in destroying, were no less revolutionary in their own way than the Jacobins had been in theirs. Nor does it significantly matter whether the ideas that are espoused are sincerely held. Some of those who idealized Germany's national origins, its medieval religion, its ancient aristocracy and noble monarchy, were undoubtedly time-servers and opportunists who used these ideas to conceal their own power-political ambitions. Gentz can be said to have belonged to this category, but it is unwise perhaps to be too dogmatic on this point. Men frequently act from mixed motives, and even when they sincerely believe in what they profess to believe they are not necessarily aware of the diverse reasons underlying their professed beliefs. Be that as it may, most of the writers, whose views we briefly surveyed, were men who ardently strove to reconcile their poetic imagination with the facts of political reality and thereby to forge a synthesis that could serve as an ideological backbone to their revolutionary aspirations.

In the preceding pages we attempted to elicit what was common to these ideological endeavours, in order to highlight their points of contact with, and divergence from, Herderian ideas. But the last thing we wished to suggest was that political Romanticism presented a solid ideological front. Few of the Romanticists were political writers first and foremost, and none, with the possible exception of Adam Müller, succeeded in elaborating a consistent political doctrine. With most of them the lines that separate politics from imagery and sheer myth were exceedingly blurred. But the shifts of emphasis vary from writer to writer. Fichte and Savigny, for example, tended on the whole towards a more pragmatic approach to politics whilst others, such as Müller and Schleiermacher, favoured more transcendental, if not oracular, modes of thought. Notwithstanding these individual differences, however, the area of agreement is substantial enough to permit us to speak of these writers as a collective group when drawing our final conclusions.

We find then that, in spite of their adherence to some of Herder's basic premises, the political Romanticists also differed from him in several significant respects. Herder's starting points were plurality and diversity, and the recognition of conflict as an integral element in social and political life. The Romanticists, on the other hand, looked upon the State as a unified organism from the very outset. What to Herder was only the *result* of countless spontaneous processes, was to the Romanticists the prerequisite condition. The organic unity of Herder was that of a relational *process of development* in which diverse interests were freely and equally partaking in an attempt to find a basis for agreement and co-operation. It was potentiality seeking realization, not enforced actuality. When Herder spoke in terms of organic metaphors, he did so in order to stress the spontaneity, the inner springs of socio-political activities. When the Romanticists made use of organic analogies, they did so in order to stress the hierarchy of status and to confer upon one form of social organization an absolute pre-eminence over every other. Even if it is conceded that the Romanticists cherished the hope that those who govern would do so in the interest of the governed, they allied this hope with complete trust in the former to be the infallible arbiters of the latter. In effect, therefore, if not always in intention, their political theories came to provide the ideological sanction for established instruments of government. In this respect Sir Ernest Barker's remarks about Hegel seem equally applicable to political Romanticism as a whole: 'Distrusting, or rather forgetting, the *process* (and the essence of liberalism is reliance upon it), it turned instead to an *organ* or instrument; and for the natural synthesis of debate it substituted the artificial synthesis of "a decreeing individual".'[41]

But these are practical considerations. On logical and theoretical grounds equal validity may be claimed for the Romanticist organic conception of functional subordination as for Herder's organic conception of functional co-ordination, for both conceptions are compatible with the image of an organism. Of course, one may legitimately question the adequacy of the organic analogy in either conception as an explanation or description of social and political structures, especially if one holds the view, as T. D. Weldon has done, that the organic analogy is to be understood not in a metaphorical but in a literal sense.[42] But this is not the point at issue. The real point at issue is whether or not the diverse claims made by the political Romanticists for the organic State are in any sense consistent with the image of an organism.

Clearly, when we think of an organism we do not think of the 'whole' as being on an ontologically higher plane that its parts. The political Romanticists, on the other hand, maintained both: (a) that the State is an organism; and (b) that it is on an ontologically higher level than its members. And they seemed to think that the first statement entailed the second, or, more precisely, they invariably argued as if the two claims were identical.[43] Similarly, it does not follow from the analogy of organism—as the Romanticists thought it did—that the State cannot be conceived in an instrumental or even pluralist sense, for there is no necessary incompatibility—as Herder seems to have realized —between the two. One can legitimately hold the State to be an organism *without* holding also that it is an end in itself. Conversely, one can legitimately uphold the belief that the State is something final in the nature of an absolute in some metaphysical or transcendental sense, without committing oneself to the view that the State is an organism. There simply is no necessary connexion between these two beliefs.

[41] Ernest Barker, *Principles of Social and Political Theory*, London, 1951, p. 23.
[42] T. D. Weldon, *States and Morals*, London, 1946, p. 34.
[43] See H. J. McCloskey, 'The State as an Organism', *Philosophical Review*, July 1963, pp. 309–24 for a fuller discussion of this point.

A further confusion arises from the Romanticists' attempt to identify the image of an organism with that of a person. For not only is the unity of a person a wholly different conception from that of the unity of an organism; it is also difficult to see how one can speak of the parts of a person in any recognizable sense. One may conceivably argue that the State is an organism made up of other co-ordinate organisms (as Herder did) or of subordinate organisms (as the Romanticists did), but it is less conceivable how one can maintain that the State as a 'person' is made up of other or lesser persons. Whilst both the organic model and the model of a person may or may not be regarded as methodologically fruitful devices of political analysis, nothing but confusion can result from the mixing or identification of these two models.

Finally, even if it is conceded that in terms of the organic model the parts can only be explained in reference to the whole, this does not imply that their *value* is derivative from the value of the whole. For clearly, ethically speaking, the members of a social whole may be more or less valuable than the whole, or of equal value. This again, Herder, in contrast to the Romanticists, seems to have realized by upholding the notions of both *Volk* and *Humanität* as equally relevant value considerations.

In the light of these observations it would seem that the political organism of the Romanticists was essentially a pseudo-organism. By making the sort of claims for the State which they did, they both distorted and obscured the image of organism as a political model. Herder, by refraining from associating such claims with the organic model was in this sense a more consistent 'organicist' than his Romanticist 'followers'. What is more, by insisting on functional co-ordination rather than subordination, he also suggested the possibility of an organic theory of the State that was both democratic and pluralistic.

On the other hand, in divorcing organicism and nationalism from radicalism and democratism, the political Romanticists exemplified, perhaps, a stronger sense of historical realism than Herder, their 'liberal' precursor. For, in doing so, they typified correctly the development of German nationalism and the essentially dynastic and 'authoritarian' forces that effected German national unification. It would, clearly, be imprudent to press this point too strongly, involving as it does the imponderables of historical causation. One thing, however, seems plain enough. Those who were most eager to appropriate Herder's philosophical vocabulary were also the first to disown his political legacy.

2. HERDER'S POLITICAL INFLUENCE OUTSIDE GERMANY

There appears to be no direct evidence to suggest that Herder's ideas made any perceptible impress on French or English political thought, in spite of the fact that the *Ideen* found an English translator during the author's lifetime.[44] It may well be true, however, that 'many who might have been affected by Herder were attracted by Hegel instead'.[45]

One major political thinker, however, was not unaffected by Herder's thought, even though it was Herder, the philosopher of history, rather than Herder, the political radical, with whom he appears to have been familiar. His name was John Stuart Mill. In his essay *On Coleridge* he speaks very highly of Herder as one of 'that series of great writers and thinkers . . . , by whom history, which was till then a "tale told by an idiot, full of sound and fury, signifying nothing", has been made a science of causes and effects; who, by making the facts and events of the past have a meaning and an intelligible place in the gradual evolution of humanity, have at once given history, even to the imagination, an interest like romance, and afforded the only means of predicting and guiding the future, by unfolding the agencies which have produced and still maintain the Present'.[46]

Mill endorsed Herder's view of education as the guardian of tradition and the herald of progress when he wrote that 'the character of the national education existing in any political society . . . (was) at once the principal cause of its permanence as a society, and the chief source of its progressiveness: the former by the extent to which that education operated as a system of restraining discipline; the latter by the degree in which it called forth and invigorated the active faculties'.[47] He wrote

---

[44] T. Churchill, *Outlines of a Philosophy of the History of Man*, London, 1800.

[45] A. Gillies, *Herder*, op. cit., p. 127. G. A. Wells (in *Herder and After*, The Hague, 1959, p. 234) puts forward as a further explanation for the neglect of Herder's thought in England the operation of two causes, 'one general and lasting, and one proximate and temporary. The first is the great industrial expansion which England experienced in the later eighteenth century, and the consequent absorption of the nation's energy in mere money-getting; and the second consists in the emergence of a strong religious reaction against the French revolution at the end of the century.'

[46] J. S. Mill, *On Bentham and Coleridge*, ed. by F. R. Leavis, London, 1950, p. 131.

[47] ibid., p. 132; it is interesting to note that although Mill is using here the terminology of Coleridge in speaking of 'permanence' and 'progressiveness', he is nevertheless applying it in an Herderian rather than a Coleridgian manner. For Mill, unlike Coleridge, does not

in a similar Herderian vein when he discussed the growth of national cultures: 'Every form of polity, every condition of society, whatever else it had done, had formed its type of national character. What that type was, and how it had been made what it was, were questions which the metaphysician might overlook, the historical philosopher could not.'[48] In his essay *On Liberty*, however, where he expressed sentiments of striking affinity to those of Herder, Mill explicitly acknowledged his intellectual debt, as far as German writers were concerned, to Wilhelm v. Humboldt only.[49] Since Humboldt himself, however, was strongly influenced by Herderian ideas,[50] Mill's expressed gratitude to Humboldt was in some measure due to Herder too.

It was primarily Coleridge who had awakened Mill's interest in German political thought. Mill had a high regard for Coleridge— 'Bentham excepted, no Englishman of recent date has left his impress so deeply in the opinions and mental tendencies of those among us who attempted to enlighten their practice by philosophical meditation', he said of him[51]—but he felt that 'in all essentials of his doctrine' Coleridge was 'anticipated . . . by the great Germans of the latter half of the last century',[52] whilst his political theories were, in Mill's view, but a 'commencement, not amounting to the first lines of a political philosophy'.[53]

Mill's judgment of Coleridge's standing as a political writer is no doubt open to question, for Coleridge, clearly, was a political thinker in his own right.[54] But there is little *political* affinity between Coleridge's outlook and that of Herder, but for the former's early republican sympathies, and it is not really surprising to learn that Coleridge expressed hostility towards Herder's ideas.[55] To be sure, Coleridge

---

identify 'tradition' and 'progress' with specific economic interests. (Cf. S. T. Coleridge, *The Constitution of Church and State*, op. cit., pp. 20–32.)

[48] ibid., p. 132.

[49] Mill, *On Liberty*, ed. by R. B. McCallum, Oxford, 1946, pp. 50, 51, 65, 93; see also his *Autobiography*, World Classics edition, London, 1924, pp. 216–17.

[50] R. Haym, op. cit., vol. I, p. 408; see also A. Gillies, *Herder*, op. cit., p. 118; and R. T. Clark, *Herder*, op. cit., p. 382.

[51] Mill, *On Bentham and Coleridge*, op. cit., p. 99.

[52] ibid., p. 103.   [53] ibid., p. 152.

[54] Of particular interest is his dialectical doctrine of 'permanence' and 'progression'. The former is held to represent the landed interests, the latter the mercantile, manufacturing, distributive and professional classes. (See S. T. Coleridge, *The Constitution of Church and State*, op. cit., pp. 20–32; and his *Lay Sermon*, op. cit., p. 414.)

[55] Whilst in 1794 Coleridge still referred to the nobility as 'that leprous stain', and also addressed a sonnet to Godwin, by 1797 he wrote: 'I abominate Godwinism!' (See Basil Willey, *Nineteenth-Century Studies, Coleridge to Matthew Arnold*, London, 1949, pp. 5, 9; and also A. Gillies, *Herder*, op. cit., p. 122.)

stressed, as Herder had done, the political significance of the Bible, as he also insisted on viewing the State as an organism. But neither his *Statesman's Manual* (1816) nor his *Lay Sermon* (1817) suggest that he desired to apply Herderian ideas in the Herderian political spirit. Their very starting points are diametrically opposed. Herder advocated reform from below whilst Coleridge addressed his *Manual* to the upper classes in the conviction that the reformation of English society must begin at the top. If he was a follower of Herder at all, he was so in a sense not very different from that in which the German political Romanticists could be regarded as Herder's successors.[56] One who *could* have been a true follower of Herder—Coleridge's erstwhile friend, William Godwin—on the other hand, hardly seems to have known of his existence.[57]

In the intellectual relationship between Coleridge and William Godwin it is very much a moot point as to who influenced whom. The likelihood is that the influence was mutual.[58] If this assumption is correct, it may not be too fanciful to suggest that the remarkable affinity between Herder's political creed and that of Godwin was not perhaps wholly accidental. For it could conceivably be attributed to Coleridge's pronounced interest in German thought and in his success in communicating this interest to others.[59] Godwin may also have learned of Herder's political views through Henry Crabb Robinson who greatly admired Herder and also went to visit him in Weimar.[60]

Godwin, like Herder, regarded political government in the estab-

[56] R. J. White, in his *Introduction to Political Tracts of Wordsworth, Coleridge and Shelley*, Cambridge, 1953, pp. xii, xiii, writes: 'No one who had read the main text of that work (*The Statesman's Manual*) could have identified his (Coleridge's) philosophy of history with that of Herder. . . . It (Herder's achievement) had very little to do with Coleridge, nor had Coleridge very much to do with it.'

[57] The same could be said of Wordsworth, whose ideas on nationality reveal an astonishing resemblance to those of Herder. For Wordsworth, as for Herder, nationality had to coincide with the State and form its natural and 'organic' basis. (See Crane Brinton, *The Political Ideas of the English Romanticists*, Oxford, 1926, pp. 56–9.) But whilst Herder's influence is uncertain, that of Rousseau is beyond doubt. It may be of interest to note, however, that Herder, towards the end of his life came to read Wordsworth's *Lyrical Ballads*, as Crabb Robinson reports in his *Diary* (I, 154) after his last visit to Herder in 1803: 'I lent him Wordsworth's Lyrical Ballads.—I found that Herder agreed with Wordsworth as to poetical language.' (Cited in Luise Schork, *Herders Bekanntschaft mit der englischen Literatur*, Breslau, 1928, p. 61.)

[58] This is suggested by F. E. L. Priestley in his edition of William Godwin's *Enquiry concerning Political Justice* (1793), published in three volumes, Toronto, 1946; see vol. III, pp. 101–6.

[59] See F. W. Stokoe, *German Influence in the English Romantic Period*, Cambridge, 1926, pp. 89–143.

[60] See F. Norman, 'Henry Crabb Robinson and Goethe', Part I, *Publications of the English Goethe Society*, vol. VI, 1930, pp. 9, 13, 20.

lished 'orthodox' form as merely a 'fatal necessity'.[61] Likewise, he
viewed all 'organization' from above with profound suspicion since he
held it to conduce to a 'fallacious uniformity of opinion'.[62] Finally,
Godwin also looked forward to a time when the need for a central
government in the accepted sense would no longer arise, but, again
like Herder, he advocated a political transformation in gradual stages
rather than one brought about by a sudden or violent revolution.[63]

There is, alas, no mention made of Herder in Godwin's work, nor
has research since provided any grounds for assuming that Godwin's
ideas were in any way directly inspired by those of Herder. I have
certainly not been able to find support for such an assumption. What
evidence there is is negative.[64] Likewise there is no evidence to suggest
that Herder had any knowledge of Godwin or his *Enquiry*.[65]

It may, of course, be argued that there is no need to postulate any
influence of Herder, since Godwin's ideas could well be regarded as the
legitimate development of certain themes that are already latent in
Locke's political philosophy. It is equally possible that for very much
the same reason Herder developed his ideas quite independently of
Godwin, that, in short, both thinkers arrived at similar ideas because
they shared a similar philosophical heritage. This, indeed, seems the
most credible verdict in the light of existing evidence, but it need not
necessarily be the final verdict.

In France, too, the influence of Herder's social and political thought
was limited. Up to the appearance of the *Ideen* in French translation in
1827, Herder was chiefly known as a literary critic and an unorthodox
theologian. His dispute with Kant did, however, draw some attention
to his philosophical writings, and by the time of his death he had
acquired sufficient reputation to be regarded as the German Fénelon.[66]

The only major French writer who seems to have studied the *Ideen*
in detail before Edgar Quinet's publication of the French translation
was Benjamin Constant who, in his *De la Religion* (1824), repeatedly
referred his readers to Herder's *Ideen*. He fully endorsed Herder's
historical approach to Christianity and expressed strong approval of
his distinction between religion as a formal doctrine and religion as a

---

[61] *Enquiry*, op. cit., vol. I, p. 222.   [62] ibid., p. 216.   [63] ibid., p. 259.

[64] Thus the most eminent Godwin scholar F. E. L. Priestley makes no mention at all of
Herder in his critical notes to Godwin's text.

[65] Godwin is not mentioned by Herder; Suphan, in his critical notes to the text, makes no
reference to Godwin either. A German translation of the *Enquiry* did not appear until 1803,
the year of Herder's death.

[66] A. Gillies, op. cit., p. 124.

moral sentiment.[67] Quinet too—whose translation of the *Ideen* was based on Churchill's English translation—expressed admiration for Herder's historical method, but at the same time he could not conceal his misgivings over what he thought was an excessive emphasis on environmental factors. For he saw in it a threat to that view of history which regarded man's development as the conquest or the control of his physical environment by the operation of his mind and the exercise of his free will.[68] It was largely as a result of this interpretation—or rather misinterpretation—of Herder's social philosophy that writers such as Michelet and Guizot turned away from Herder even before they had come to read him.[69]

In the sphere of political thought and sociology—as distinct from philosophy of history—there is hardly any evidence to suggest that even where affinities exist, as for example, in the writings of Condorcet, Saint-Simon, Auguste Comte, or (despite fundamental disagreements) De Maistre, they can be attributed to Herderian influences. This is not really as surprising as it may seem. These writers—just as Godwin in England—were in a position to build upon traditions that were well-established in their own country and hence they felt little need to look elsewhere for inspiration. Herder's ideas were so much part of these same traditions, that they supported rather than influenced the socio-political trend of thought in England and France.

It was in South and Eastern Europe that Herder's ideas caused the greatest political stir. Professor A. Gillies has drawn attention to the impact which Herder's philosophy of nationalism and his concept of *Humanität* had on the political thought and activity of Giuseppe Mazzini. 'Almost everywhere in Mazzini's writings', he remarked, 'may be found sentences that forcibly recall Herder.'[70] Of the extracts adduced in support of this statement, the following may be cited. It reads almost like a translation of Herder's own lines: 'That which is true of each individual with regard to the other individuals forming a part of the society to which he belongs, is equally true of every people

---

[67] Constant, op. cit., p. 149, quoted in G. A. Wells, op. cit., p. 251.

[68] Quinet, *Idées*, Paris, 1827, p. 511.

[69] H. Tronchon, *La Fortune intellectuelle de Herder en France*, Paris, 1920, pp. 440 ff. But even those who had warmly welcomed Quinet's edition of the *Iaeen* and had given it serious attention, as Victor Cousin, for example, had done, regretted that, by giving insufficient recognition to the scope of human initiative in the shaping of social development, Herder had helped to undermine what in actual fact—as Cousin realized—he wished to strengthen: man's faith in progress and perfection. (See R. Flint, *History of the Philosophy of History*, Edinburgh, 1893, pp. 455-7, and G. A. Wells, op. cit., pp. 255-7.)

[70] A. Gillies, *Herder*, op. cit., p. 128.

with regard to humanity. . . . Every people has its special mission, which will co-operate towards the fulfilment of the general mission to humanity. That mission constitutes its nationality. Nationality is sacred.'[71]

In the development of Slav nationalism, in particular, Herder's ideas played a vital part; so much so, in fact, that Herder has been acclaimed as the spiritual father of the Slav national revival.[72]

Of the diverse Slavonic peoples the Czechs are the most western ethnic group. Not surprisingly, therefore, they were more strongly affected by the European Enlightenment than their geographically more distant cousins. They were, as a result, not only the first to proclaim Herder's gospel of national self-determination, but also foremost among those anxious to realize its socio-cultural and democratic implications. Fully accepting Herder's maxim that a people's claim to political recognition must be grounded in its consciousness of a collective cultural heritage, Czech national leaders devoted their efforts to the cultivation of the Czech language and to urging their countrymen to take an active interest in their history and literary traditions. With this emphasis on language and history, it was no accident that philologists and historians came to play such an important rôle in the early stages of the Czech national revival. Indeed, the development of most Slav national movements shared this characteristic with the Czechs.

It is interesting that the Slovaks, though linguistically closest to the Czechs, chose to interpret the nationalist creed in a more expansive sense. Being geographically less isolated from other Slavonic groups, they were more anxious to stress the features which united them with, rather than those that distinguished them from, the rest of the Slavonic world. Whereas Czech philologists like Josef Dobrovský (1753–18.9) and Josef Jungmann (1773–1847) were primarily interested in furthering the Czech language and 'purifying' it from Germanisms, Slovak scholars like Pavel Josef Šafařík (1795–1861) and Jan Kollár (1793–1852) emphasized the common Slav heritage and the need for all Slavs to unite. Henceforth nationalist agitation oscillated between this wider, Pan-Slavist conception and the more narrow, particularist interpretation of nationalism. But whilst the latter interpretation was still held to be compatible with the continued existence of the Austrian Empire

---

[71] G. Mazzini, *Life and Writings*, 6 vols., London, 1890–1, vol. III,. pp. 31–3, quoted in A. Gillies, *Herder*, op. cit., pp. 128–9.
[72] See A. Fischel, *Der Panslawismus bis zum Weltkrieg*, Berlin, 1919, p. 113; see also Janko Janeff, 'Herder und die Slawen', *Monatsschrift für höhere Schulen*, vol. XXXVII (1938), p. 91, R. R. Ergang, op. cit., pp. 256–63, and Carleton J. H. Hayes, loc. cit., p. 734.

('Austro-Slavism'), the Pan-Slavist conception implied a revolutionary re-orientation towards Russia as the messianic liberator of the Slav world and its future gravitational centre.[73]

Both the 'messianic' and the 'revolutionary' elements in Pan-Slavism appealed to the Russians. They helped to provide the inspirational source of an ideology that was as welcome to the proselytizing ambitions of the Russian Orthodox Church as it was later to those of the Russian Communist Party.

Two further important schools of political thought in Russia drew inspiration from Herderian ideas: the 'Westerners', with Belinsky and Herzen at their head, and the Slavophiles under Komyakov, the brothers Kireyevski, and others. Herder's conviction that European civilization needed a new lease of life, coupled with his belief that the rejuvenation would come from Russia, once its 'unspoilt' peoples had become conscious of their mission,[74] exercised a deep influence over the leaders of these two movements. In spite of differences in their political orientation, both Westerners and Slavophiles upheld Herder's image of the Russians as a fresh, resourceful, and unspoilt nation, as they also shared his faith in its native genius and in its ability to accomplish one day its own regeneration and by so doing, that of the Slav world as a whole.[75]

A number of writers have described the impact of Herderian thought on the growth of Polish, Serbo-Croat, Ukrainian and other Slav national movements, and there is, therefore, no need to enlarge on this subject here.[76] In all these movements, Herder's call to explore native

---

[73] Pan-Slavism existed of course in many different forms, and different definitions and interpretations abound. (See, for example, M. Weingart, *Slovanská vzájemnost*, Bratislava, 1926 pp. 5–200; H. Kohn, *Pan-Slavism*, Indiana, 1953; A. Fischel, op. cit.; B. H. Summer, *Survey of Russian History*, London, 1944, p. 242; H. Seton-Watson, *The Decline of Imperial Russia*, London, 1952, pp. 90–3.) But all writers on Pan-Slavism agree that emphasis on linguistic affinity was the most dominant characteristic. (I am indebted to Dr. J. F. N. Bradley of the University of Manchester for his advice on the Pan-Slav movement. In his article 'Czech Pan-Slavism Before the First World War', *Slavonic and East European Review*, vol. XL, no. 94 (December 1961), pp. 184–205, he describes the growing importance of Pan-Slavism in Czech nationalism towards the end of the nineteenth century.)

[74] See footnote 74 to p. 103.

[75] N. V. Riazanovsky, in his *Russia and the West in the Teaching of the Slavophiles*, Cambridge, Mass., 1952, regards Slavophilism as being simultaneously a Russian phenomenon and an aspect of Pan-Slavism.

[76] The following may be found informative: R. Schierenberg, *Der Politische Herder*, Graz, 1932, pp. 65–92; Matth. Murko, *Deutsche Einflüsse auf die Anfänge der böhmischen Romantik*, Graz, 1897, pp. 2 ff.; J. Jakubec and A. Novak, *Geschichte der tschechischen Litteratur*, Leipzig, 1913, p. 157; Konrad Bittner, 'Herder und die Tschechen', *Geist der Zeit*, Berlin, 1939, p. 229; Janko Janeff, loc. cit., pp. 91–7; and his 'Das nationale Erwachen der Slawen und der Panslawismus', *Deutsche Monatshefte*, 1939–40, pp. 42 ff.

traditions in literature, to collect folk-songs and to study folk-lore was assiduously followed.

But by far the most important source of Herder's inspirational power was, without doubt, his chapter on the Slavs in the *Ideen*. In it he expressed the hope that the 'now so backward, but once so industrious and happy peoples, will in the end awake from . . . (their) long listless slumber and, having shaken off the chains of slavery, will enjoy the possession of . . . (their) beautiful lands from the Adriatic Sea to the Carpathian Mountains, and from the Don to the Moldau'.[77] The chapter appeared as early as 1795 in a Latin translation in a work (*Bibliotheca slavica*) by the Czech philologist Václav Durých (1735– 1802), and soon afterwards it was published also in Czech, Slovak, Polish, Croat and Ukrainian translations.[78] When, in June 1848, the Slav Congress met, it adopted a Manifesto couched in terms almost identical to those which Herder used in the Slav-chapter of the *Ideen*.[79] Its chief architect was František Palacký (1798–1876), one of the greatest of Slav historians and an enthusiastic admirer of Herder.[80]

The importance which is attached to Herder's influence on the growth of political nationalism among the subject peoples of the Habsburg Empire may be gauged by its having been considered as one of the major forces that led to the break-up of the Danube-Monarchy.[81] We regard this as a somewhat exaggerated estimation of the potency of Herder's ideas; at the same time it cannot be denied that these ideas contained some highly inflammable material. But it required an explosive situation before it could constitute a real danger. It also required a man like Thomas G. Masaryk to ignite it.

Yet of all the forms which nineteenth-century nationalism assumed, Masaryk's was the least aggressive. If there ever was a man genuinely anxious to put into practice what Herder had only dimly visualized, it was this professor-statesman and founder of one of the most democratic successor States to Austria-Hungary. Like Mazzini and Palacký, Masaryk sincerely strove to further the cause of both *Volk* and *Humanität*.

---

[77] XIV, 280.   [78] K. Bittner, loc. cit., p. 233.

[79] K. Bittner, loc. cit., p. 238; see also Janko Janeff, 'Das nationale Erwachen der Slawen', loc. cit., p. 53. This Congress has been described as the first of the great landmarks in the political phase of Slav nationalism which saw its aim in the linking of national and democratic aspirations. (See R. Schierenberg, op. cit., p. 92.)

[80] Palacký called Herder the 'apostle of *Humanität*', and referred to him as his favourite author. (V. J. Nováček, *Fr. Palackého korespondence a zápisky*, Praha, 1898–1911, vol. I, p. 13.)

[81] R. Schierenberg, op. cit., p. 77.

Masaryk's writings and his practical political work not only bore witness to an unusual grasp of, and regard for, Herder's conception of nationalism,[82] but they also revealed a remarkable degree of affinity with the democratic and republican sentiments of Herder's political creed.

Masaryk rejected the political organism of Hegel and the Romanticists, but he shared Herder's view that social development and political activity did not consist in 'mechanical' operations.[83] He rejected also the postulate that power or force was the essence of political government.[84] The State, he argued, was a community, consisting of 'similar individuals', whose political association was not the result of physical force or common racial characteristics, but rather the expression of a psychological need.[85] Like Herder, Masaryk identified the chief source of this 'psychological need' with the national consciousness of a *Volk*. He described the nature of this consciousness as the 'feeling of belonging together, of forming a distinct group among other national groups that constitute mankind', primarily on the basis of a common language and common literary and cultural traditions.[86]

Political development, Masaryk held, was essentially a matter of *Bildung*, i.e. the 'conscious forming of people, the fashioning and imaginative moulding of actual life'.[87] Not revolution, not the violent overthrow of institutions, but patient reform of the people, of men's 'heads and hearts' was the only way of effecting real and lasting changes in political life. Human progress was the result of tenacious and unobtrusive effort, of piecemeal improvements. Revolutionary changes, though they appeared to happen suddenly, had in reality been long prepared in obscurity.[88] Unspectacular work, not dramatic heroic feats,

---

[82] Masaryk had a great admiration for Herder in whom he saw 'the most important teacher of the Slavs at the time of their national revival'. (T. G. Masaryk, *Česká otázka* (1895), Praha, 1924, p. 229; the English rendering of the title would be 'The Czech Question'.)

[83] T. G. Masaryk, *Otázka sociální* (1898), 2 vols., Praha, 1946, vol. I, pp. 197–8. (This work is a penetrating analysis of Marxism.)

[84] ibid., vol. II, p. 124: 'The State must have an ethical basis.' Similarly, ibid., pp. 33, 101, 133; and vol. I, p. 237.

[85] Masaryk, *Otázka sociální*, op. cit., vol. I, p. 285; see also ibid., p. 251. Masaryk, like Herder, regarded psychology as the basic social science to which socio-political questions were ultimately reducible. (See his *Versuch einer Concreten Logik*, Wien, 1887, §§ 64 and 67.)

[86] Masaryk, *Russland und Europa*, Jena, 1913, 2 vols., vol. I, § 59; see also his *The Problem of Small Nations in the European Crisis*, London, 1916, ch. 1.

[87] Karel Čapek, *Hovory s T. G. Masarykem*, Praha, 1936, p. 139.

[88] Masaryk, *Otázka sociální*, op. cit., vol. II, pp. 304–5.

not romantic revolutionism or martyrdom, not cataclysmic upheavals, was, for Masaryk, the only sure means of achieving a political transformation of society.[89] The State, he argued, was not the 'god-like, omniscient and omnipotent institution that Hegel held it to be; it was a human institution, very human indeed, with all the imperfections of those who organized it'.[90] Like Herder, he thought of politics essentially in terms of social culture. The practical work of political leaders was the discovery and furtherance of social and cultural values that would give purposive direction to a society. Not domination and privilege, but service and the scrupulous observation of the maxim never to treat a fellow-being as a means only, were the characteristics which Masaryk wished to see associated with political leadership.[91]

We could go on adducing more instances of the remarkable parallelism of thought in these two men, of their dislike of 'metaphysics', intuitions and instincts—'instinct—that is moral chaos',[92] of their desire to eliminate such philosophical dualisms as between mind and matter, reason and feeling, subjectivism and objectivism, or of their pluralistic approach to the problem of historical causation.[93] But we must resist this temptation. We must beware also of conveying the impression that Herder's ideas were the sole, or even the dominant, influence on Masaryk's sociology and political philosophy. Whilst Masaryk was conscious of Herder's rôle in the history of Slav nationalism as also of his debt to Herder's philosophy of *Volk* and *Humanität*,[94] he was hardly aware of the many other points of contact between himself and Herder. Clearly, Herder's influence was but indirect in those instances, diffused as it had become in the works of many, and, in particular, in the writings of Czech and Slovak nationalists of the preceding generation. The extent of the political affinity between Herder and Masaryk would suggest, however, that, in spite of the century that separated the times of their intellectual activity, many of Herder's ideas had lost none of their appeal and relevance.

It would seem, then, that it was not in the country of its birth that Herder's socio-political thought left its deepest imprint. Those who

---

[89] Masaryk, *Otázka socialní*, op. cit., vol. II, pp. 231–2.

[90] Masaryk, *Světová Revoluce*, Praha, 1925, § 129.

[91] K. Čapek, op. cit., p. 302.

[92] Masaryk, *Otázka socialní*, op. cit., vol. II, p. 142.

[93] Other points of contact are discussed by A. Gillies, 'Herder and Masaryk: Some Points of Contact', *Modern Language Review*, vol. XL, 1945, pp. 120–5.

[94] K. Čapek, op. cit., p. 301; see also K. Bittner, 'Herder und die Tschechen', loc. cit., p. 430.

could have been Herder's successors were in view of the political conditions of post-Napoleonic Germany unable or unwilling to see the relevance of its liberal and democratic implications to the problems with which their country was faced.

BIBLIOGRAPHY

A. PRIMARY SOURCES

(i) HERDER'S WORKS, LETTERS, AND MEMOIRS

Herder, J. G., *Sämtliche Werke*, hg. von B. Suphan, 33 vols., Berlin, 1877–1913. (All references in the text are made to this edition.)
Dobbek, Wilhelm (ed.), *Herders Briefe*, Weimar, 1959.
Düntzer, H. and Herder, F. G. von (ed.), *Herders Reise nach Italien*, Gießen, 1859.
Aus Herders Nachlaß, 3 vols., Frankfurt a.M., 1856–7.
Von und an Herder, 3 vols., Leipzig, 1861–2.
Herder, Maria Caroline von, *Erinnerungen aus dem Leben J. G. von Herders*, ed. by J. G. Müller, 2 vols., Tübingen, 1820.
Herder, Emil Gottfried von (ed.), *Herders Lebensbild*, 3 vols., Erlangen, 1846.
Hoffmann, O. (ed.), *Herders Briefwechsel mit Nicolai*, Berlin, 1887.
Herders Briefe an Hamann, Berlin, 1889.
Müller, Johannes von, *Briefwechsel mit J. G. Herder und Caroline von Herder* (1782–1808), ed. by K. E. Hoffmann, Schaffhausen, 1952.
Schauer, H. (ed.), *Herders Briefwechsel mit Caroline Flachsland*, 2 vols., Weimar, 1926–8.
Herders Dresdener Reise, Dresden, 1929.
Wagner, K. (ed.), *Herders Briefe an J. H. Merck*, Darmstadt, 1835.
Briefe von und an J. H. Merck, Darmstadt, 1835.
Bibliotheca Herderiana, Vimariae, 1804.

(ii) OTHER WORKS

Blackwell, Thomas, *Enquiry into the Life and Writings of Homer*, second edition, London, 1736.
Coleridge, S. T., *The Statesman's Manual*, London, 1816.
Lay Sermon, London, 1817.
The Constitution of Church and State, London, 1829.
Fichte, J. G., *Reden an die deutsche Nation*, *Werke*, 8 vols., ed. by I. H. Fichte, Leipzig, 1845–6, vol. VII.
Gatterer, J. C., *Allgemeine Historische Bibliothek*, Göttingen, 1769.
Gentz, F., *Briefwechsel zwischen F. Gentz und A. Müller*, Stuttgart, 1857.
Gierke, O., *Natural Law and the Theory of Society*, trans. by E. Barker, Cambridge, 1934.
Godwin, William, *An Enquiry concerning Political Justice*, London, 1793, ed. by F. E. L. Priestley, 3 vols., Toronto, 1946.

Gottsched, J. C., *Erste Gründe der Weltweisheit*, Leipzig, 1733.

Hartley, David, *Observations on Man, His Frame, His Duty, and His Expectations*, 2 vols., London, 1749.

Hegel, G. W. F., *Vorlesungen über die Philosophie der Weltgeschichte, Werke*, ed. by G. Lasson, Leipzig, 1920-1, vol. I.
    Naturrecht und Staatswissenschaft im Grundrisse, trans. by T. M. Knox, *Hegel's Philosophy of Right*, Oxford, 1942; corr. edition 1953.

Hume, David, *A Treatise of Human Nature*, London, 1738.

Kant I., *Idee zu einer allgemeinen Geschichte in weltbürgerlicher Absicht, Schriften*, Preuss. Akademie der Wissenschaften edition, Berlin, 1923, vol. VIII.

Leibniz, G. W., *Monadology*, and *Nouveaux Essais, Die philosophischen Schriften*, ed. C. I. Gerhardt, 7 vols., Berlin, 1875-90.

Lessing, G. E., *Die Erziehung des Menschengeschlechts, Werke*, ed. by Paul Rilla, Berlin, 1956, vol. VIII.

Locke, John, *An Essay concerning Human Understanding*, ed. by A. C. Fraser, 2 vols., Oxford, 1894.

Luther, Martin, *Schriften*, Weimar, 1853, vol. II.

Masaryk, T. G., *Česká Otázka*, Praha, 1924.
    Versuch einer Concreten Logik, Wien, 1887.
    Otázka socialní (1898), 2 vols., Praha, 1946.
    Russland und Europa, 2 vols., Jena, 1913.
    The Problem of Small Nations in the European Crisis, London, 1916.
    Svetová Revoluce, Praha, 1925.

Michels, Robert, *Political Parties*, London, 1915.

Mill, J. S., *On Bentham and Coleridge*, ed. by F. R. Leavis, London, 1950.
    On Liberty, ed. by R. B. McCallum, Oxford, 1946.
    Autobiography, World Classics edition, London, 1924.

Montesquieu, C. de, *De l'esprit des lois*, trans. by Thomas Nugent, London, 1752, vol. I; and the more recent translation by Franz Neumann, New York, 1949.

Moritz, C. P., *Anton Reiser*, trans. by P. E. Matheson, London, 1926.

Möser, Justus, *Werke*, ed. Abeken, 10 vols., Berlin, 1842-3.

Müller, Adam, *Elemente der Staatskunst*, 3 vols., Berlin, 1809.
    Ueber König Friedrich II, Berlin, 1810.

Novalis, *Werke*, ed. C. Seelig, 5 vols., Zürich, 1945.

Novalis Briefwechsel, ed. by J. M. Raich, Mainz, 1880.

Priestley, Joseph, *An Essay on the First Principles of Government, and on the Nature of Political, Civil and Religious Liberty*, London, 1768; second edition, 1771.
    Disquisitions relating to Matter and Spirit, London, 1777.
    Miscellaneous Observations Relating to Education, Cork, 1780.
    Lectures on History, London, 1826 (first edition, 1788).

Pütter, J. S., *Handbuch der teutschen Reichshistorie*, Göttingen, 1772.
    Vorläufige Uebersicht des teutschen Staatsrechts, Göttingen, 1788.

Rousseau, J. J., *The Social Contract and Discourses*, trans. and ed. by G. D. H. Cole, London, 1913.

Emile, or Education, trans. by Barbara Foxlex, Everymans Library edition, London, n.d.

Savigny, F. C. von, *Vom Beruf unsrer Zeit für Gesetzgebung und Rechtswissenschaft*, Heidelberg, 1814.

System des heutigen Römischen Rechts, 9 vols., Berlin, 1840–51.

Schlegel, Friedrich, *Werke*, 15 vols., Wien, 1846.

Schlözer, A. L. von, *Stats Anzeigen*, 17 vols,. Göttingen, 1783–92.

Stats Gelartheit, Göttingen, 1793.

Shaftesbury, *Characteristicks of Men, Manners, Opinions, Times*, third edition, London, 1723 (first edition, 1711).

Thomasius, Christian, *Einleitung zu der Vernunfft-Lehre*, Halle, 1691. (Edition cited in the text is that of 1699.)

Historie der Weiszheit und Thorheit, Halle, 1693.

Außübung der Vernunfft-Lehre, Halle, 1705.

Ernsthaffte, aber doch Muntere und Vernünfftige Thomasische Gedancken und Erinnerungen über allerhand auserlesene Juristische Händel, 4 vols., Halle, 1720–1.

Tindal, Matthew, *Christianity as Old as the Creation*, London, 1730.

Toland, John, *Christianity Not Mysterious*, London, 1696.

Voltaire, *Oeuvres*, ed. Lequieu, Paris, 1820, vol. XI.

Wolff, Christian, *Vernünfftige Gedancken von der Menschen Thun und Lassen*, Halle, 1720.

Vernünfftige Gedancken von dem gesellschaftlichen Leben der Menschen, fourth edition, Frankfurt and Leipzig, 1736.

Jus Naturae Methodo Scientifica Pertractum, Francofurti et Lipsiae, 1740–50, vol. VIII.

Institutiones Juris Naturae et Gentium, Halae et Magdeb., 1750.

Grundsätze des Natur- und Völkerrechts, Halle, 1754.

B. SECONDARY SOURCES

(i) HERDER STUDIES AND BIOGRAPHIES

Barnard, F. M., 'The Hebrews and Herder's Political Creed', *Modern Language Review*, vol. LIV, 1959.

'Herder's Treatment of Causation and Continuity in History', *Journal of the History of Ideas*, vol. XXIV, 1963.

'Herder and Israel', *Jewish Social Studies*, vol. XXVIII, 1966.

Berlin, Isaiah. 'Herder and the Enlightenment', in Earl R. Wasserman (ed.), *Aspects of the Eighteenth Century*, Baltimore, 1965.

Bittner, Konrad, 'Herder und die Tschechen', *Geist der Zeit*, Berlin, 1939.

Herders Geschichtsphilosophie und die Slawen, Reichenberg, 1929.

Clark, Robert T. Jr., 'Herder's Conception of "Kraft" ', *Publications of the Mod. Lang. Assoc. of America*, 1942.

Herder, Berkeley and Los Angeles, 1955.

Dobbek, W., *J. G. Herders Humanitätsidee als Ausdruck seines Weltbildes und seiner Persönlichkeit*, Braunschweig, 1949.

Ergang, R. R., *Herder and the Foundations of German Nationalism*, New York, 1931.

Gillies, A., 'Herder's Essay on Shakespeare: "Das Herz der Untersuchung"', *Modern Language Review*, vol. XXXII, 1937.

'Herder's Approach to the Philosophy of History', *Modern Language Review*, vol. XXXV, 1940.

'Herder's Preparation of Romantic Theory', *Modern Language Review*, vol. XXXIX, 1944.

'Herder and Masaryk: Some Points of Contact', *Modern Language Review*, vol. XL, 1945.

Herder, Oxford, 1945.

Hatch, Irvin Clifton, 'Der Einfluß Shaftesburys auf Herder', *Studien z. vergl. Literaturgeschichte*, Berlin, 1901.

Hayes, Carleton J. H., 'Contribution of Herder to the Doctrine of Nationalism', *Amer. Historical Review*, vol. XXXII, 1927.

Haym, R., *Herder, nach seinem Leben und seinen Werken*, 2 vols., Berlin, 1880.

Janeff, Janko, 'Herder und die Slawen', *Monatsschrift für höhere Schulen*, vol. 37, 1938.

Kühnemann, E., *Herder*, third edition, München, 1927.

McEachran, F., *The Life and Philosophy of J. G. Herder*, Oxford, 1939.

Müller, Johann Georg, *Aus dem Herderschen Hause*, ed. by Jakob Baechtold, Berlin, 1881.

Pascal, Roy, 'Herder and the Scottish Historical School', *English Goethe Society*, vol. XIV, 1939.

Probst, Ernst, *Herder als Psychologe*, Inaug. Dissertation, Bern, 1925.

Rasch, Wolfdietrich, *Herder*, Halle, 1938.

Rouché, Max, *La Philosophie de l'histoire de Herder*, Paris, 1940.

Schierenberg, R., *Der Politische Herder*, Graz, 1932.

Schock, Luise, *Herders Bekanntschaft mit der englischen Literatur*, Breslau, 1928.

Schütze, Martin, 'The Fundamental Ideas in Herder's Thought', *Modern Philology*, June 1920–November 1923.

Siegel, Carl, *Herder als Philosoph*, Stuttgart and Berlin, 1907.

Simpson, Georgina R., *Herder's Conception of 'Das Volk'*, private edition, University of Chicago Libraries, 1921.

Stadelmann, Rudolf, *Der Historische Sinn bei Herder*, Halle, 1928.

Tronchon, H., *La Fortune intellectuelle de Herder en France*, Paris, 1920.

Wells, G. A., 'Herder's Determinism', *Journal of the History of Ideas*, 1958.

Herder and After, The Hague, 1959.

Wiese, Benno von, 'Der Gedanke des Volkes in Herders Weltbild', *Die Erziehung*, 1939.

Volk und Dichtung von Herder bis zur Romantik, Erlangen, 1938.

'Volkstum und Geschichte bei Herder', *Zeitschrift für Deutsche Bildung*, 1934.

(ii) OTHER WORKS

Adams, H. P., *The Life and Writings of Giambattista Vico*, London, 1935.

Aris, Reinhold, *History of Political Thought in Germany* (1789–1815), London, 1936.

Avineri, Shlomo, 'The Problem of War in Hegel's Thought', *Journal of the History of Ideas*, vol. XXII, 1961.

'Hegel and Nationalism', *The Review of Politics*, vol. 24, 1962.

Barker, E., Introduction to, and translation of, O. Gierke's *Natural Law and the Theory of Society*, Cambridge, 1934.

Principles of Social and Political Theory, London, 1951.

Barnard, F. M. 'Christian Thomasius: Enlightenment and Bureaucracy', *American Political Science Reveiw*, vol. LIX, 1965.

'Metaphores, Laments and the Organic Community', *Canadian Journal of Economics and Political Science*, vol. XXXII, 1966.

Barraclough, G., *The Origins of Modern Germany*, Oxford, 1949.

Becker, Carl L., *The Heavenly City of the Eighteenth-Century Philosophers*, Yale, 1932.

Bendix, Reinhard, *Max Weber*, London, 1960.

Berger, Friedrich, *Menschenbild und Menschenbildung*, Stuttgart, 1933.

Berlin, Isaiah, *The Age of Enlightenment*, New York, 1956.

Historical Inevitability, London, 1954.

Two Concepts of Liberty, Oxford, 1958.

Biedermann, Karl, *Deutschland im Achtzehnten Jahrhundert*, 3 vols., second edition, Leipzig, 1880.

Boehn, Max von, *Modes and Manners*, trans. by Joan Joshua, London, 1935. Vol. IV, (*The Eighteenth Century*).

Bradley, J. F. N., 'Czech Pan-Slavism Before the First World War', *Slavonic and East European Review*, vol. XL, 1961.

Brinton, Crane, *The Political Ideas of the English Romanticists*, Oxford, 1926.

Bruford, W. H., *Germany in the Eighteenth Century*, Cambridge, 1935.

Brüggemann, Fritz, *Das Weltbild der deutschen Aufklärung*, Leipzig, 1930.

Aus der Frühzeit der deutschen Aufklärung, second edition, Leipzig, 1938.

Bühler, Johannes, *Deutsche Geschichte*, vol. IV, Berlin, 1950.

Bury, J. B., *The Idea of Progress*, London, 1920.

Čapek, Karel, *Hovory s T. G. Masarykem*, Praha, 1936.

Cassirer, Ernst, *Leibniz' System*, Marburg, 1902.

Freiheit und Form, Berlin, 1916.

Die Philosophie der Aufklärung, Tübingen, 1932.

The Platonic Renaissance in England, trans. by James P. Pettergrove, London, 1953.

The Logic of the Humanities, trans. by Clarence Smith Howe, New Haven, 1961.

The Myth of the State, Yale, 1946.

An Essay on Man, Yale, 1944.

Cobban, Alfred, *National Self-Determination*, London, 1944.

Collingwood, R. G., *The Idea of Nature*, London, 1945.

The Idea of History, London, 1946.

Croce, Benedetto, *The Philosophy of Giambattista Vico*, trans. by R. G. Collingwood, London, 1913.

Dietze, H., *Geschichte des deutschen Handels*, Leipzig, 1923.

Dilthey, Wilhelm, 'Das achtzehnte Jahrhundert und die geschichtliche Welt', *Deutsche Rundschau*, 1901.

Emmet, Dorothy, *Function, Purpose and Powers*, London, 1958.

Fischel, A., *Der Panslawismus bis zum Weltkrieg*, Berlin, 1919.

Fleischmann, Max, *Christian Thomasius*, Halle, 1931.

Flenley, Ralph, *Modern German History*, London, 1953.

Flint, R., *History of the Philosophy of History*, Edinburgh, 1893.

Gardiner, Patrick (ed.), *Theories of History*, Illinois and London, 1959.

German Studies, Festschrift to L. A. Willoughby, Oxford, 1952.

Gooch, G. P., *Germany and the French Revolution*, London, 1927.

Gundolf, Friedrich, *Romantiker*, Berlin, 1930.

Haering, Theodor L., *Hegel, sein Wollen und sein Werk*, Leipzig and Berlin, 1929.

Halstein, G., *Die Staatsphilosophie Schleiermachers*, Leipzig, 1923.

Hampshire, Stuart, *Spinoza*, London, 1951.

The Age of Reason, New York, 1956.

Hartung, Fritz, *Deutsche Verfassungsgeschichte vom 15. Jahrhundert bis zur Gegenwart*, Leipzig and Berlin, 1928.

Haym, R., *Die romantische Schule*, Berlin, 1870.

Hazard, Paul, *La Crise de la Conscience Europeenne*, Paris, 1935.

La Pensée Européenne au XVIIIème Siècle, Paris, 1946.

Heigel, K. Th., *Deutsche Geschichte vom Tode Friedrich des Großen bis zur Auflösung des alten Reiches*, Leipzig, 1899.

Hempel, Ernst, *Justus Mösers Wirkung auf seine Zeitgenossen*, Inaug. Dissertation, Freiburg, 1931.

Hettner, H., *Geschichte der deutschen Literatur im XVIII Jahrhundert*, Braunschweig, 1926.

Huber, E. R., *Deutsche Verfassungsgeschichte*, vol. I, Stuttgart, 1957.

Huizinga, J., *Im Bann der Geschichte*, Basel, 1943.

Janeff, Janko, 'Das nationale Erwachen der Slawen und der Panslawismus', *Deutsche Monatshefte*, 1939–40.

Jaspers, Karl, *The Origin and Goal of History*, trans. by Michael Bullock, London, 1953.

Jouvenel, Bertrand de, *Sovereignty*, trans. by J. F. Huntington, Cambridge, 1957.

Kaiser, Gerhard, *Pietismus und Patriotismus im literarischen Deutschland*, Wiesbaden, 1961.

Kedourie, Elie, *Nationalism*, London, 1960, rev. ed., 1961
Knapp, G. F., *Die Bauernbefreiung und der Ursprung der Landarbeiter*, Leipzig, 1887.
Kohn, H., *Pan-Slavism*, Indiana, 1953.
Korff, H. A., *Geist der Goethezeit*, 2 vols., Leipzig, 1923-30.
Laslett, Peter (ed.), *Philosophy, Politics and Society*, Oxford, 1956.
Lechler, G. V., *Geschichte des Englischen Deismus*, Stuttgart and Tübingen, 1841.
Lemberg, Eugen, *Nationalismus*, 2 vols, Hamburg, 1964.
Longee, Robert W., 'German Romanticism and Political Thought', *The Review of Politics*, vol. 21, 1959.
Magnan, Fauchier-, Adrien, *The Small German Courts in the Eighteenth Century*, trans. by Mervyn Savill, London, 1958.
Martin, Kingsley, *French Liberal Thought in the Eighteenth Century*, second edition, London, 1954.
McCloskey, H. J., 'The State as an Organism', *Philosophical Review*, 1963.
Mehlis, G., *Schelling's Geschichtsphilosophie*, Heidelberg, 1907.
Meinecke, Friedrich, *Die Idee der Staatsräson in der Neuen Geschichte*, München and Berlin, 1924.
— *Die Entstehung des Historismus*, 2 vols., München and Berlin, 1936.
Merton, Robert K., *Social Theory and Social Structure*, revised edition, Free Press of Glencoe, 1957.
Morley, John Viscount, *Diderot and the Encyclopaedists*, 2 vols., London, 1923.
Murko, Matth., *Deutsche Einflüsse auf die Anfänge der böhmischen Romantik*, Graz, 1897.
Norman, F., 'Henry Crabb Robinson and Goethe', Part I, *Publications of the English Goethe Society*, vol. VI, 1930.
Parry, Geraint, 'Enlightened Government and its Critics in Eighteenth-Century Germany', *The Historical Journal*, vol. VI, 1963.
Pascal, Roy, *The German Sturm und Drang*, Manchester, 1953.
Popper, Karl, *The Open Society and its Enemies*, 2 vols., second edition, London, 1952.
— *The Poverty of Historicism*, second edition, London, 1960.
Reiss, H. S., *The Political Thought of the German Romantics*, 1793-1815, Oxford, 1955.
Renner, B., *Die nationalen Einigungsbestrebungen F. K. Mosers*, Königsberg, 1919.
Riazanovsky, N. V., *Russia and the West in the Teaching of the Slavophiles*, Cambridge, Mass., 1952.
Rörig, F., *Ursachen und Auswirkungen des deutschen Partikularismus*, Berlin, 1937.
Rose, William, *Men, Myths, and Movements in German Literature*, London, 1931.
Russell, Bertrand, *A Critical Exposition of the Philosophy of Leibniz*, London, 1937.

Sampson, R. V., *Progress in the Age of Reason*, London, 1956.

Saw, Ruth Lydia, *Leibniz*, London, 1954.

Schmitt, Carl, *Politische Romantik*, München and Leipzig, second edition, 1925.

Schnabel, Franz, *Deutsche Geschichte im Neunzehnten Jahrhundert*, 4 vols., Freiburg, second edition, 1948–51.

Schweitzer, Albert, *Kultur und Ethik*, München, 1923.

Selle, Götz von, *Die Georg August Universität zu Göttingen*, Göttingen, 1937.

Seton-Watson, H., *The Decline of Imperial Russia*, London, 1952.

Shafer, Boyd C., *Nationalism, Myth and Reality*, London, 1955.

Smith, Ronald Gregor, *J. G. Hamann*, London, 1960.

Stephen, Leslie, *History of English Thought in the Eighteenth Century*, 2 vols., London, 1876.

― *English Literature and Society in the Eighteenth Century*, London, 1904.

Stokoe, F. W., *German Influence in the English Romantic Period*, Cambridge, 1926.

Summer, B. H., *Survey of Russian History*, London, 1944.

Treitschke, Heinrich von, *Deutsche Geschichte im neunzehnten Jahrhundert*, ed. by H. Heffter, 2 vols., Leipzig, 1934.

Troeltsch, Ernst, 'Naturrecht und Humanität in der Weltpolitik', in *Deutscher Geist und Westeuropa*, ed. by Hans Baron, Tübingen, 1925.

Unger, R., *Gesammelte Studien*, 2 vols., Berlin, 1929.

Walsh, W. H., *An Introduction to Philosophy of History*, London, 1951. ·

Walzel, Oskar, *German Romanticism*, trans. by A. E. Lussky, New York–London, 1932.

Wedgwood, C. V., *Truth and Opinion*, London, 1960.

Weingart, M., *Slovanská vzájemnost*, Bratislava, 1926.

Weldon, T. D., *States and Morals*, London, 1946.

Wesendonck, Hermann, *Die Begründung der neueren Geschichtsschreibung durch Gatterer und Schlözer*, Leipzig, 1876.

White, R. J., *Political Tracts of Wordsworth, Coleridge, and Shelley*, Cambridge, 1953.

Wiese, Benno von, *Politische Dichtung Deutschlands*, Berlin, 1931.

Willey, Basil, *The Eighteenth Century Background*, London, 1940.

― *Nineteenth-Century Studies, Coleridge to Matthew Arnold*, London, 1949.

INDEX

Schlözer, August Ludwig von, 5n., 10, 22, 23–24, 26, 72, 155
Schubart, Christian Friedrich Daniel, 3, 18n.
Seckendorff, Veit Ludwig von, 19
Semler, Johann Salomo, 13, 14
Shaftesbury, Anthony Ashley Cooper, 3rd Earl of, 14, 16–17, 18, 54n., 55, 90
Smith, Adam, 19
Solon, 31
Sonnenfels, Josef von, 27
Spalding, Johann Joachim, 13, 14, 15
Spener, Philipp Jakob, 13
Spinoza, Benedict de, 7, 10, 11, 45–46, 50
Stein, Heinrich Friedrich Karl, Baron vom, 159n.
Sulzer, Johann Georg, 17
Suphan, B., xix, 154n., 170n.

Thomasius, Christian, 7–10, 29, 72

Tindal, Matthew, 89
Toland, John, 89
Trapp, Ernst Christian, 28n.
Treitschke, Heinrich von, 27
Troeltsch, Ernst, xviii n.
Trotsky, Leon, 116n.

Vico, Giovanni Battista, 110n.
Voltaire, François Marie Arouet de, 72, 111n., 125n., 129, 132

Weber, Max, xix, 82n.
Wesendonck, Hermann, 23
Wieland, Christoph Martin, 99
Winckelmann, Johann Joachim, 110n.
Wolff, Christian, 7, 12–14, 16, 20–22, 23, 72
Wordsworth, William, 169n.

Zeno, 130